MW01123543

# ISLAM, DEMOCRACY AND DIALOGUE IN TURKEY

*For mum and dad*

# Islam, Democracy and Dialogue in Turkey
## Deliberating in Divided Societies

BORA KANRA
*Australian National University, Australia*

ASHGATE

Published by
Ashgate Publishing Limited
Wey Court East
Union Road
Farnham
Surrey, GU9 7PT
England

Ashgate Publishing Company
Suite 420
101 Cherry Street
Burlington
VT 05401-4405
USA

www.ashgate.com

**British Library Cataloguing in Publication Data**
Kanra, Bora.
　　Islam, democracy and dialogue in Turkey : deliberating in
　　divided societies.
　　1. Islam and secularism--Turkey. 2. Communication in
　　politics--Turkey. 3. Islam and politics--Turkey.
　　4. Democratization--Turkey. 5. Consensus (Social
　　sciences)--Turkey.
　　I. Title
　　324'.09561-dc22

**Library of Congress Cataloging-in-Publication Data**
Kanra, Bora.
　　Islam, democracy, and dialogue in Turkey : deliberating in divided societies /
by Bora Kanra.
　　　　p. cm.
　　Includes bibliographical references and index.
　　ISBN 978-0-7546-7878-6 (hardback) -- ISBN 978-0-7546-9733-6
(ebook) 1. Deliberative democracy--Turkey. 2. Social learning--Turkey. I. Title.
　　JQ1809.A15.K36 2009
　　320.9561--dc22

2009023287

ISBN　9780754678786 (hbk)
ISBN　9780754697336 (ebk)

**Mixed Sources**
Product group from well-managed
forests and other controlled sources
www.fsc.org Cert no. SGS-COC-2482
© 1996 Forest Stewardship Council

Printed and bound in Great Britain by
TJ International Ltd, Padstow, Cornwall

# Contents

# List of Tables

# List of Abbreviations

AKP    Adalet ve Kalkınma Partisi – Justice and Development Party
ANAP  Anavatan Partisi – Motherland Party
AP     Adalet Partisi – Justice Party
BBP    Büyük Birlik Partisi – Grand Unity Party
BKP    Başkent Kadın Platformu – Capital Women's Platform
BSKP  Barış İçin Sürekli Kadın Platformu – Women's Platform for Peace
CHP    Cumhuriyet Halk Partisi – People's Republican Party
DP     Demokrat Parti – Democrat Party
DSP    Demokratik Sol Parti – Democratic Left Party
DYP    Doğru Yol Partisi – True Path Party
FP     Fazilet Partisi – Virtue Party
ID     Islamic Discourse
IHD    İnsan Hakları Derneği – Human Rights Association
IP     İşçi Partisi – Workers Party
IT     Ittahat ve Terakki – Unity and Progress
KD     Kemalist Discourse
LLD    Liberal Left Discourse
MHP   Milliyetçi Hareket Partisi – Nationalist Movement Party
MNP   Milli Nizam Partisi – National Order Party
MSP   Milli Selamet Partisi – National Salvation Party
ND     Nationalist Discourse
NDR   National Democratic Revolution
OSF    Osmanlı Sosyalist Fırkası – Ottoman Socialist Party
PKK   Partiya Karkerên Kurdistan – Kurdistan Workers' Party
RP     Refah Partisi – Welfare Party
SHG   Sivil Haklar Girişimi – Civil Rights Initiative
SP     Saadet Partisi – Felicity Party
TIP    Türkiye İşçi Partisi – Turkish Workers Party
TKP   Türkiye Komunist Partisi – The Communist Party of Turkey
TSIP   Türkiye Sosyalist İşçi Partisi – Socialist Worker's Party of Turkey
TSF   Türkiye İşçi Çiftçi Sosyalist Fırkası – Workers' and Farmers' Socialist Party of Turkey

# Acknowledgements

No work can be completed without the intellectual and moral support of colleagues and friends. For fruitful discussions, comments and guidance I am indebted to Selen Ayırtman, Seyla Benhabib, Mary Dietz, Keith Dowding, John Dryzek, Akasha-Rose Emmanuel, Nancy Fraser, Bob Goodin, Paul 't Hart, Carolyn Hendriks, Akira Inoue, Doris Kordes, Nelly Lahoud, Christian List, John Nethercote, Jensen Sass, Nic Southwood, Joelle Vandermensbrugghe and David West. I am solely responsible for any mistakes.

This research was supported by Australian Research Council Discovery Grant DP0773626, for which I am grateful. I also wish to express my gratitude to the participants of discussion groups and the interviewees who volunteered to contribute to the Q study in Turkey. The support of the Faculty of Communication, University of Ankara, and the Department of Political Administration, İzzet Baysal University, was also crucial for the success of Q study in Turkey. I thank both universities for their generous support. Parts of this book were previously published as 'Democracy, Islam and Dialogue: the Case of Turkey', *Government and Opposition*, vol 40 (4), 2005.

Bora Kanra
Canberra, May 2009

# Chapter 1

# Introduction

After more than a decade of intense debate, the normative idea of deliberative democracy has established itself as a viable foundation for designing democratic institutions. Yet the debate continues. The more diverse the social context, the more difficult it is to develop a sustainable framework for deliberative democracy. Some difficulties stem from the usual predicaments any project about democracy faces, such as existing power relations and inequalities in various forms; others are generated by ambiguities in deliberative theory itself.

Development of the idea of deliberation as a practical programme requires, in the first instance, further investigation of the increasingly diverse nature of modern societies. This is particularly true for those societies sharply divided on religious, ethnic and cultural lines. The issue is how to establish a properly functioning deliberative environment when those divisions represent a fundamental barrier to resolving differences over controversial issues.

Deliberative theory presupposes that in order to guarantee proper rules of engagement during deliberation, basic individual rights – freedom of expression, freedom of religious practice – have been established as governing normative principles. This is so not only for the deliberative process itself but also for the society at large. An established liberal culture is a prerequisite for the success of deliberative practice. Yet if deliberation requires a well-established, mature liberal culture, deliberative theory offers little to improve the conditions of those societies divided and trapped in a cycle of non-democratic rule. The first question for deliberative theory is whether it has a place in such societies at all. If the answer to this question is yes, the theory needs revisit its major assumptions in this context.

For example, insufficient attention paid to the internal differences of deliberative theories and the tension this insufficiency creates in the design of a deliberative framework. The internal difference question can be associated with the different phases of deliberation as decision-making and social learning. Deliberation is generally treated as a decision-making procedure. This inclination overlooks another important phase of deliberation. It is oriented to social learning and understanding rather than decision-making. An aim of this book is to explore and advocate the importance of recognising the social learning phase of deliberation and to argue that for development of democratic governance in divided societies, social learning is as important as decision-making.

The first task of this study is to establish the differences between social learning and decision-making stages of deliberation. Social learning needs to be acknowledged in its own terms, with its own claims, in order to free its deliberative potential from the terms of decision-making. This analysis forms the basis of a comparison of the theories of Habermas and Rawls. A dialogical account of deliberation is essential to appreciate the concept of social learning. A monological account of deliberation, as in Rawls, does not grasp the different dimensions of deliberation sufficiently because it neglects the fact that individual preferences could only be formed in relation to the preferences of others. Hence a monologic account of deliberation fails to conceive deliberation as a continuing learning process. Habermas's theory of communicative action, by contrast, provides important insights into the social learning aspect of deliberation. Despite his emphasis on social learning, Habermas, nevertheless, does not sufficiently elaborate its role in deliberative practice. Instead he subordinates the social learning dimension of deliberation to an analysis of the formal role that decision-making procedures play in institutional settings. This shortcoming largely derives from his requirement of strict rationality in deliberative settings. This consideration of social learning also embraces the work of other theorists such as Gadamer, McCarthy, Benhabib, Young and Dryzek.

The questions under study in this book are vividly illustrated in Turkish politics. In Turkish politics there is a relentless contest between secular and Islamic ideas. Chapter 3 provides a background to the existing conditions in the Turkish political sphere where secular and Islamic ideas are contested relentlessly. Turkey is one of those societies where ethical, religious and cultural divisions cut deep. It is one of the very rare examples in the Islamic world where Islam successfully coexists with a secular system.

In Turkey, a country of diverse social fabric, Islam sits in the background of the secular regime established by Mustafa Kemal Atatürk in 1923. In this regime the paradigms of the Qur'an have no visible influence in the conduct of public affairs. Kemal's dramatic steps towards secularisation transformed the circumstances in which religion and politics interact in Turkey. Having lost its dominant position, for the first time, Islam had to play a defensive role against an unfriendly state. This required a different type of interaction between Islamic and Kemalist secular forces of the society, changing continuously according to the social and political circumstances of the time.

It is the dynamics of this interaction that makes Turkey a unique case study of the different ways in which deliberative processes can function. The divisions between secular and Islamic lines in Turkey have become increasingly antagonistic following the rise of the Islamic Refah Partisi (RP) – Welfare Party, into the ranks of government during the 1990s. Tensions between the army and the RP leadership led to the resignation of the RP from the government in 1998. Instead of a decline, however, Islamic politics made a strong comeback in the 2002 general elections following formation of a new party, Adalet ve Kalkınma Partisi (AKP) – Justice and Development Party, founded by a group of elite RP members disenchanted with the orthodox Islamic politics of the RP.

The AKP owes its electoral success to a paradigm shift towards a democratic rights discourse in Islamic politics. This shift, apart from its fundamental effects on democratic development in Turkey, testifies to the importance of social learning in divided societies. A healthy dialogue oriented to social learning and mutual understanding between Islamic and secular forces within the Turkish public sphere could enhance the possibility that an adequate framework for reconciling differences can be established. Chapter 2 will start with a preliminary discussion about the relationship of Islam and democracy. It will include some thoughts on how a Habermasian framework might offer a remedy for reconciling the principles of a democratic polity with some Islamic concepts and will conclude with an outline of the evolution of Islam's relationship with the Turkish secular state.

Chapter 4 provides a background for a Q study conducted in Turkey prior to the 2002 general elections to analyse the discourses of the Turkish public sphere. Developed by William Stephenson from the 1930s, Q methodology is a useful tool to map out a typology of different perspectives pertinent to the area of research deriving from its focus on systematic examination of personal experiences. Through this typology it becomes possible to examine the relationship between different perspectives, and thus to identify the points of convergence and/or divergence among them.

This is the main reason that Q methodology has been chosen to analyse the varying relations between the perspectives of the Turkish public sphere. The aim of the Q study was to determine the kinds of discourses about democracy, Islam and secularism in the Turkish public sphere and then identify how they converged and/ or diverged from each other. The critical moments of convergence and divergence on how each discourse perceives and identifies a problem reveals important clues that can lead to development of a new framework in which differences can be reconciled. This framework will then be used to map possible ways of developing an understanding between discourses.

Chapter 5 presents the findings of the Q study in Turkey. After factor analysis, the Q study indicated the existence of four main discourses present in the Turkish public sphere: Kemalist Discourse, Nationalist Discourse, Liberal Left Discourse and Islamic Discourse. The chapter analyses the findings about each discourse by examining the meaning of each statement for each discourse. Before interpreting statements, background of each discourse relevant to the findings of the Q study is explained. This is a historical account aiming at tracing the roots and evolution of each discourse in the Turkish public sphere in order to display the complexity of the relationship between discourses. The link between past and present of each discourse is explained in this section. Combining the historical origins of each discourse with their present position in relation to the topic at hand provides important insights as to why social learning and understanding aspects of deliberation are crucial to relating each group to the common ground to which they belong. Discovery of potential moments of reconciliation is closely tied to development of a healthy dialogue between opposing sides. The competitive disposition that decision-making procedures prompts between conflicting groups does not usually allow development of the kind of dialogue that is necessary for establishing trust and/or empathy. Historical origins of each discourse testify to the fact that there are, indeed, more commonalities between secular and Islamic discourses of Turkey than is usually thought.

The Q study findings provide important clues about why in a divided society such as Turkey, deliberation oriented to social learning and understanding could play a vital role. The findings show that divisions between secular and Islamic discourses in Turkey are not necessarily insurmountable. Even so, achieving an understanding of commonalities between discourses requires an emphasis on implementation of the right deliberative framework – deliberation oriented to social learning and understanding. Analysis of the findings demonstrates why divisions of the Turkish public sphere can be better reconciled within the social learning dimension of deliberation rather than processes oriented to decision-making.

Chapter 6 analyses each discourse from a different perspective. This time similarities and differences between discourses will be looked at in comparison to their attitudes towards some themes that commonly appeared in the statements such as dialogue for mutual understanding, the scarf, Kemalism and secularism, the state and the army, the media, democracy and Islam. Through this topic-based analysis, points of convergence and divergence from one discourse to another can be further clarified.

Chapter 7 elaborates on the prospects of democratic development in Turkey on the basis of an important finding of the Q study. As revealed in Chapter 4, the Q findings detect some similarities between liberal left and some Islamic groups. These two groups show signs of converging in conceptualisation of a democratic order based on the protection of individual rights. The basis of this proximity between Islamic and liberal left groups is a paradigm shift that occurred first within the left and then among Islamic groups. In the period after the 1980 coup, some sections of the left, trying to recover from the relentless onslaught of the army, switched from their traditional class-based politics to a new paradigm based on acknowledgement of basic individual rights. A similar shift occurred in the late 1990s within the ranks of Islamic politics, ironically again caused by the army. In 1998, following an ultimatum by the army indicating that the political manifestation of Islam reached an intolerable level of threat to the secular system, some groups within mainstream Islamic politics decided not to use Islam as the basis of their political discourse. Instead, they redefined the vision of their politics on the basis of individual rights, as in the case of liberal left groups. The paradigm shift by both groups represented a vital turning point for the future of democratic politics in Turkey. The fact that two different sections of Turkish society, traditionally hostile to one another, are now able to develop a similar view of democratic politics is of fundamental importance for the future forms of democracy in Turkey. The reflections of this move in the public sphere, in the form of broad alliances, are not yet commonplace. The genesis of an alliance between these groups is, nevertheless, already at work. Therefore the purpose of Chapter 7 is to analyse this crucial development within the ranks of the left and Islamic politics. An historical account on how the concept of individual rights has evolved in both Islamic and leftist ranks is tested in the case of Barış İçin Sürekli Kadın

Platformu (BSKP) – Women's Platform for Peace, an anti-war alliance formed with the participation of a very diverse political and cultural representation of groups, ranging from Muslim women and Kemalists to leftists and homosexuals. The case of the BSKP provides a real life experience of how the social learning aspect of deliberation can bring about a better understanding between conflicting perspectives by establishing trust and enhancing general acceptance of democratic principles.

Chapter 8 returns to the principal theoretical theme of the book. It first evaluates social learning one more time in the light of Seyla Benhabib's *The Claims of Culture* (2002). A preliminary framework, the Binary Deliberation Model, is then introduced to argue for an alternative way of institutionalising social learning. It investigates how social learning can be linked to formal decision-making procedures in a collaborative and productive way.

# Chapter 2
# Deliberation as Social Learning

## Social Learning versus Decision-making

Deliberation, in the theories of deliberative democracy, is often treated as part of a formal decision-making process. This approach fails to appreciate the full benefits of the deliberative process. It fails to see that deliberation also runs as an opinion-formation process oriented to learning. This differs substantially from the decision-making process in terms of its structural and cognitive elements.

The scope of deliberation covers a vast range of human activity, yet its primary carrier, in an operational sense, is the cognitive activities of individuals, searching for a sense of consistency in their dealings with the issues at hand. Consistency is the logical link between positions individuals develop during deliberation and the cognitive skills they choose to evaluate these positions. In this sense participants apply different logic, hence cognitive skills, to the different stages of deliberation, which in terms of their aim and their orientation can be conceptualised in two distinct categories: social learning and decision-making.

Social learning is the first stage that individuals engage within a genuinely deliberative environment. The aim of interaction between participants is to develop an understanding of each other's claims. In other words, the purpose of deliberation becomes one of evaluation of other perspectives. The orientation towards learning and understanding indicates that social learning processes operate at a distinctively different dimension in terms of their logic as well as institutional design.

The main skill that participants apply to the process at this stage is cognitive objectivity. Participants put themselves into each other's shoes in order to look at the various claims on the agenda from an objective perspective. Hence, interpretation of differences becomes the focus of the deliberative practice and reaching agreement does not assume a priority during deliberation. The lack of pressure to make a decision also bestows a different set of spatial and temporal properties upon social learning. Most importantly, deliberation does not operate under formal time and space constraints as in most decision-making oriented procedures. This paves the way for a more inclusive and more informal deliberative framework in which differences can be expressed in a variety of more satisfactory ways. The social learning phase of deliberation, therefore, is primarily a hermeneutic practice. It fits well into Gadamer's notion of 'the fusion of horizons', in which the traditional and the new converge to form a new perspective on the issue at hand (Gadamer 1989). In the fusion of horizons, nobody is fully detached from their subjective views, but then arrive at a new juncture through learning without specifically striving for a rational agreement. Since it is oriented to broaden the scope of understanding, both the flow of information and the impact of deliberation make a horizontal move among participants.

If participants are not, however, seeking a decision, what is the merit of discussion? Theorists of deliberative democracy give various answers to this question. Warnke maintains that, 'in the first place, we come to understand perspectives other than our own; in the second place, we often learn from them' (2001: 313). Fearon (1998) echoes Warnke's succinct summary of the benefits of discussion. He highlights several reasons why deliberation, even only for the sake of exchanging ideas, has a value. Fearon's argument does not deal directly with the social learning aspect of deliberation, but nonetheless reinforces the idea that, when deliberation works with an orientation to learning, it could 'improve the likely implementation of the decision'. Fearon also argues that the quality of discussion helps to gain the legitimacy of final decision in the eyes of the group, thereby contributing to group solidarity. In a similar vein, Bohman (1998) maintains that unrestricted public discussion increases the democratic quality of the decisions because it takes into account all existing positions.

Fennema and Maussen (2000) also underline the importance of public discussion 'as more dispersed and less institutionalised forms of public debate' distinct from the regulated arena of public deliberation that is linked to decision-making. They conceive public discussion as a learning process and contend that public discussion should be as unrestricted as possible so that different positions become visible in the public eye. Fennema and Maussen suggest that this broad inclusiveness could not only contribute to the overall quality of decisions in the long run, but could also counter some arguments against deliberation on the basis that it favours the articulate (Mansbridge 1980, Fraser 1992, Sanders 1997). Deveaux (2003) also reflects on the benefits of locating the source of democratic legitimacy outside formal political deliberation. For Deveaux, the informal dimension of deliberation reflected in 'acts of cultural dissent, subversion, and reinvention in a range of social settings' is an important part of democratic activity since democratic legitimacy cannot be exhausted by formal political processes alone.

For development of democratic governance in multicultural settings the social learning phase of deliberation is particularly important both in terms of its intrinsic qualities and as a prerequisite to effective decision-making. It is relatively difficult for different groups in a divided society to converge on common ground successfully without prior attention to the social learning phase. Groups can develop an understanding of each other without being pressed to reach agreement. When ethical and cultural differences are considered without the immediate pressure of decision-making during the social learning phase, the unique qualities of deliberation can then flourish freely and potentially enhance the outcome of any later decision-making procedure. An example of this will be presented in the case study on Women's Platform for Peace in Turkey in Chapter 7.

In contrast to social learning, deliberation as decision-making aims at a specific decision. This is usually a formal process oriented to making decisions under some limited time and space conditions. At the end of the process participants are forced to make a decision through voting, consensus, or some other kind of agreement. The main difference between social learning and decision-making, then, is their orientation to understanding and agreement respectively. An important consequence of decision-making procedures is that the urgency of reaching a decision overwhelms opinion-formation and prevents a broadening of learning. A highly precious element of deliberation, time, is characteristically limited in decision-making procedures, thus limiting the sharing of information. In this sense, the hermeneutic function of social learning ceases its operation and retreats to the background since deliberation moves into a different stage. With this, the logic and the internal dynamics of deliberation also change. The flow of information follows a vertical pattern towards achievement of a final outcome in contrast to horizontal movement in social learning. This shift in the way deliberation functions results in subordination of understanding and learning under the pressure of reaching agreement.

Probably the most important consequence of the shift from social learning to reaching agreement (or from understanding to decision-making) occurs at the level of personal engagement between participants. Orientation towards decision-making undermines the role of cooperative interaction by triggering an inclination towards protecting the existing configuration of interests, thus leading to a strategic power struggle among participants. Dryzek (2005), for instance, argues that decision-making processes might exacerbate the possibility that deliberation could turn to an identity contest, if decision-making is linked to sovereignty challenge. The case study on Women's Platform for Peace in Turkey in Chapter 7 is a good example of Dryzek's assertion. The contest between Kemalist and Islamic women led to an immediate breakdown even before the decision-making phase of communication. A focus on identities, therefore, rather than constructive engagement would surely have a detrimental impact on the quality of the deliberation. Fung (2003), on the other hand, raises the point that in decision-making oriented procedures, participants only take deliberation seriously if they believe it will have influence. In this sense, decision-making oriented procedures encourage strategic calculations rather than learning.

The strategic use of deliberation within decision-making processes is also highlighted by Sunstein (2002). He argues that under the pressures of decision-making, members of a deliberating group could polarise their pre deliberation tendencies towards a more extreme point instead of moving towards agreement. He points to research that the more participants attend to deliberation as a like-minded group emphasising their group identity, the less chance there will be that their original position will be moderated by deliberation. When this occurs there is clearly less chance that deliberation could display the kind of interaction favoured by an attitude towards understanding. This point also indicates that the more members of a group are subject to peer pressure and group expectations, the less they interact with an attitude towards understanding others. As Mackie (2006) observes, people, acting as part of an interest group, rarely admit to changing their minds during a deliberative practice, but admitting becomes relatively easy in a subsequent forum with different participants.

Sunstein, on the other hand, observes that his findings are at odds with Fishkin's Deliberative Opinion Polling (DOP) conducted in several countries (Fishkin 1995). DOP, in which small groups of participants from different backgrounds are asked to deliberate about various issues, has found no systematic tendency toward polarisation, even though it was identifiable in some cases. After analysing the differences between his cases and the DOP's, Sunstein concludes that the difference stems from the institutional design of the deliberative procedures. In DOP cases, a large pool of information, including participants from various backgrounds, were available. The most important, though, is that there was no pressure for decision-making at the end of deliberation. Those factors, according to Sunstein, have considerably reduced the possibility of group polarisation in DOP cases.

**Establishing Dialogic Necessity**

The deliberative framework based on the distinction of different phases of deliberation, as discussed above, envisages that the members of collective bodies develop an understanding of their differences on the issues common to them. Defining social learning as perspective taking immediately highlights the intersubjective nature of deliberation – individuals learn how to tackle the fragmented nature of the social world in reciprocal relations with others.

This reciprocal relationship invokes a certain mode of interaction in which participants accept that their action carries a dialogic substance. When they sincerely attempt to understand each other they operate on an intersubjective basis. The dialogic action of participants dealing particularly with deep divisions is crucial for societies such as Turkey where secular and Islamic claims are contested relentlessly on a daily basis. Analysing this action mode, therefore, is important in order to highlight the dynamics of deliberation oriented to social learning. As Elster (1998) asserts, the idea of deliberative democracy simply rests on argumentation, not only because it proceeds by argument, but also because it can only be justified by argumentation. Thus, any theory which puts deliberation at the centre of its framework logically needs to establish its foundation through an analysis of argumentative speech.

Habermas's theory of communicative action is, in this sense, ground breaking. It specifically focuses on the intersubjective nature of human communication, which can then be used to derive conclusions for a democratic polity. Establishing deliberation as a dialogical process helps Habermas to construct his framework on the basis of presuppositions of dialogue, which he inherently links to human speech. The framework that Habermas draws provides important insights on the social learning aspect of deliberation, more specifically on the kind of role that social learning plays in human communication. The analysis of the dialogic conditions of deliberation is also important to distinguish it from other deliberative frameworks which are monologically constructed. In the next section, based on a critique of the Rawlsian framework, I shall argue that any democratic theory that does not appreciate the dialogic character of deliberation fails to appreciate the social learning capacity of deliberation. It is, thus, essential that an understanding of the difference between a dialogic and monologic account be established.

In his ground breaking *The Theory of Communicative Action*, Habermas (1987) investigates construction of a common social world through analysis of different stages of socialisation. Drawing from Mead's theory of socialisation, Habermas argues that the fundamental ideas of morality, such as equality of respect and common good, are digested into the moral consciousness of individuals through a social learning process achieved through each individual's dialogue with others. Habermas's emphasis on the intersubjective and dialogic conditions of moral development provides a resourceful basis for the social learning capacity of deliberative processes. For instance, the Q study results, to be discussed in detail in Chapter 5, highlight some important commonalities between secular and Islamic discourses in Turkey. These commonalities, however, remain unknown to all parties until a communication process oriented to learning is established. The fact that development of moral consciousness goes hand in hand with recognition of other world views; that in order to reach this stage it is necessary to look at the world from others' points of view; and all this constitutes a constructive learning process, paves the way to formulation of a framework in which the social learning aspect of deliberation could be rescued from its neglected position. Failing to do so results, one way or another, in a monological account of deliberation, as in Rawls, whose Kantian model of individuals is capable of making rational decisions in their solitude. A critique of Rawls, therefore, is important not only for distinguishing a dialogic account of deliberation from a monologic one, but also for showing why establishing deliberation as social learning as an analytic category is essential.

## Why a Monological Account of Deliberative Democracy is Insufficient: Rawls

The importance of Habermas's emphasis on the dialogic conditions of moral development stems from the fact that his move represents a shift from a subject-oriented to an intersubjective paradigm, advocating the communicative action of individuals as the main premise for testing the legitimacy of rules. The engagement between Rawls and Habermas shows the importance of this paradigm shift. My intention here, though, is not to provide a full analysis of Rawls's theory. It is to underline briefly the benefits of deliberation as social learning by showing why a monological account of deliberation is insufficient to capture the full meaning of the deliberative process. Rawls's treatment of the subject, which hardly moves away from Kant's transcendental interpretation, plays an important role in explaining why a monological account restricts itself by the rules of decision-making procedure. It is not capable of expanding the scope of deliberation to the sphere of social learning.

The role of the subject is central because its characteristics determine the nature of the deliberative process. If the subject is not captured within its continuously evolving interactive environment with others, that is, that individuals come upon themselves in an ever-expanding fashion in their communicative interaction with others; that the identity of individuals could only be formed in relation to other identities and in this sense it is a continuing learning and justification process, then it is less likely that the deliberation will be conceived as a learning process. Rawls's subjects, in this sense, are fully matured in that they have the ability of being both reasonable and rational, while empowered with a capacity for a sense of justice and a conception of the good (Rawls 1993). Their interaction with the outside world occurs usually in an experimental manner. They come upon themselves mainly through mediation of objects around them. In this sense, their reciprocal relationship is driven by 'the idea of mutual advantage understood as everyone's being advantaged with respect to each person's present or expected future situation as things are' (1993: 16-17).

The function of reciprocity in Rawls's account is a pragmatic task to understand other's position and to choose the best alternative to serve individual advantage (1993: 49-42). Rawls ties this pragmatism mainly to what he perceives as 'the practical impossibility of reaching agreement on the truth of comprehensive doctrines' (1993: 63). Hence, Rawls's individuals in deliberation hardly move away from their existing frame of reference. Deliberation in this sense is a matter of mainly checking the compatibility of others' views with their's, and accepting them in an overlapping fashion if they are suitable. In this framework, Rawls leaves little room for the moral development of the individual's ego. His reference to the social learning aspect of deliberation is limited to a monological learning process as the accumulation of knowledge about the practical world.

Rawls makes an attempt to capture the dialogic significance of moral development. Ironically he uses, as also does Habermas, Piaget and Kohlberg. In the light of Piaget's work, he maintains that acquiring a moral point of view 'rests upon the development of intellectual skills required to regard things from a variety of points of view and to think of these together as aspects of one system of cooperation' (1973: 468). It is true that for Piaget, as Rawls conceives, the essence of moral development is to acquire the multiplicity of world views available within the social context to which individuals belong. Equally important for Piaget is acceptance of this process as an ever-evolving cognitive development; as he asserts, 'every reciprocal action between individual subjects mutually modifies them. Every social relation is thus a totality in itself which creates new properties while transforming the individual in his mental structure' (quoted in Habermas 1984: 69). In this sense, cognitive development is not only the understanding and construction of an external world, but also decentring ego through its reflective conceptualisation of the social world by discursively negotiating moral norms. Thus, only through an intersubjectively structured justification of norms can ego evolve to be an autonomous identity. However, Rawls grasps Piaget's work only from his pragmatic angle as 'the art of perceiving the person of others, that is, the art of discerning their beliefs, intentions and feelings' (1973: 469). He fails again to appreciate fully the dialogic role of learning.

Rawls's analysis could satisfy the requirements of decision-making oriented deliberative practices in which subjects aim to choose the best option available among alternatives. It is, however, inadequate from the point of social learning. In order for a person to define themselves oin relation to others, the intersubjective core of a socially produced self requires not only understanding others but also internalising their perspectives, including their comprehensive doctrines. Habermas elaborates this moment lucidly:

> Under the pragmatic presuppositions of an inclusive and noncoercive rational discourse among free and equal participants, everyone is required to take the perspective of every one else, and thus project herself into the undertakings of self and world of all others; from this interlocking of perspectives there emerges an ideally extended we-perspective from which all can test in common whether they wish to make a controversial norm the basis of their shared practice (1995b: 117).

The source of the problem for Rawls is that his framework is constructed on the basis of a Hobbesian distrust, which conceives individuals as 'warring factions', rather than capable of acting cooperatively towards a mutual understanding. That is why he aims to construct a platform that 'excludes the knowledge of contingencies which sets men at odds and allows them to be guided by their prejudices' can be excluded (1973: 19). Yet it is precisely this mistrust that renders his theory as a monological one based on a contract, the rules of which are pre-established before any argument takes place between the concerned parties. He maintains 'the aim of the contract approach is to establish that taken together they impose significant bounds on acceptable principles of justice' (1973: 18).

In order to achieve this, Rawls formulates the idea of 'the veil of ignorance'. This blocks out participants' knowledge about their existing social conditions, their role and place within the social system, as well as their specific goals, desires and interests to ensure that these contingencies do not interfere with the process of decision-making. With the veil of ignorance Rawls believes that:

> [S]ince the differences among the parties are unknown to them, and everyone equally rational and similarly situated, each is convinced by the same arguments. Therefore we can view the choice in the original position from the standpoint of one person selected at random (1973: 139).

The whole purpose of this exercise for Rawls is that people arrive at a consensus under a fair and impartial framework: 'no one knows his situation in society nor his natural assets, and therefore no one is in a position to tailor principles to his advantage' (1973: 139). Yet the very nature of this framework leads to a certain kind of consensus where ideas overlap (overlapping consensus) without necessarily going through a justification process since, in the original position, participants are not given the opportunity to evaluate the differences between themselves and then reach a consensus.

Habermas points to this logical flaw in Rawls's framework. Habermas argues that the constraints through which the original position is designed limits participants as moral persons 'who possess a sense of justice and the capacity for their own conception of the good, as well as an interest in cultivating these dispositions in a rational manner'(1995b: 112). On the other hand, according to the idea of overlapping consensus, the same participants are supposed to understand 'the highest-order interests' such as all citizens are free and equal as well as reasonable and rational, in order to realise social unity. Therefore, the participants find themselves in a peculiar dilemma in which they 'are supposed both to understand and to take seriously the implications and consequences of an autonomy that they themselves are denied' (1995b: 112).

The crucial point is that the way Rawls justifies his deliberative framework overlooks the social learning aspect of deliberation simply because he ignores the dialogic unity of social learning and decision-making in favour of a strict decision-making regime among the formal bodies of 'public reason' such as parliamentary debates, judicial decisions, elections, administrative acts and pronouncements. With this, Rawls undermines the actual potential of informal deliberative practices oriented to understanding and social learning more than decision-making. Rawls's public reason, therefore, is deprived of the benefits of a more reflexive and discursive deliberative practice, which continuously reconstructs itself through an open-ended, continuing communication process. Habermas warns that even though Rawls intends to establish an intersubjectively applied procedure through his original position, the potential gains of his attempt are scattered because of the constraints he sets on the amount of information participants can exchange. Thus his attempt remains inadequate since he imposes 'a common perspective on the parties in the original position through informational constraints and thereby neutralizes the multiplicity of particular interpretive perspectives from the outset' (1995b: 117). Imposing a perspective in a rather monological fashion could also jeopardise the impartiality of judgment for they do not 'withstand revision in light of morally significant future experiences and learning processes' (1995b: 118).

Habermas's emphasis on the importance of learning process leads back to the main point of the argument that the social learning aspect of deliberation is a corollary to a dialogically formulated deliberative framework. Rawls's individuals are not adequately equipped to conceive deliberation as a learning process since their autonomy is monologically constructed, that is, it does not grow from intersubjective relationship with others. Even in the midst of collective action with others, what motivates Rawls's individuals is mainly choosing the best alternative to their advantage. What goes down with this is the fact that deliberation is an intersubjectively structured, dialogic act in which the autonomy of individuals is shaped through a continuously evolving mutual understanding and learning process between parties. Failure to capture this moment results also in failure to distinguish the fundamental distinction between social learning and decision-making aspects of deliberation. Unfortunately, such a failure does not bring much good news to divided societies. In the case of Turkey, for instance, it is hard to envisage seculars and Islamists coming to terms about their differences under a Rawlsian framework. The Rawlsian veil might work under certain circumstances where issues only with a practical focus and without direct reference to foundational views are discussed between seculars and Islamists. Yet the real challenge appears when the issues at stake are somehow related to their doctrinal foundations. As will be shown later, this is well exemplified in the saga over the headscarf. Hiding the normative attachments of headscarf behind a Rawlsian veil to foster agreement would not produce a positive outcome simply because people would find endorsing a concept in the public domain hard if they reject the same concept in their private lives. The only possibility that remains is to render conditions under which learning and understanding of differing claims are given priority without restricting expression of views.

## Habermas and the Presuppositions of Speech

The critique of Rawls's monological account has shown that a proper appreciation of deliberation requires a clear analysis of the type of action that individuals enter during their dialogue. The importance of this analysis stems both from the need for a better understanding of the whole process in terms of its inner dynamics, and from the fact that the integrity of any deliberative framework is dependent upon an explanation about what makes the actual procedure a legitimate one. In this sense, Rawls was mistaken in choosing monologically-imposed devices to explain the legitimacy of a dialogic practice; a kind of methodological mishap.

Habermas, by contrast, grounds his whole argument in a paradigm shift from subjective independent reasoning to intersubjective dialogue by situating the burden of judgment within the actual communication process. In this framework, the legitimacy of the deliberative procedure depends entirely on an individual's dialogic action. In order to do this Habermas had to prove that the communicative action of individuals carries a normative content, which in turn ensures the legitimacy of the process. Habermas finds the point of appraisal in the presuppositions of human speech.

> A communicatively achieved agreement has a rational basis; it cannot be imposed by either party, whether instrumentally through intervention in the situation directly or strategically through influencing the decisions of opponents. Agreement can indeed be objectively obtained by force; but what comes to pass manifestly through outside influence or the use of violence cannot count subjectively as agreement. Agreement rests on common *convictions* [emphasis in original] (1984: 287).

Habermas posits two main points. Firstly, communication is the main medium to establish coordination of social activity. Secondly, communication aimed at coming to agreement has to satisfy a certain level of rationality which is already embedded within the structures of language. Indeed, without referring to a model of speech, Habermas asserts, the process of understanding remains unresolved. Thus, he adds, understanding can be fully appreciated 'only if we specify what it means to use sentences with a communicative intent' (1984: 287).

It is through this communicative intent that language assumes the role of coordinating the actions of individuals. Habermas argues that the structure of language is in fact oriented to reaching understanding, which is mutually presupposed by participants in their dialogue. In other words, when individuals come together with a communicative intent their action is driven by some pragmatic rules of language. Habermas calls these rules 'universal pragmatics' and asserts that they are unavoidable as long as the focus of communication is maintained towards reaching a shared agreement. If a person wants to participate in a dialogue with a sincere intention of reaching agreement, that person cannot avoid raising some validity claims corresponding to different speech acts. So, when they claim that whatever they want to communicate has a true content, their speech corresponds to constative speech acts (verbs such as assert, describe). Meanwhile, they claim that their speech is right with respect to prevailing norms and values, corresponding to regulative speech acts (verbs such as order, prohibit). They also would want to express themselves truthfully so that others can trust them by referring to their intentions and feelings, which correspond to representative speech acts (such as admit, conceal). And, finally, their speech should claim that whatever they raise is intelligible, that is, comprehensible to others. Those four claims to different validities (truth, rightness, truthfulness and comprehensibility) and corresponding categories of speech acts constitute the basis for the pragmatic presuppositions of an argumentative speech driven by a rational discourse. The most important of these presuppositions are, according to Habermas:

a.  Publicity and inclusiveness: No one who could make a relevant contribution with regard to a controversial validity claim must be excluded;
b.  Equal rights to engage in communication: Everyone must have the same opportunity to speak to the matter at hand;
c.  Exclusion of deception and illusion: participants have to mean what they say; and
d.  Absence of coercion: communication must be free of restrictions that prevent the better argument from being raised or from determining the outcome of the discussion (in Rehg and Bohman 2001b: 34).

This is surely an idealised form of communication (counterfactual in Habermas's term), which could only occur 'if and only if, for all possible participants, there is a symmetrical distribution of chances to choose and apply speech-acts' (quoted in Thompson and Held 1982: 123). At the same time, however, they are unavoidable since 'someone who seriously takes part in an argument de facto proceeds from such presuppositions' (2001b: 35). What is important in this formulation is that participants envisage argumentation as free from repression and inequalities if they are sincere in their attempt to reconcile their differences. Since agreement only arises as a common conviction it presupposes the voluntary and equal participation of subjects. In other words, the premise for a communicatively achieved agreement is the acceptance of its legitimacy by the participants. Therefore, whoever wants to engage in discourse with a serious intention makes some normative presuppositions which regulate action towards the creation of legitimate outcomes. In this sense, deliberative procedures can operate on the basis of internal rules that are implicit in the structure of language. The qualities of the procedure, then, can be determined by the internal dynamics of the process itself without resorting to an epistemic criterion outside the procedure. Thus, as opposed to the constraints Rawls suggests, Habermas relies on the procedure itself to ensure a legitimate outcome.

With this, Habermas's framework lays the ground for developing a deliberative environment oriented to learning and understanding, that is, the process of understanding could indeed be as legitimate as a decision-making process since both ultimately rely on the same premise – the rules of argumentative speech. Deliberation in either form can produce fair results in the eyes of participants as long as they act sincerely. This is particularly important for groups feeling marginalised such as Muslims living in secular societies. As I will discuss in the next chapter, Habermas' intersubjective framework can offer a trustworthy option for the members of Muslim communities to engage dialogically with secular-minded or non-Muslim people.

However, despite this important opening in his theory, Habermas shifts his attention to the formal bodies of deliberation such as parliament, administrative bodies and the legal system particularly in his later work. He does this by developing a two-track model in which he assigns a division of work between opinion formations within the public sphere and will formation within formal bodies of decision-making (1996). Within this framework, while the broad, encompassing activities of the public sphere become home for social learning oriented practices operating within 'an open and inclusive network of overlapping, subcultural publics' (1996: 307), the formal bodies of deliberation as the sphere of 'democratically institutionalized will-formation' represents the institutional base for decision-making.

One of the implicit motives driving Habermas's two-track model is his commitment to the link between the purpose and the rational properties of deliberation. As I will discuss in detail later in the section on Gadamer, what concerns Habermas is that if the presupposition of reaching consensus were dropped from dialogue, then the deliberative process would lose its rational sense and become something else other than rational argumentation. In this sense, he conceives rational argumentation as the main alternative against coercion and manipulation. Therefore, the forms of rational argumentation protected within the formal deliberative institutions are essential for maintaining a non-fragile democratic polity. The result is decoupling opinion formation from decisions, where the core of decision-making power is delegated to formal deliberative bodies. With this, the role of citizens, who are supposed to be 'the authors of the law', is limited to acting as a sensory device only, since 'civil society can directly transform only itself, and it can have at most an indirect effect on the self-transformation of the political system' (1996: 372). His statement, 'discourses do not govern' (1992: 452), demonstrates clearly what concerns him. They can surely influence the administration 'in a siege-like manner', yet 'communicative power cannot supply a substitute for the systematic inner logic of public bureaucracies' (1992: 452). To put it more succinctly:

> Social movements, citizen initiatives and forums, political and other associations, in short, the groupings of civil society, are indeed sensitive to problems, but the signals they send out and the impulses they give are generally too weak to initiate learning processes or redirect decision-making in the political system in the short run (1996: 373).

'The authors of the law', then, hope to influence decision-making processes through some indirect means such as elections and the media. Hence Habermas shifts his attention to formal procedures within the administrative bodies where a practice of rational debate is assumed as the rule. With this move, though, Habermas leaves a vast terrain of deliberative activity unattended. The issue here is not so much whether he is still interested in the informal discursive activities in the public sphere (surely he is), but whether this shift in his orientation is sufficient to utilise the rich, but untapped sources of deliberative activity outside the formal bodies of deliberation.

This shortcoming of Habermas's theory has been brought to attention by some democratic theorists such as Thomas McCarthy, Seyla Benhabib, Iris Young and John Dryzek. They have made some inroads into the idea of less formal forms of deliberation. These theorists expand the understanding of deliberation through their emphasis on the less restricted, more inclusive, informal phases of deliberation. But their contribution is usually limited by lack of emphasis on the social learning aspect of deliberation in their methodological design. Deliberation, in this sense, is still tied to the terms of decision-making procedures, preventing a full appreciation of social learning phase of deliberative activity.

*McCarthy's Challenge to Habermas*

McCarthy was one of the first political theorists to highlight the tension in Habermas's thought caused by the strict rationality requirement in communicative settings (1978). McCarthy's critique provides some valuable conceptual tools to devise an alternative approach for differentiating between social learning and decision-making aspects of deliberative processes. McCarthy's critique focuses on Habermas's conceptualisation of rationally motivated agreement and argues that Habermas perceives rationality from a rather narrow perspective. The reason, according to McCarthy, is that Habermas ties rational agreement too strictly to his theory of communicative action, positing that practical reason always acts towards reaching a consensus in dialogue (1991). McCarthy argues that in order for Habermas's discourse ethics to serve as a realistic normative ideal for democratic theory in pluralistic societies, his emphasis on the scope of rational, moral consensus should be fine-tuned by looking at the potential disagreements in the matters of ethical concern more carefully (1998). McCarthy's argument departs from the point where Habermas identifies three analytically distinguishable discourses in decision-making procedures as pragmatic, ethical, and moral (Habermas 1995a). These discourses are all related to the question 'What should I do?' but taking a different meaning depending on the kind of problem.

Pragmatic discourses, according to Habermas, are about practical, empirical matters such as policy issues. They are oriented to reaching preestablished goals by weighing up the efficiency of various strategies. In this sense their validity is gained from the degree of their applicability. Ethical discourses, on the other hand, are related to norms and values derived from a specific life story, which take the question of 'What should I do?' from the point of 'Who I am', 'Who I want to be' and 'What kind of life I want to pursue'. In ethical discourses, reason and will condition each other reciprocally since 'justifications become rational motives for changes of attitude' (1994: 11). In moral discourses, finally, the orientation to self-understanding in ethical questions shifts to an interpersonal level where the justification and application of norms stipulating reciprocal rights and duties becomes the main motive in answering the question, 'What should I do?' In this sense, contrary to ethical discourses, moral discourses 'require a break with all of the unquestioned truths of an established, concrete ethical life, in addition to distancing oneself from the contexts of life with which one's identity is inextricably interwoven' (1994: 12). In Habermas's framework, the question of justice or rights is allocated to moral discourses since, to claim validity, they need to undergo a universal test. They are not related to a specific form of life because they try to answer the question, 'What should I do?', with reference to 'What is equally good for all?' This reference to 'all' requires that moral questions should be debated under the strict condition of universalisability.

McCarthy raises his objection at this point and argues that, owing to his strict universalisability requirement, Habermas's separation of discourses inadequately deals with the fact that discourses are part of the concrete stories of different traditions and self-perceptions. McCarthy also points out that Habermas is aware of the predicament his analysis creates. Writing about abortion, for instance, Habermas readily acknowledges that 'descriptions of the problem of abortion are always inextricably interwoven with individual self-descriptions of persons and groups, and thus with their identities and life projects. Where an internal connection of this sort exists, the question must be formulated differently, specifically, in ethical terms' (1994: 59). Yet, if this is true for abortion, it is the fact of pluralist societies that they are continuously challenged by similar types of problems. The most important societal problems causing deep divisions belong to the same category. For instance, in the case of Turkey, the division between Muslims and seculars cuts through the layers of ethical and moral disputes concurrently. As McCarthy asserts, these disputes 'could not be resolved consensually at the level at which they arose' (1998: 127). Then, it is hardly a feasible proposal that the democratic practice weighs heavily towards rational consensus trying to realise a universal justification of norms through one right answer. Hence, McCarthy argues that it is necessary 'to go beyond this either/or and try to capture the dialectical interdependence *in practice* of these *analytically* distinguishable aspects' [emphasis in original] (1998: 127). Along this line he suggests that if something has to be decided from the standpoint of justice, the scope of 'all' should be limited to the particular members of the society in question, to a particular time and place, yet should be inclusive of the whole range of interpretive and evaluative perspectives related to the topic in question. Being able to deal with persistent ethical and political differences then requires the utilisation of 'cultural resources and institutional arrangements different from those suited to domains in which there is only one right answer to every well-formulated question' (1998: 152).

The key concept for McCarthy is mutual accommodation as an alternative way of dealing with persistent ethical and political differences, operating on the basis of mutual respect and consideration of the humanity of others. Through mutual accommodation, differences can become part of a cooperative, harmonious and mutually supportive sphere of relations. This is a procedural framework in which rational acceptance does not come from 'the force of the better argument' alone, but more from the acceptance that they abide by the rules of engagement which they conceive as fair 'even when things do not go their way'. In this sense, McCarthy suggests a two-track version of justification of outcomes: direct and indirect justification. Habermas's formulation of rational consensus can apply in direct justification, that is, directly justified outcomes are accepted by all – possibility of one single answer.

On the other hand, indirectly justified outcomes 'are accepted by different parties for the same procedural reasons, but different substantive ones' (1998: 146), hence disagreements of a reasonable nature can coexist. McCarthy concludes:

> It seems best, then, to acknowledge and analyse independently a type of ethical-political dialogue aimed not at negotiated compromise, not at substantive agreement, and not at ethical-political consensus, but at forms of mutual accommodation that leave space for reasonable disagreements. We can imagine cultures that nourish the corresponding values and virtues, and practices that are predicated not on the assumption of one right answer but on respect for, and a desire to accommodate, ineliminable difference. We can imagine them because we already rely upon them in areas of our lives where it is important for us to maintain harmonious, cooperative, and mutually supportive relations with people with whom we do not always agree, whom we cannot always convince or be convinced by, and whom we do not want simply to outsmart. In multicultural democracies, they will inevitably play a larger role in political life as well (1998: 153).

With this, a sphere of dialogue based on mutual understanding, distinct from strategic use of decision-making procedures, becomes the focus of McCarthy's argument. He comes very close to suggesting a framework based on a distinction between opinion formation and the decision-making dimensions of deliberation. Yet McCarthy moves no further and stops evaluating what the independent type of ethical-political dialogue he suggests entails in terms of its analytic features. He makes the need clear for the practices of an open-ended, mutual accommodation based processes with no ultimate consensus orientation. However, he elaborates neither the dynamics nor the logic of these practices in terms of what evidently makes them different from, or how they can be related to, the practices of decision-making processes.

In fact McCarthy's scheme carries an ambiguity towards his treatment of decision-making since it leaves the fundamental question of how to make democratically legitimate decisions open. It is this ambiguity that leaves him susceptible to the kind of charge that Habermas lays. In reply to McCarthy, Habermas asserts that 'given McCarthy's premises, he cannot explain how democratic legitimacy is even possible' (1998: 395). Habermas considers that if democracy is accepted as a solution to fair decision-making, then reaching agreement ultimately becomes the apex of this practice. Habermas's insistence upon rational agreement can be seen as a methodological requirement in that, without referring to rational agreement, no theory can define fair decision-making procedure as the crux of a genuine democratic polity. That is, that the focus on decision-making and rational agreement is directly correlated and Habermas, in this sense, is consistent with his line of argument. Therefore, the dilemma does not so much stem from seeking rational agreement but more from imposing this requirement on all dimensions of deliberative practice, hence not allowing for a proper development of a different domain in which different kinds of communicative activities orient themselves more towards understanding than rational agreement.

In deliberative theory, this domain corresponds to deliberation as social learning where opinion formative, interpretive actions of participants, distinct from decision-making, become the main paradigm through which the open-ended, inclusive features of deliberation oriented to understanding free themselves from the specific rules of engagement in decision-making practices. Within this domain, the resources of social learning are allocated to where they belong in order to achieve an orientation to understanding rather than functioning in the service of decision-making procedures only. Any attempt to broaden the framework of deliberation would be bogged down unless this shift in the orientation of deliberative practice is made clear, that is, a specific argument decoupling it from the references of decision-making is developed.

*Hermeneutics Reconsidered: Gadamer's Fusion of Horizons*

A specific argument for social learning from the perspective of deliberative theory requires an elaboration of how its interpretive, hermeneutic character can actually coordinate the process of deliberation. For this, Gadamer's hermeneutics and Habermas's engagement with it offer valuable insights. Habermas acknowledges that in building his communicative model of action he has taken all the functions of language equally into account, including Gadamer's hermeneutics (1984: 95). His extensive engagement with Gadamer in the early stages of his theory was critical to establishing his framework. Particularly in more recent work, however, the role of Gadamer's hermeneutic approach has gradually retreated to the background, with no clearly specified function. In order to revitalise the role of the interpretive, as well as inclusive and open-ended characteristics of learning processes that are crucial for divided societies, Gadamer's hermeneutics needs to be revisited.

A likely outcome of applying a demanding level of rationality would be to undermine the important role that social learning could play within deliberative settings. It is normal to expect a competent level of rational attentiveness during a decision-making process, yet it could equally be limiting, as well as misleading, if this level is expected to govern deliberation oriented to social learning. This brings us back to the importance of acknowledging differences in the logic of different deliberative processes. In those settings where the initial aim is to develop an understanding of other parties, it is participants' interpretations of various life stories that play a more functional role. In their dialogic engagements, when participants seek to understand each other, they have to open themselves up in order to explain their positions and to understand what the other stories are. This does not necessitate an agreement, but an interpretive, hermeneutical sensitivity towards others, aiming at what Gadamer calls a 'fusion of horizons' (1975).

In the fusion of horizons, participants make themselves understandable to each other without relinquishing their original position, trying to find a common point rather than converting to an alternative position. Gadamer conceives understanding as 'part of the process of the coming into being of meaning' (1975: 147) in which nothing appears to be perfect rather than a continuous adaptation of different views. In their hermeneutical endeavour individuals try to situate themselves within the broader horizon of the context they are in. Their primary aim is to understand what is given to them and what constitutes the meaning and the importance of it. For that, they do not have to disregard their original hermeneutic position. They do, however, need to open themselves to the opposite claims and allow them to enter into a dialogic conversation (1975: 289). In this sense, understanding always operates with a practical aim in mind and the fusion of horizons works as a test of the claims of each horizon. It is only by this process that individuals come to an understanding of themselves and situate themselves correctly within 'one great horizon'.

> When our historical consciousness places itself within historical horizons, this does not entail passing into alien worlds unconnected in any way with our own, but together they constitute the one great horizon that moves from within and, beyond the frontiers of present, embraces the historical depths of our self-consciousness (1975: 271).

In this framework, Gadamer drops away the dichotomised relationship between understanding and misunderstanding in a way that no communication process is seen to be perfect and complete. They are, even so, inclusive of all features that are part of the identity structures of individuals. Gadamer thus introduces one of his fundamental contributions to hermeneutic theory. He asserts that prejudices are also part of individuals' identities. They are constitutive of the meaning of each horizon to the extent that they effectively shape the existing boundaries of horizons. Accordingly, he maintains that no process of understanding can be conceived properly without acknowledging the role of prejudices. In his words:

> A consciousness formed by the authentic attitude will be receptive to the origins and entirely foreign features of that which comes to it from outside its own horizons. Yet this receptivity is not acquired with an objectivist 'neutrality': it is neither possible, necessary, nor desirable that we put ourselves within brackets. The hermeneutical attitude supposes only that we self-consciously designate our opinions and prejudices and qualify them as such, and in so doing strip them of their extreme character. In keeping to this attitude we grant the text the opportunity to appear as an authentically different being and to manifest its own truth, over and against our own preconceived notions (in Rabinow and Sullivan 1979: 151-152).

What is at issue here for Gadamer is that one interprets and understands what is given from a selective perspective bound by personal social and cultural circumstances. Understanding operates under the auspices of a certain frame of reference and the gap between different reference points could only be narrowed down through the dialogic practices of a community. In this sense, the immediate interest behind hermeneutics is not to develop a critique of existing circumstances but instead coming to an understanding through dialogue about the issues of common interest. The importance of Gadamer's framework for divided societies such as Turkey will become immediately evident when the findings of the Turkish study is presented in the next coming chapters. At first instance, divisions between secular and Islamic worldviews will appear highly problematic. However, as will be seen, in the background lies a large pool of commonalities emanating from a common heritage, yet to be discovered. Interpretation of these common points requires a dialogic process oriented to understanding. Gadamer's emphasis on working on commonalities towards a fusion of horizons offers a framework in which interpretation of differences also becomes possible.

This is exactly where Habermas feels uneasy about the hermeneutic tradition. He is concerned that the lack of critical touch in the interpretive actions of participants would turn dialogue to only a simple act of speech with no immediate reference to a future direction assimilating language 'to stylistic and aesthetic forms of expression' (1984: 95). Predictably, Habermas's concern here is related to mobilising the rationality potential residing within the communicative action of individuals. He asserts 'reaching an understanding functions as a mechanism for coordinating actions only through the participants in interaction coming to an agreement' (1984: 99). In other words, if the dialogue is not oriented to reaching agreement in a way that the rational assets of communication are overlooked as in hermeneutic practice, then it would fail to capitalise on its own critical potential.

It is ironic that the resolution of Habermas's concern lies in his own theory. That is, if the universal pragmatics of speech presuppose a rational attitude towards differences among participants, then a dialogue oriented towards understanding should ultimately be able to develop a rational and critical attitude during deliberation. As he acknowledges:

> Participants, however diverse their backgrounds, can at least intuitively meet in their efforts to reach an understanding. In all languages and in every language community, such concepts as truth, rationality, justification, and consensus, even if interpreted differently and applied according to different criteria, play *the same grammatical role* [emphasis in original] (1996: 311).

This role is for the members of different cultural groups being able to take a reflexive, rational attitude toward their own cultural traditions. Habermas also asserts that under the conditions of modern societies, in which a positive law and secularised politics are achieved, even religious or metaphysical worldviews would lose their fundamentalist character, simply because they have to compete with other world views 'within the *same* universe of validity claims' [emphasis in original], assuming the presuppositions of secularised thought (1996: 551, n59). The underlying assumption here is that the rational and critical thinking is embedded within the pragmatics of daily communication to the degree that all traditions are capable of developing a self-reflective, critical discourse whereby they can distinguish between what is true and what they hold to be true as long as they subject themselves to the presuppositions of argumentative speech (Habermas 1995). Yet, if this is the case, it becomes difficult to justify Habermas's critique of Gadamer that hermeneutic interpretation is prone to lose the critical edge required for making universally valid justifications.

The difficulty does not seem so much to stem from the difference in what they say, but more from the focus of Habermas's analysis. Under Habermas's scheme, the critical potential that the hermeneutic action carries is mostly elaborated from, thus subordinated to, the conditions of formal deliberative practices. If the difference between understanding and agreement in his framework was clear enough, that is, if he distinguished the deliberative sphere of understanding oriented to social learning from the formal decision-making oriented deliberative procedures, then Gadamer's hermeneutic could have found its proper place within the informally structured practices of deliberation.

In fact, Gadamer is as close to Habermas as he can be in relation to the interaction between understanding and agreement. He, too, argues that understanding involves primarily coming to an agreement. It is a dialogically reached agreement in the sense that it involves a process which takes others' claims seriously, defines and tests them against one's own prejudices and reaches a new understanding of the issue at hand. As Warnke (1987) points out, Gadamer perceives understanding as an appropriation process through which participants reach a 'better' position by becoming able to see strands of agreement and disagreement at the end. That is why Gadamer defines hermeneutic understanding as a learning experience broadening the horizons of participants. The result of this process goes beyond the original positions of participants, reflecting a transformation to a new view and a new stage of the tradition (Warnke 1987: 104). In other words, the critical dimension that Habermas is concerned with is embedded within the conditions of dialogue between different traditions in Gadamer. Each tradition carries its own critical reflection into the dialogue. Unlike Habermas, Gadamer does not emphasise a strong orientation towards agreement; instead, he substantially relaxes the dose of rational behaviour in favour of a more informal exchange between parties.

Gadamer's framework provides an essential ingredient for the social learning point of view. His hermeneutic emphasis on the dialogic character of understanding complements the role of social learning in deliberative processes. The challenge for deliberative theory is to encompass the essentials of Gadamerian and Habermasian frameworks within the same framework. The features of Gadamer's hermeneutics serve deliberation as social learning well. Similarly, Habermas's theory, particularly in his early work, has enough room to accommodate a hermeneutic approach. The passage below testifies well to how Habermas's critical theory and hermeneutics can interact:

> For those acting in the first person singular or plural with an orientation to mutual understanding, each lifeworld constitutes a totality of meaning relations and referential connections with a zero point in the coordinate system shaped by historical time, social space and semantic field. Moreover, the different lifeworlds that collide with one another do not stand *next to each other* without any mutual understanding. As totalities, they follow the pull of their claims to universality and work out their differences until their horizons of understanding 'fuse' with one another, as Gadamer puts it [emphasis in original] (in Outhwaite 1994: 358).

As Axel Honneth (1995) explains, Habermas reaches the fundamental premise of his theory, that is, human subjects are united with one another through the medium of linguistic understanding, through a study of hermeneutic philosophy. In his later works, however, his concentration on the formal deliberative procedures oriented to decision-making impedes him from benefiting from this early insight. Thomas McCarthy (1978) has rightly pinpointed this tendency by stating that the critical theory of Habermas is becoming more formal and universal and less hermeneutical and situational.

In a similar vein, Richard Bernstein (1983, 1985) highlights the difference between Habermas and Gadamer by pointing to an inherent tension in Habermas's thought. Bernstein argues that the way Habermas structures his argument leaves only two alternatives: either universal criteria will be established as a rational basis for evaluating the plausibility of competing interpretations of different world views (horizons in Gadamer) or there will be no escape from relativism. Habermas's answer to this dilemma is to develop a communicative ethics grounded in the intersubjective structures of social production with a strong emphasis on a rational basis required for testing competing claims.

Bernstein maintains that Gadamer's hermeneutic theory avoids this dilemma because of his different emphasis on the process of understanding which shows that making comparative judgments is possible without necessarily appealing to such strong universal criteria. Bernstein in this sense perceives Habermas and Gadamer as complementary rather than competing. He claims that Gadamer's hermeneutic can be employed to obtain a better understanding of what Habermas is doing. On the other hand, Habermas provides a more comprehensive and plausible interpretation of current historical circumstances than does Gadamer.

The importance of Gadamer for my argument lies in his assertion that traditions are not self-contained and completely isolated from others. Hence, it is always possible to find different ways of surpassing the boundaries of each tradition so long as there is a sincere dialogue seeking to comprehend the claims of other traditions. What is required is no more than a deliberative environment oriented to learning in which the primary role of dialogue is hermeneutic understanding. This becomes particularly important in countries like Turkey where sharp divisions between secular and Islamic claims to the truth cut across society. The key point is that when divided traditions meet each other, their first task is to develop an understanding of one another to overcome different interpretations of the issues at hand. This is clearly a hermeneutic task which does require establishment of its own deliberative sphere freed from the pressures of decision-making procedures, open to reasonable disagreements without converging on one answer.

*Expanding the Scope of Deliberative Practice: Benhabib*

The role of hermeneutics in deliberative practices has been echoed in the theory of Seyla Benhabib. Benhabib maintains that the emphasis on rationality in democratic theory is a consequence of the universalist tendencies that appeared in moral theory as a response to the challenges of modernity. Following the dawn of modernity, Benhabib (1987) argues, moral theory underwent a differentiation process between moral and ethical issues for the defence of the autonomy of the self, leading to a differentiation between 'the generalised' and 'the concrete' other. This move was mainly motivated by the desire of the emerging bourgeoisie to find a universally applicable system of norms. This was essential in order to overcome the problems of men living under the purely egoistic conditions of 'the state of nature'. Morality was emancipated from ethical worldviews and justice alone became the centre of moral theory.

A consequence of this development was that while the issues of justice were dealt with extensively within the moral domain of the public sphere, an entire domain of human activity related to ethical self-understanding of men was confined to the limits of the private sphere and put beyond the light of justice. The generalised other, born as a result of this dichotomy, required viewing each individual as a rational being abstracted from the concrete identity of the other. Its moral dignity was constituted not by acknowledgement of differences from others, but by comprehension of what was common to all. Its interaction with others was regulated primarily by formal public and institutional rules.

Benhabib argues that only by focusing on what is common, the generalised other reflects only one side of the self and ignores paying attention to the individual needs of the others. The concrete other, then, expands the boundaries of the generalised other by dealing with each individual's personal histories constitutive of their concrete identities, including their emotional state of affairs. In contrast to the generalised other, the concrete other abstracts itself from the question of what is common and focuses on comprehending the needs of others, their motivations, desires and background stories. Within this model, procedures are geared to bridging the gap between formal and informal politics by focusing on ordinary people's everyday deliberations. In Benhabib's words:

> [T]he procedural specifications of this model privilege *a plurality of modes of association* in which all affected can have the right to articulate their point of view. These can range from political parties, to citizens' initiatives, to social movements, to voluntary associations, to consciousness-raising groups, and the like. *It is through the interlocking net of these multiple forms of associations, networks, and organizations that an anonymous 'public conversation' results. It is central to the model of deliberative democracy that it privileges such a public sphere of mutually interlocking and overlapping networks and associations of deliberation, contestation, and argumentation* … today our guiding model has to be that of a medium of loosely associated, multiple foci of opinion formation and dissemination which affect one another in free and spontaneous processes of communication [emphasis in original] (1996: 73-74).

Benhabib's formulation points to a direction where certain characteristics of deliberation as social learning become clearly visible. Deliberation is seen as a continuing process of argumentation oriented to understanding occurring at different levels of public sphere. She further qualifies her model as 'non coercive and non final processes of opinion formation in an unrestricted public sphere' (1996: 76).

It is not difficult to discern that with her differentiation of the generalised other from the concrete other, Benhabib moves towards a hermeneutic elaboration of the interaction between individuals based on mutual understanding. The universalist tendencies in contemporary moral theory, Benhabib argues, recapitulate the old Kantian dilemma by depriving noumenal selves from being properly individuated, which results in a monological model of moral reasoning. For instance, under conditions of Rawls's veil of ignorance, 'the *other as different from the self* disappears' [emphasis in original] (1987: 165) and differences become irrelevant. Instead, she argues for an interactive universalism, advocating a model of communicative need interpretation and acknowledging the dialectic unity of the generalised and the concrete other. The underlying premise for this framework is the fact that members of individual communities develop their self-consciousness in reference to the contingent life histories of others in that the discourses of need interpretations reveal a historical dimension in which the history of the self and the history of collective are intertwined.

Benhabib adds that the relationship between the generalised and the concrete other is not only confined to the past and the present since they carry a practical intent related to future. As she asserts, 'What such discourses can generate are not only universalistically prescribable norms, but also intimations of otherness in the present that can lead to the future' (1987: 169). Benhabib calls this process 'historically self-conscious universalism' in which the principles of deliberative polity, universal respect and egalitarian reciprocity are arrived 'from *within* the normative hermeneutic horizon of modernity' [emphasis in original] (1992a: 30). It would be quite normal to assume that this horizon, similar to Gadamer's, involves all presuppositions and assumptions of discourses reflecting the background stories of every community. Benhabib, however, distances herself from Gadamer's hermeneutic through a critique similar to that of Habermas. She maintains that because Gadamer does not provide a clear account of what constitutes the validity of moral judgment, his theory lacks a critical yardstick to distinguish between traditions in terms of their worthiness (1992a: 135).

Benhabib's understanding of Gadamer appears to be affected by an ambiguity in her treatment of the internal differences of deliberation as in the case of McCarthy. Benhabib certainly provides a more inclusive alternative since she clearly focuses on the importance of informal ways of deliberating within the public sphere. But she does not explain why, most of the time, the logic of these informal interactions differs from the formal ones. Instead, in her model, the process of understanding, or the hermeneutic circle, appears to be subordinated to decision-making processes, that is, she identifies the social learning aspect of deliberation within the terms of decision-making processes.

This is quite apparent in her criticism of Iris Young. Benhabib (1996) opposes Young's formal identification of different aspects of deliberation. In Benhabib's view, Young's formal inclusion of various other modes of communication, such as greeting, story telling and rhetoric, as well as rational argumentation, is both unnecessary and implausible. Benhabib maintains that these modes of communication may have their place within the informally structured daily communicative practices, yet she claims that insisting on their formal recognition results in building an undesired opposition between the modes of communication and critical argumentation. This is quite a puzzling conclusion by Benhabib in the sense that it renders her previous affirmation of an 'anonymous public conservation', based on 'free and spontaneous processes of communication', indeterminate in terms of its critical potential. The ambiguity increases even more when she states that the kinds of communicative modes that Young defends do not suit the public language of institutions and legislatures, which appeals to public reasons, consonant with the specific rhetorical structure of law (1996: 83). Benhabib clearly prefers to allocate the defining role in deliberation to the formal institutions rather than spheres of informal communication. She ties her understanding of anonymous public conversation to the terms of decision-making bodies.

This shift towards defining deliberation mainly in decision-making terms undermines Benhabib's attempt to overcome the strict universalisability requirement of discourse ethics. The main dilemma arises because a consistent way of arguing for the informal circles of deliberation requires a clear division of work between understanding and agreement oriented phases of deliberation. So long as the emphasis in deliberative processes remains within the confines of the terms of the decision-making process there seems methodologically no consistent way out of this dilemma. This is perhaps the main reason that Habermas does not change his position in relation to the role that rational agreement plays in his theory. He, therefore, manages to maintain the consistency of his argument.

The solution Benhabib offers to relax the conditions of rational agreement makes a loop and ends up being tied to the same terms again. From a social learning perspective, Benhabib surely takes the right step to relax the universalisability requirement in order to initiate 'an anonymous public conversation'. But failing to demarcate clearly what differentiates 'multiple foci of opinion formation and dissemination' from decision-making processes reduces the impact of her emphasis on 'non final processes of opinion formation'.

The way out of this dilemma is to acknowledge the different modes of communication formally and then situate the kinds of rationality within each communicative sphere they belong to. It is only through this way that the benefits of Young's 'greeting, rhetoric and storytelling', or any other informal mode of communication for that matter, can be utilised fully.

## *Outside the Boundaries of Formal Deliberation: Young*

Ironically, though, Young's attempt to broaden the boundaries of deliberation through the inclusive features of her communicative democracy falls victim to the same dilemma. In her account of deliberative democracy, Young displays a clear awareness of the role of different modes of communication in deliberative practices and tries to broaden the scope of inclusion. She states that:

> A theory of democratic inclusion requires an expanded conception of political communication, both in order to identify modes of internal inclusion and to provide an account of more inclusive possibilities of attending to one another in order to reach understanding (2000: 56).

To achieve the desired level of expansion, Young introduces three categories of greeting, rhetoric and narrative in addition to formal argument. She indicates that these additional categories are also important to counter-balance some exclusionary characteristics in formal argumentative speech. For instance, lack of competence in articulation of argument, being too emotional or passionate, or lack of orderly conduct, could result in some contributions to being excluded from serious consideration, 'not because of what is said, but how it is said' (2000: 56).

The inclusion of different possibilities of communication helps to broaden the scope of deliberative practices for two main reasons. First of all, through a more personal expression of participants' needs and desires, deliberative processes would become more context sensitive since the gap between public and private reasoning will narrow, prompting a clearer climate among participants for understanding one another's meanings and intentions, consequently fostering the conditions of social learning.

Second, it would relax the strict conditions of universality, and thus rationality, by taking into account understanding more than agreement. The move towards understanding constitutes a step into the domain of hermeneutic action, raising the possibility of demarcating a distinction between two different levels of deliberation as social learning and decision-making.

Young fails to appreciate this opportunity. Her analysis does not fully articulate those differences. Her acknowledgement of different modes of communicative styles does not show how those different styles correspond to different modes of deliberation. Instead, as in Benhabib, Young considers her alternative as a contribution to decision-making processes. Her reference to those alternative modes of communication through the decision-making processes, remains inadequate in freeing the benefits of her argument from the limits of what currently governs theories of deliberation.

Because of this problem, Young's theory becomes vulnerable to the kind of critique that Benhabib raises. Benhabib is right in the sense that under the terms of the decision-making process, it is hard to envisage a deliberative process sustaining Young's type of communicative styles. The restrictions of the decision-making process, as outlined earlier, would eventually squeeze these alternative modes of communication out of the deliberation process. This is a natural consequence of the fact that these alternative modes belong to a different deliberative sphere oriented more to the hermeneutic cycles of understanding and learning rather than decision-making. Young's attempt to broaden the scope of deliberation, therefore, remains under-developed. In order to utilise adequately the role that her alternative communication styles play the differentiation of deliberation between social learning and decision-making modes should be properly established.

*Decoupling Social Learning from Decision-Making: Dryzek*

John Dryzek (1990, 2000) has made an important contribution to deliberative theory as a social learning experience. The importance of Dryzek's framework is twofold. Firstly, he recognises the social learning aspect of deliberation as distinct from decision-making by pointing to the different ways in which the deliberative process functions. Secondly, and more importantly, he suggests that decoupling these two phases of democratic process is a viable alternative for reconciling different views particularly when tough identity issues are at stake. This is certainly what is needed in order to maintain the methodological consistency discussed above.

Under his scheme, which he calls discursive democracy, Dryzek posits democracy as a dynamic, open-ended project in which discourses engage each other in a timeless and spaceless fashion. Envisaging democratic process as contestation of discourses enables Dryzek to devise a framework based on the dialogic qualities of deliberation. Resembling Habermas's 'subjectless form of communication', Dryzek's discourses do not possess agency in that they cannot be reduced to a well-defined, individualistic set of values. They reflect, instead, different dimensions of individuals depending on the discursive circumstances. In his words:

> A discourse is a shared means of making sense of the world embedded in language. Any discourse will always be grounded in assumptions, judgements, contentions, dispositions, and capabilities. These shared terms of reference enable those who subscribe to a particular discourse to perceive and compile bits of sensory information into coherent stories or accounts that can be communicated in intersubjectively meaningful ways. Thus a discourse will generally revolve around a central story line, containing opinions about both facts and values (2000: 18).

Defining discourses over the boundaries of individual identities, that is, on the basis of what constitutes their identity instead of what they want, enhances the possibility that individuals can transcend their binding group identities and express themselves freely and reflexively. Dryzek's discursive model is broadly inclusive in the sense that the contestation of discourses is not restricted only to reasoned argument. Many other kinds of communication, including gossip, jokes and rhetoric, are allowed to take place in the process as long as they are reflective, non-coercive and capable of linking the particular experiences with some more general point or principle. Discursive democracy in this sense is the sum of intersubjective communication across discourses within the public sphere and not limited to decision-making procedures only.

For Dryzek (2005), the idea of reciprocity does not grow out of the moment of decision in democratic practice, but from public deliberation construed as social learning. He asserts that under the pressure of decision-making, especially when a decision is reached by voting, the democratic process turns into a contestation of identities. Particularly in divided societies, 'the game becomes one of ensuring that the state is defined to make sure that one's favoured identity will always and inevitably win key votes' (2005: 226). In other words, contestation of identities, instead of contestation of discourses, rules the process of deliberation in the form of 'a raw clash of identities', rendering a reflective attitude less possible.

Dryzek posits his solution. He suggests focusing on deliberation to function mainly within the boundaries of the public sphere, and decoupling deliberation and decision moments of the democratic process. He maintains that 'reflection is a diffuse process, taking effect in the relative weight of competing discourses *over time*' [emphasis in original] (2005: 229), hence locating contestation of discourses in the public sphere as a social learning experience would enhance the possibility that individuals would be able to reflect on their preferences. This situation, according to Dryzek, 'is less fraught than that in hot deliberation, where reflection can only take effect in the choices of individuals under the gaze of both opponents and those with a shared identity' (2005: 229). Dryzek refers here to Mackie's observation (2006) that people resist admitting that they change their minds in deliberative forums, although, at another time and place with different participants, admission becomes easier and more likely.

With his emphasis on decoupling social learning phase of deliberation from decision-making phase, Dryzek takes an important step towards the analytical treatment of internal differences in deliberative practices. Even though, in this initial stage, his theory does not fully elaborate how he envisages a workable arrangement between the two different phases of deliberation, it is now possible for Dryzek to argue the benefits of deliberation oriented to social learning through its own parameters without reverting back to premises where the rules of decision-making dominate. In other words, Dryzek is now one step closer to overcoming the dilemma that has marred the theories of McCarthy, Benhabib and Young. The ontological shift that this step requires is also within the vicinity of Dryzek's framework. His argument in favour of contestation of discourses in a timeless and spaceless fashion brings attention to the analysis of the pockets of deliberative activities in various forms and shapes oriented to mutual understanding.

What has been discussed in this chapter so far shows that deliberative theory is due for a new approach through redesign of deliberative practice. This becomes particularly apparent when the social learning aspect of deliberation is brought into the foreground. Deliberative activity is the sum of two different but complementary stages: social learning and decision-making. Deliberative theory in general treats the decision-making stage as the focus of deliberative activity. This is true even in the cases of theorists who make great inroads into the informal zones of deliberation. Their attempts underline the importance of deliberative activity outside the formal territory of decision-making procedures. The way they conceptualise deliberative practice, however, is still tied to the parameters of decision-making procedures. In this sense, they do not offer a clear plan to salvage social learning from the pressures of activities oriented to decision-making.

A plan as such involves allocating social learning its own sphere decoupled from decision-making procedures. This is not to suggest that social learning and decision-making become mutually exclusive activities. On the contrary, they still function together. But they do so in a more efficient way in that interpretive, hermeneutic qualities of social learning freed from the strict time and space requirements of decision-making procedures prosper in their own space. This is one of the main aims of the binary deliberation model that I will discuss in Chapter 8. The binary deliberation model not only promises better conditions for dialogue oriented to understanding between opposing parties, but also could affect the quality of decisions due to enhancement in the reflective thinking of participants. The importance of this move will be seen more clearly in the following chapters investigating the relationship between secular and Islamic groups in the Turkish public sphere.

# Chapter 3
# Background to the Case of Turkey

In Chapter 2 I have argued for a new deliberative framework based on analytic separation of the social learning phase from the decision-making phase. This separation is specifically important in societies where ethical, religious and cultural divisions cut deep. Recognition of deliberation as social learning opens up a more adequate space for members of these societies to deal more effectively with differences separating them. Turkey is one such society, not only because of its diverse social fabric, but also because it is a rare instance in the Islamic world where Islam coexists with a secular system in which religious rules play no role in the conduct of public affairs. In Turkey, Islam sits at the background of the secular regime established by Mustafa Kemal in 1923.

The impact this dramatic move on Turkish society is not the aim of my analysis. For better or worse, though, those dramatic steps towards secularisation transformed the circumstances in which religion and politics interacted in Turkey. Having lost its dominant position, for the first time, Islam had to play a defensive role in relation to an unfriendly state. This required a different type of interaction, changing continuously according to the dynamics of the time. It is the dynamics of this interaction that makes Turkey a good case to study in terms of the alternative ways that deliberative processes function.

The importance of experience in Turkey has become even more significant with the decisive victory of the Islamic-leaning Adalet ve Kalkınma Partisi (AKP) – Justice and Development Party in the 2002 and 2007 general elections. For the first time in the 80-year-old history of the Republic, Turkey is now governed by an Islamic-leaning party. All types of fears and controversies that preoccupy most secular minds have come to the surface. Division on religious and secular lines has always been sharp in Turkey, yet the decisiveness of the AKP's victory almost caused a sense of despair among secular-minded Turks.

The AKP's victory came in the midst of increasingly bitter conflict between the Army and representatives of Islamic politics. To the secular eye, the election results were a defiance of the secular principles of the Republic. Secular Turks were not alone in being troubled by the AKP's election victory. Particularly following the 2002 election results, a strong measure of astonishment was also observable in the Western world struggling to recover from the impact of the September 11, 2001 attacks in the Unites States. While the main concern for secular Turks was fear of losing the long secular tradition and perhaps being forced to live under some Islamic rules, the West was preoccupied with the question of whether Islamic fundamentalism was about to flourish in a country perceived as exemplary in combining secularism and Islam.

Despite the AKP leadership's continuous conciliatory gestures, indicating no intention to alter Turkey's existing secular system, in the eyes of Kemalists the AKP still remains a threat to the inherited system. Cumhuriyet Halk Partisi (CHP) – People's Republican Party, the only opposition party in parliament and the main political voice of the Kemalist line, claims that the AKP has a hidden agenda to overturn the secular system. The Deputy Chairman of the CHP, Ali Topuz, on one occasion, declared that the CHP was now engaging in a guerrilla war against the Government to protect the secular system. The Army has expressed similar view, if not so aggressively. Thus, the level of formal politics in Turkey has shown deep divisions between Islamic and secular groups.

There is only a small possibility that these divisions, endemic to Turkish social and political life, can be reconciled within the boundaries of formal politics. Although the commonalities between Islamic and secular lines are larger than one could expect, making those commonalities functional in the sense that they contribute to formation of a democratic polity around which different groups could gather regardless of background, requires an alternative way of conceiving the democratic process. Deliberation oriented to social learning and understanding offers this possibility. Turkey's current dilemma, between Islamic and secular politics, may be resolved if the social learning model of deliberation can secure a place in the public sphere to function towards enhancement of mutual understanding between conflicting groups.

The examples of dialogue and cooperation at grassroots levels between some groups that traditionally are not considered as allies are already at work within Turkey's vibrant public sphere. Examples of this are the cooperation between Islamic and secular groups, most notably between some leftist and Islamic women's organisations, to be examined below. Those interactions are not common practice, but they nevertheless suggest scope for a new democratic politics in Turkey. The Q study findings in Turkey will show that the root of this unlikely alliance is a paradigm shift towards individual rights in both Islamic and left politics. This shift has not been properly comprehended by either secular or Islamic sections of Turkish society. It is therefore important that development of interaction between secular and Islamic groups should be investigated. This would not only help to appreciate why social learning plays a crucial role in social development but would also reveal the conditions for a new type of politics for both Islamic and secular sections of the Turkish community.

Before these matters can be addressed directly it is necessary first to consider the relationship between Islam and democracy, and in particular whether Islam can accommodate itself to a secular order. This requires looking at the arguments defending the possibility of compatibility between Islam and democracy in the liberal Islamic tradition in general. Arguments about the possibility of a relationship between Islam and democracy will be briefly surveyed as a foundation for discussion of Islam's interaction with democratic values. The chapter will conclude with examination of the relationship between Islam and the state in Turkey, particularly developments within Islamic politics since formation of the AKP.

## Islam and Democracy

It has long been argued that from a liberal point of view, the problem for a Muslim, whose sole aspiration is to become selfless in the service to God, is how to establish an autonomous, worldly notion of sovereignty without challenging God's. There is an extensive literature on the topic but, in a nutshell, critiques point out the fundamental role the principle of *tawhid* plays in Islam. As the very foundation of Islamic belief, the *tawhid* refers to the oneness of God, that is, He is the greatest, He is unique and transcendent, and has no equals. With the *tawhid*, for a Muslim, anything other than God becomes secondary. So, for instance, the dual structure of public and private in any imagined democratic society is at best blurred but most probably impossible since the *tawhid* only envisages a monolithic code of orders to reflect the unity of God and His believers (*umma*). The divine order covers any aspect of life to such a degree that it becomes meaningless to separate religion from politics, the state and the law. In line with this argument, Roy (1994), for instance, claims that the *tawhid* principle has been interpreted in such a way that the divine oneness of God must also be reflected in the society where no segmentation in any form, social, ethnic, tribal (even national), and no political authority detached from God, are allowed. Thus it is concluded that Islam, as an inclusive, total order, excludes any secular space, even a contingent one simply because it does not recognise any sovereign other than God. Using similar logic, Huntington expressly claims that 'the underlying problem for the West is not Islamic fundamentalism. It is Islam' (1996: 217).

A major objection to this type of critique is that only focusing on the textual interpretation of the Qur'an pays little attention to the contextual reality in which Islam evolves. It does not reflect the diversity in Islam, and undermines attempts of many Islamic scholars endeavouring to develop an alternative reading of Qur'an. It fails, for instance, to explain the attempts made by a large number of states, such as Turkey, Malaysia and Indonesia, to create a legal arena based on fundamental human rights; nor does it explain why Islamic fundamentalism has not been able to find mass support among Muslims. Esposito and Voll (1996), for instance, analyse the evolution of Islamic states in different Islamic countries and conclude that these experiences reflect the great diversity of the Islamic world. Within his diversity, Stepan (2001) shows that in countries like Indonesia, Pakistan, Bangladesh, Turkey and even post-1997 Iran, Islamic fundamentalism is retreating rather than advancing. Halliday (2003) also argues that Islam does not pose a threat to the West simply because it is not about inter-state relations, but about how Muslims organise themselves.

In a more recent study of religion and politics worldwide, comparing two World Values Survey data from 1995 to 2001, Norris and Inglehardt (2004) found no evidence to suggest that there is a 'clash' concerning political values as suggested by Huntington. Instead, their findings point out that Islamic societies, in their attitude toward democracy, display surprising commonalities with the West. On the other hand, Norris and Inglehardt indicate that a cultural 'clash' is widely observable since religious legacies still play a significant role in shaping cultural values in contemporary societies. The primary fault line between the West and Islamic communities, according to Norris and Inglehardt, is not related to democratic government, but to issues based mainly on gender equality and sexual liberalisation. They conclude: 'the central values separating Islam and the West revolve far more centrally around *Eros* than *Demos*' [emphasis in original] (2004: 134).

In the light of these critiques, paying attention to the democratic dimension in Islam becomes critical. The (in)compatibility between Islam and democracy is well researched.[1] Scholars investigating liberal interpretations of Islam have extensively argued that Islam does allow separation of divine and worldly affairs. Khurshid Ahmad (1976) maintains that the Islamic way of living subscribes to the view that individuals are responsible for their own actions and that everybody is personally accountable to God. He cites several verses from the Qur'an, such as 'Man shall have nothing but what he strives for' (53:39) and 'God does not change the condition of a people unless they first change that which is in their hearts' (13:11), to assert that God only revealed the broad principles of an ethical life and left people free to apply these principles according to their conditions.

Similarly, Little (1988) argues that the Qur'an clearly considers religious belief as a deeply inward, personal matter, a matter of the heart leading to tolerance of religious diversity. He also quotes several verses from the Qur'an: 'To you your religion and to me my religion' (Sura 109); 'To each among you, have we prescribed a Law and Open Way. And if God enforced His Will, He would have made of you all one people' (Sura 5/48); 'Let there be no compulsion in religion' (2/256). Little maintains that these and many other verses in the Qur'an confirm the differentiation of the spiritual and civic realms in Islamic thought. What is more, he argues, both Western and Islamic traditions share a common framework in reference to freedom of conscience and religious liberty, thus rendering current human rights formulations also relevant to cultures beyond the West.

Consistently with Little's argument El Fadl (2004) maintains that this common framework, providing a direct link between Islam and democracy, can be found in Islam in the formulation of justice in human life. The concept of justice in Islam, according to El Fadl, celebrates human diversity and cooperation and 'incorporates that diversity into the purposeful pursuit of justice and creates various possibilities for a pluralistic commitment in modern Islam' (2004: 20).

Another Islamic scholar, Ashgar Khan (1986), speaks even more confidently about the division of religious and political affairs in Islam. He asserts that, in an Islamic setting, the state cannot even be termed Islamic, precisely because the Qur'an contains no reference to an Islamic state with a particular kind of structure or ideology. He concludes that 'in the absence of a definition of the nature of the state in either the Qur'an or the Ahadith, it is not only possible but essential for Muslims to evolve appropriate forms of government, keeping in view the

---

1    Some examples: Surush 2000, Sharif 1999, Esposito and Voll 1996, Kabuli 1994.

social, economic and political imperatives of the time' (1986: 80). Muhammad Iqbal, in like manner, asserts that 'the Republican form of government is not only thoroughly consistent with the spirit of Islam, but has also become a necessity in view of the new forces that are set free in the world of Islam' (1986: 260).

March (2007) investigates the issue from the point of whether it is reasonable for Muslims to accept the terms of Western citizenship in a pluralist liberal society without contradicting their Islamic foundations. With his argument March takes the debate into the territory of political theory. He argues that even though the idea of Muslim citizenship in non-Muslim states is deeply problematic from the traditional scriptural point of view, there still exist plenty of resources within authentic Islamic values that can legitimately foster a social contract between Muslims and a non-Muslim liberal democracy. Among these resources March specifically points to the duty of upholding contracts, reinforcing that Muslims should respect and follow all laws in a non-Muslim state when they voluntarily accept its protection. Honouring contracts that Muslims enter is clearly demanded by the Qur'an in some well-known verses such as 'Fulfill God's covenant when you have entered into it and break not your oaths after asserting them' (16:91); or 'Fulfill every contract for contracts will be answered for (on the Day of Reckoning)' (17:34). March indicates that there is also a strong tradition in Islamic jurisprudence that opposes forming meaningful cooperation with non-Muslims. Nevertheless, these principles of loyalty are commonly articulated in our present day by both Sunni and Shi'ite sources. They consider contemporary visas and naturalisation process as legally and morally binding agreements and urge Muslims to avoid any action damaging their state of citizenship 'even when it is engaged in conflict with a Muslim force or entity' (2007: 246). This loyalty, however, comes with one proviso, that Muslims are not forced to accept conditions that directly contradict Islamic principles. In other words, once the liberal principle of religious freedom is guaranteed, March sees a real possibility for Muslims signing a social contract with a politically liberal non-Muslim state.

March's argument is related to the management of a plural society under a liberal framework. Ramadan (2001) contributes to the argument from the Islamic point of view. He argues that political orientations of Islam from the very early days of its inception allowed non-Muslims to participate fully in the social and political life of the society they lived under a Muslim majority. Non-Muslims were eligible for election to government posts without any discrimination as well as having total autonomy over their private affairs including religious and cultural traditions. Their autonomy in private affairs often extended to legal regulation allowing them to form their own judiciary independent from the rulings of Muslim clerics.

The pluralist aspect of Muslim tradition, particularly in the form of the Ottoman's *millet* system, caught the eye of another political theorist, Will Kymlica. He (1996) defined the Ottoman *millet* system as the most developed form of the group-rights model of religious tolerance. In Kymlica's view, although *millet* system was not necessarily liberal in Western sense, it was generally humane and tolerant of group differences, and hence offered a more superior form of religious tolerance than John Rawls's contemporary political liberalism.

These examples show that Islamic tradition includes rich and diverse examples for managing cultural and religious plurality. Diversity of these examples expands even further in the modern era. From Asia Pacific to the Middle East various Muslim nations have developed different responses to challenges of modernity by incorporating democratic principles into their social and political frameworks. As part of this transformation process, the relationships between Islam and democracy have also been extensively debated among Turkey's Islamic intelligentsia, whose arguments have not only analysed this relationship in general terms but also focused on the special circumstances of Turkish Islam.[2]

One theme that appears consistently in their arguments is Islam's natural affinity with a democratic framework. The Qur'an, Turkish Islamic scholars argue, does not make explicit reference to any kind of governing structure or style, yet it asserts certain norms to reflect the will of people in political and administrative affairs. *Shurah* (consultation) is one of those rules, which should play a central role in governing people. The Qur'an commands Muslims to make decisions after consultation. Because they are the agents of God (vice-regents) they should be consulted by the ruler as a matter of respect. In this regard, *shurah* represents a general right for people, carrying a progressive potential in any discussion on Islam and democracy. Similarly, *ijma* (consensus) has been an important concept particularly in development of Islamic law. Even though it has been mostly used to indicate consensus among *ulema* (Islamic scholars) rather than among the general community, the concept of *ijma* can be directed towards establishment of a legitimate political order. Above all, the Qur'an orders that God's authority can only be assigned to the community of individual believers (*umma*), in any ideal Islamic society only the people are supposed to be sovereign. Even the authority of the Prophet Muhammad in this sense is restricted to being a messenger.

Apart from these general arguments about the compatibility of Islam and democracy, the distinctive characteristics of Turkish Islam have also been dealt with extensively. Mardin (2006) relates distinctiveness of Turkish Islam to the influence of positivism on the Ottoman administration. Branding it as 'Turkish Islamic Exceptionalism' Mardin argues that the Ottomans incorporated the principles of positivist thinking, which created secular West, long before 19th century reforms of *Tanzimat*. The nature of these reforms will be discussed later. What is important in Mardin's argument is that the influence of positivism created a 'peculiar mix of state and religious discourse' in the Ottoman empire in which Islam 'had only had scattered moments of hegemony' (2006: 4). Mardin asserts that this unique character of Ottoman religious structure has been largely overlooked because of the concentration of Islamic studies on the Islam of Arabs.

---

2   Some examples: Arslan 1996, 1999, Uyanık 1999, Alper 2000, Yaran 200, Bulaç 2001, Güler 2002.

Similarly, Çaha (1999) argues that under the Ottoman rule a civil code (*kanun*) always ran parallel to the religious code (the *Shari'ah*). Particularly in the 19th century, the civil code had become gradually more dominant in relation to the conduct of public affairs, restricting application of the religious code mainly to the private affairs. Çaha points out that since the Ottomans had never been dominated by the West, they did not develop any strong anti-Western sentiments and adopted principles of Western-style governing without much hesitation, such as a constitutional parliamentary system based on democratic individual rights. This alone represents one of the most important reasons that Turkey today displays a different picture compared to other Islamic countries.

The role of *tasavvuf* in development of Islam in Turkey is another theme raised by Islamic scholars. Mehmed Aydın (1994), a minister in the current AKP government, argues that the *tasavvuf* (Sufii) tradition in Turkey has greatly enhanced the role of dialogue in Islamic tradition. Sufiis, through dialogue with God, always perceive themselves to be engaging in an equal and sincere learning process, contrary to a master-servant type of relation prevailing in most theological (scriptural) traditions. Ali Bulaç (1991), in line with Aydın's argument, observes that the conditions of dialogue traditionally exist within Turkish society. He argues that the main task in Turkey now is to discern points of convergence between different views through dialogue. Bulaç maintains that the Islamic rule is not only geared to the demands of a pluralistic society, but also orders the practice of Islam accordingly. The Qur'an acknowledges that there are other ways of living than those advanced by Islam and that judging those will ultimately be done by God himself on Judgement Day; thus there should be no compulsion in religious matters. Bulaç concludes that the actual task is to discern the point of convergence between different views through dialogue. Once the common way is established it becomes the basis for a social contract between the parties involved.

Mardin (2006) also points to the importance of *Nakşibendi* movement and their incorporation of *Sufii* orders into their ranks in the creation of Turkish Islam. Particularly during the 19th century, *Nakşibendi* networks were expanded all over Anatolia. They were instrumental in maintaining 'an Islamic civility' when Ottoman administration was helpless to prevent a continuing inter-tribal conflict and anarchy in Anatolia. Mardin maintains that this *Nakşibendi* lineage is directly linked to the ascendance of the AKP in today's Turkey (2006: 10-18). An extension of *Nakşibendi* networks, Fetullah Gulen's liberal Islamic movement influential among the AKP ranks has been part of this liberal tradition in Turkey (Çaha and Aras 2000, Yavuz and Esposito 2003).

These are only few examples of the abundant literature refuting the incompatibility between Islam and democracy. None of them suggests that building a framework, in which both Islam and democracy work cooperatively, is an easy task. Since establishment of Emevi dynasty in the 7th century, there has been almost no example of a properly functioning democratic system in the Western sense within the Islamic world. Perhaps more importantly, the challenges that a democratic polity poses for the Islamic way of living still have not been resolved properly in the minds of many Muslims. These include universal individual rights, particularly in sex and gender. In relation to women's place in Islam, at least it might have been possible to claim that there has been an increasing awareness about gender equity, which are consistently brought to the agenda by Islamic women's organisations (Tuksal 2000, Göle 2002). On the other hand, gay and lesbian rights appear to be an awkward issue for Islamic politics as the Qur'an explicitly prohibits homosexual relationships.

Nevertheless, the arguments outlined above in favour of compatibility between Islam and democracy show that Islam does have resources available to be utilised for a democratic polity, but only in different forms depending on the historical circumstances in which Islam evolves. In other words, the context is important in interpreting textual references in the Qur'an. This is the key to appreciating the dynamics of Islam in relation to its interaction with social and political surroundings.

In this sense, Gellner's analysis of the development of Islam as a social order is a promising starting point. Gellner (1981) points to the different ways in which Christianity and Islam evolved, arguing that from the beginning Christianity contained an understanding of a separation between religious and political affairs, since it grew out of a context dominated by Roman rule. The political structure of Palestine, at the time of Christ, was directly subordinated to the Roman Empire through a governor. For Christianity there was no other solution but to constrain theocratic aspirations with some political modesty, which meant acknowledging the difference between civil and religious law, formulated in the New Testament as 'render to God that which is God's and to Caesar that which is Caesar's'. Gellner concludes, 'a faith which begins, and for sometime remains, without political power, cannot but accommodate itself to a political order which is not, or is not yet, under its control' (1981: 2).

Islam's development, on the other hand, followed a completely different pattern. Its success was so rapid that it owed nothing to any sovereign, thus inhibiting 'the handing over of some sphere of life to non-religious authority'. Indeed, there was no Caesar in the Arabian Peninsula in Muhammad's time. Political power was grounded in different customs and beliefs disseminated in a sporadic fashion. The challenge for Muhammad was to introduce a new political system to unify the anarchic rivalry among different tribes, rather than to work out ways to handle the pressures of a strong central authority. The consequence was simultaneous development of political and religious spheres in which the rules of politics were readily subordinated to the rule of Islam.

Arkoun (1994) views development of Christianity and Islam in a similar vein and asserts there are in fact no differences among the Judaic, Christian and Islamic way of internalising the authority of the Revelation. Speaking of a separation between the realms of power in civic and religious terms is, in a theological sense, not conceivable. He contends, without taking into account the historical conditions of the day, that establishing any contrast between Christianity and Islam would be too hasty, superficial and unacceptable.

Gellner's and Arkoun's analyses highlight the fact that the development of Islam as a blueprint of social order is the product of certain historical circumstances. If the circumstances change, a change in the dialogue between the state and Islamic forces should also be expected. Gellner's contextual sensitivity does not go any further than pointing to the conditions under which Islam flourished. The rest of his argument leads to the conclusion that Islam cannot be secularised.[3] Nevertheless, his emphasis on the contextual sensitivity of Islam can be helpful in understanding why Islam can take different shapes under different circumstances. Development of Islam under the secular regime of the Turkish Republic constitutes a good example in support of this assertion. However, before examining the example of Turkey, I will revisit Habermas's framework to explore its potential in developing a productive engagement between Western and Islamic ideas.

## Further Reflections on Islam–Democracy Relationship

The shortcomings of Habermas's framework in shaping an analytical treatment of social learning and decision-making aspects of deliberation have already been canvassed. Nevertheless, Habermas's framework still plays an important role in providing a foundation for a discursively functioning public sphere, particularly to tackle the problems of division or cleavage. The intersubjective nature of Habermas's theory, focusing on what he calls 'the subjectless form of communication', could, for instance, provide a better environment for dialogue with members of Islamic communities. When this is coupled with some characteristics of decision-making in Islamic tradition, a better than expected picture of the relationship between Islamic and democratic traditions perhaps become possible.

Habermas has long argued that, under the increasingly pluralistic conditions of modernity it is no longer possible to apply a single ethical standard to a legitimately functioning political order (Habermas 1990, 1994, 1996, 2001). He maintains that the complexity of modern societies and their systemic divisions resulted in the formation of a decentred public sphere in which the self-understanding of different groups relies on a different set of value systems. He asserts that a viable democratic model should step out of monologically structured frameworks in which legitimacy is imposed either *a priori* or from the outside rather than to arise from the practices based on reasoned discussion of actual people. Habermas calls this the 'discourse theory of democracy' which refers to a discursive environment in which no one should be able to claim a privileged position to determine an outcome.

What is important in this framework is Habermas's paradigm shift from a subject-based theory to a theory of intersubjectivity where 'the subjectless form of communication' becomes the only sovereign regulating the democratic process. In his words:

---

3 Also see Ernest Gellner (ed.) 1994. *Conditions of Liberty: Civil Society and its Rivals*, London: Hamish Hamilton.

> Once one gives up the philosophy of the subject, one needs neither to concentrate sovereignty concretely in the people nor to banish it in anonymous constitutional structures and powers. The 'self' of the self-organising legal community disappears in the subjectless forms of communication that regulate the flow of discursive opinion and will-formation in such a way that their fallible results enjoy the presumption of being reasonable. This is not to denounce the intuition connected with the idea of popular sovereignty but to interpret it intersubjectively. Popular sovereignty, even if it becomes anonymous, retreats into democratic procedures and the legal implementation of their demanding communicative presuppositions only in order to make itself felt as communicatively generated power (1996: 301).

With adoption of this intersubjective paradigm Habermas seems to offer a promising way of resolving the issue of sovereignty in a Muslim mind. Tying sovereignty to a worldly subject has always been a difficult dilemma for Muslims. Unlike Christianity, for whom Christ is the Son of God, and as such God Himself (God the Son), in Islam the prophet Muhammad only represents God's authority. He is a messenger, one among other believers. This is where Habermas's intersubjectively-designed subjectless framework might be able to offer some comfort. When the deliberative moment, that is, the discursive practices of people, takes over the authority from any subjectively asserted *a priori* formulations, it will leave the place for a new sovereign, in the form of an equally structured dialogue between participants carrying different convictions about what is good or bad. What this means for a Muslim is that, under the guidance of 'the subjectless form of communication', the concern of being subdued to an authority other than God might be considerably attenuated.

More recently, Habermas clarified his position further regarding the role of religion in the public sphere. Referring to the growing influence of religion throughout the world, Habermas argues that achieving 'the normative expectations of the liberal role of citizens' under a liberal constitutional framework requires a mutual learning process between secular and religious citizens (2006: 4). An important part of this process is not to restrict the kinds of reasons that religious people might offer in public debates. This is necessary, Habermas contends, simply because 'the normative expectation that all religious citizens when casting their vote should *in the final instance* let themselves be guided by secular considerations is to ignore the realities of devout life, an existence led *in light of belief* [emphasis in original] (2006: 9). The toleration of religious justifications therefore is not only necessary for development of epistemic qualities enabling a person to relate themselves reflexively to others, but also for the moral justification of the political authority of the state. For that, Habermas affirms, 'the liberal state must not transform the requisite *institutional* separation of religion and politics into an undue *mental* and *psychological* burden for those of its citizens who follow a faith' [emphasis in original] (2006: 9). If this is achieved then citizens of a certain faith would be able to learn epistemic attitudes necessary to translate secular values into their own vocabulary.

The impetus towards dialogue could then make some Islamic resources available for deliberation. Islamic concepts such as shurah and ijma might be incorporated into deliberative practice. As mentioned previously, *shurah* (consultation) and *ijma* (consensus) are frequently mentioned in the liberal Islamic literature to indicate the democratic potential within Islam. This is not to suggest that these concepts are used in the same way as the Western concepts into which they are translated. In Islam, they have a broad meaning and are mainly used among *ulema* (Islamic scholars), particularly for the application of Islamic law. However, it is important to acknowledge that they carry a substance for rational dialogue which can be utilised for cross-cultural practices between Islamic and liberal Western values. *Shurah*, for instance, has long been a central tenet of Islamic polity. The Qur'an commands Muslims to make decisions after consultation, because they are the agents of God (vice-regents). While they seek perfection in their decisions, they should also be consulted by the ruler as a matter of respect. In this regard, *shura* represents a general right for people potentially playing a central role in any discussion of Islam and democracy. For Ramadan, *shura* provides the space for Muslims to manage pluralism in their communities.

Similarly, *ijma* has been an important concept particularly in development of Islamic law. Even though it has been mostly used to indicate consensus among *ulema* (Islamic scholars) rather than among the general community, Esposito and Voll (1996) claim that Islam has the resources to direct *ijma* towards establishment of a legitimate order. Since there is no explicit reference to any kind of governing structure in the Qur'an, the legitimacy of the state primarily depends on the principle of *ijma* to the extent that a legitimate order should reflect the will of people. Note that this is consistent with Ashgar Khan's assertion supporting the division of religious and political affairs in Islam, as discussed previously. Hence, it is possible to predict that if the popular usage of *ijma* becomes a common procedure in Islamic settings, a deliberative framework would be one step closer to a Muslim mind.

With these possibilities in mind, Adanalı (2000), a Turkish scholar of Islam, discusses integrating Habermas's framework into the practice of the *Kelam* tradition in Islam. *Kelam* refers to rational argumentation mainly used among Islamic intelligentsia to interpret Qur'anic verses and to defend Islam against other beliefs. Adanalı, drawing a parallel between *Kelam* as a dialogic process and Habermas's theory of communicative action, argues that the Habermasian framework can very well be utilised within the *Kelam* tradition to develop a less orthodox interpretation of the Qur'an (2000: 69). Adanalı goes no further than making a suggestion. He does not develop a framework to show how this interaction could be achieved in actual circumstances yet he still foresees a possibility in two different traditions converging.

Absence of an ecclesiastical structure in Islam could also contribute positively to the debate. Since Islam does not recognise any authority between the individual and the God, no one or no institution can claim arbitrary power over *umma* as representative of God's sovereignty within the political sphere. With the *tawhid* principle, for a Muslim, any source of power, either material or spiritual, claiming sovereignty over people is, at least in theory, meaningless. The consequence of this could very well be a relatively egalitarian societal structure, a fundamental condition for the Habermasian framework. This could be particularly useful in the face of a common critique which claims that Habermas's discourse theory is susceptible to the influence of asymmetrical power relationships during deliberation.

These features of Islamic culture resonate reasonably well with the essential ingredients of deliberative democracy. It is then possible to establish channels of communication between Islamic and Western world views to negotiate their conflicting claims. But turning this possibility into a real practice requires the support of suitable deliberative settings. In the case of Turkey, it is most unlikely that the possibility of communication between the two could flourish under the conditions of decision-making. In order to test each other's validity, the claims should be severed from the pressures of decision-making and brought into the realm of social learning where deliberative practice freely flows not for decision-making but for the sake of understanding.

## Islam and the State Relationship in Turkey

I have earlier argued that Islam and democracy are not mutually exclusive and the political form assumed in Islamic societies depends upon the circumstances of the day. In this sense, in Turkey, the conditions under which Islam has been interacting with the state since the foundation of the Republic provides valuable insights into the political capacity of Islam to deal with surrounding social and political conditions. I will now examine the relationship between Islam and the state following emergence of the new Turkish Republic after the collapse of the Ottoman Empire in 1923. The immediate aim is simply to depict the contours of the interaction of Islam with a secular system to which it is subordinated. The relationship between Islam and the Turkish Republic developed in five stages between establishment of the Turkish Republic and the present day.

### *The Five Stages of Islam and the State Relationship*

Proclamation of the Kemalist Republic in 1923 ushered in a new era for Islam in Turkey. Islam now had to adapt to a new political structure. Having for the first time since establishment of the Ottoman Empire lost its dominant position, Islam had to defend itself against an unfriendly state. This required a different type of interaction which changed continuously according to the dynamics of the time. The unique relationship between Islam and the secular state in Turkey is captured succinctly in Gellner's observation that 'Islam is unique among world religions, and Turkey is unique within the Muslim world' (1997: 233).

Each of the five main stages indicates a different level of engagement in Islam's interaction with the Kemalist state. The five stage categorisation of Islam's evolution under the Turkish Republic provides background to my argument that the social learning model of deliberation could play a crucial role in divided societies such as Turkey. This background will also lay a foundation for appreciation of the findings of the Q study contained in the next chapter.

The first stage runs from 1923, the inception of the Republic, to 1946, the year following the end of the Second World War. This was a period of retreat by Islam, particularly during Mustafa Kemal Atatürk's rule. Separation between religious and political affairs was the most dramatic and forceful step taken by the Kemalist forces in their endeavour to establish a Western style regime. The radical shift towards secularisation was grounded in equally radical changes at bureaucratic, legal and legislative levels. These changes included abolition of the Sultanate and the Caliphate in 1924, banning of all religious sects in 1925, adoption of the secular civil code of law from Switzerland and the Dress and Headgear Law in 1926, abolition of religious courts and religious titles in 1928, and a constitutional amendment in 1937 declaring that the Turkish Republic was a secular state. Simultaneously, the state tried to contain the influence of Islam. All religious activities were placed under state supervision and the Directory of Religious Affairs was established. Largely removed from the political sphere, Islam retreated to the private sphere where it continued to maintain a strong presence. In terms of interaction between Islam and the state, it was a one-way traffic, since Islam was placed under control of the state. The secularisation process aimed at strict control not only over religious entities but also defining what 'correct' religion is (Parla and Davison 2004).

The end of the single party rule in 1946 marks the beginning of the second stage. Following establishment of Demokrat Parti (DP) – Democrat Party, the first multi party elections were held in 1946. The DP presented the first opportunity for the religious segment of Turkish society, mainly rural, to gain a foothold within the public arena. Islamic groups, some of them influential sects such as *Nakşibendis*, quickly gathered around the newly-established DP. Though it lost the first multi-party election in 1946, the DP continued to gain the support of Islamic voters and was successful in the 1950 election. The DP government, in accordance with undertakings to its Islamic constituency, relaxed some rules concerning religious practice and education. More importantly, it opened the doors of the public service to some well-educated religious people, mostly coming from rural areas. This was a turning point in relations between the religious periphery and the secular centre. This interaction was helpful in bridging the gap between the Kemalist elite and the rural population, which was usually looked upon as being uneducated and backward (Mert 2001).

For a decade the DP, in a sense, became the public face of Islam. It was ousted military coup in 1960. The leader of the DP, Adnan Menderes, and his two deputies, were charged with treason and executed in 1961. The rest of the party executive was jailed on similar charges. The Army asked İsmet İnönü, the leader of the

CHP (Mustafa Kemal's secular party), to form a government and work on a new constitution. Though this was not the intention of the Army, this new Constitution, usually considered as the most democratic so far, provided more opportunities for religious groups to appear legally in the public realm mainly because of its provision for extended rights to set up civil associations (Mazıcı 2002).

Meanwhile, the followers of the DP formed a new party, Adalet Partisi (AP) – Justice Party. The AP openly acknowledged the DP tradition and legacy. The AP, as the DP used to, appealed to religious voters and successfully gained their support to win the general election of 1965 by a big margin. The AP Government continued the DP's tolerant approach to Islam, opening up the party and public institutions to committed Muslims.

1970 marks the start of the third stage, the beginning of political Islam's long walk to the power. Until the 2002 general elections, this was mainly the work of one Islamic party, though it had to change its name several times following military interventions. Name changes notwithstanding, the party's staff and organisational structure usually remained the same.

In 1970, the first Islamic party, Milli Nizam Partisi (MNP) – National Order Party, was founded. With the MNP, the Islamic tradition finally succeeded in representing itself in its own terms in the political system. Islamic discourse was now a legitimate part of the political sphere. Within a short period of time the MNP had branches throughout Turkey. This rapid growth was halted in 1971 by a second military coup. During the transition government which followed, the Constitutional Court abolished the MNP. But only one year later, the MNP supporters formed a new party, Milli Selamet Partisi (MSP) – National Salvation Party, which was again supported by Islamic groups. The 1973 general election was a big success for the MSP. With 11 percent of the votes, they won 48 seats in Parliament. Because no party had a majority a coalition government was necessary. After lengthy negotiations, the MSP agreed to form one with the CHP. This coalition collapsed in 1975, but the MSP managed to be part of a succeeding coalition with the AP and ultra nationalist Milliyetçi Hareket Partisi (MHP) – Nationalist Movement Party, the Nationalistic Front Coalition. Unlike the first coalition with the CHP, this time the MSP was part of a right wing government, which lasted until another military coup in 1980.

During its time in those coalition governments, the MSP, as the political face of the Islamic Discourse, was careful not to be distinguished as representing a challenge to the secular system. The main intention of the leadership was to create a base within the state; hence they rigorously tried to hold as many positions as possible within the state bureaucracy. The electoral success of the MSP had a definite impact on other right wing parties, which all tried to adjust their discourse according to the Islamic tone developed by the MSP. Islamic references used in Turkish politics increased considerably.

A fourth stage commenced with the military coup of 1980, triggered by the rapid, and almost uncontrollable, increase in clashes between left and right wing groups threatening the stability of the regime. In the early hours of 12 September

1980, the Army launched a coup and took control of all political and administrative institutions including the Parliament. Most party leaders and politicians, including the Prime Minister, were arrested. This was followed by an onslaught on militant political groups. The Army's main target was left wing organisations but some right wing and Islamic militants, who instigated the pre-coup violence, were also singled out.

The fourth stage, the period from 1980 and 1997, witnessed the ascendancy of Islam in Turkish politics. For the first time, Islam tried to be increasingly more assertive, sometimes even aggressive, in its dialogue with the state, particularly between 1995 and 1997. Ironically though, crucial support for Islam came from an unexpected source – the Army.

The aim of the 1980 military coup was elimination of leftist organisations, seen as a real threat to the unity of the state and the nation. Since the Army did not see Islam as a threat, most leaders of the MSP arrested after the coup were soon released. The Army's choice to control the ideological vacuum created by the defeat of the left was Islam. Strong Islamic themes marked most public speeches of the Army leadership. The Chief of the Staff, General Kenan Evren, is remembered even today for his emphasis on the importance of Islam in maintenance of national unity. Religious classes in public schools were made compulsory. In the first years after the coup, leftist staff members in schools, universities and the public service were dismissed and replaced by religious people. The same trend continued under Anavatan Partisi (ANAP) – Motherland Party Government, which won the first general elections after the coup in 1984. In fact, the most prominent members of the ANAP, including the leader, Turgut Özal, were members of the MSP before the military coup.

In 1982, the remaining members of the MSP formed another party, Refah Partisi (RP) – Welfare Party. After a relatively slow start, the RP obtained 9.8 percent of the votes in the 1989 elections, then almost doubled its vote in the 1994 local elections. With 19 percent of the votes, the RP won local councils throughout Turkey, including in Istanbul and the capital city Ankara. Finally, in the 1995 general elections, it became the largest party in Parliament after collecting 20 percent of the general vote and formed a coalition government with Doğru Yol Partisi (DYP) – True Path Party, which was established by the AP followers after the military coup.

The leader of the RP, Professor Necmettin Erbakan, became prime minister. This was a turning point in the sense that the RP, perhaps with the confidence gained by winning the support of large numbers, adopted a more aggressive style in its discourses. Issues arising from conflict between Islamic and modern ways of living came on to the political agenda. For instance, in universities, admission of female students wearing the headscarf became a battleground for how to draw a line between Islamic and secular values. This was accompanied by an increasing number of critiques of the secular regime and Kemalism. The RP's contentious style finally prompted the National Security Council to issue an ultimatum on 28 February 1997, forcing the RP to resign from the government. A few months later, the Constitutional Court abolished the RP. This represented a turning point in the relationship between RP, the state and the Army. Since 1997, while some of the RP followers tried to develop a different vision of Islamic politics as an alternative to the RP's aggressive rhetoric, the Army put an end to its tolerant approach to Islam.

1997 to 2002 formed the fifth stage in Islam's relation with the Republic. Soon after abolition of the RP, the party faithful formed another party, Fazilet Partisi (FP) – Virtue Party and contested the 1999 general elections. The result was disappointing in comparison with the RP's success in 1995, a reflection of the discontent of Muslims with the confrontational style of the RP. The FP only managed to become the third party in Parliament after Demokratik Sol Parti (DSP) – Democratic Left Party and the MHP.

The FP's misfortune continued with another decision of the Constitutional Court that their formation replicated too much of the old RP and hence they had to be closed down. As usual, a new party was quickly established, Saadet Partisi (SP) – Felicity Party. However, the long running internal divisions within the party, which started with the abolishment of the RP, finally surfaced. After bitter debates in different party forums the liberal wing of the party resigned from the SP and formed the AKP. The result of this move was remarkable. Established less than a year before the general elections in November 2002, the AKP managed to draw support not only from the SP's Islamic grassroots, but also from other conservative but secular parties, most notably the ultra right wing, nationalist MHP. It won the election with 34 percent of votes, twice as many as the CHP, the Kemalist secular party, and secured one of the biggest majorities in the history of the Turkish Parliament. Meanwhile, the SP, claiming to be the real standard bearer of the long running tradition of Islam's political struggle in Turkey, accused the AKP of betraying this tradition, but had to satisfy itself with only 2 percent of the votes.

*The AKP's Paradigm Shift*

The current political climate in Turkey shows that this result represented a fundamental shift in Turkish politics both in terms of voters' behaviour and party politics. As one television commentator suggested, 'nothing would be the same again in Turkey' in terms of Islam's relationship with the secular state. The major change in this framework occurred mainly in the Islamic discourse, which decided to remove Islam from being the backbone of their politics to define itself differently, based on the liberal idea of individual rights. The AKP's remarkable achievement was a clear sign of a rethinking process by Islamic forces in a secular setting. It was likewise an acceptance, by the majority of the Turkey's Muslim community, of AKP's more liberal attitude. It testifies to an Islamic party's capacity to adapt eventually to its environment.

A break from the rhetoric of more than 30 years of Islamic politics was crucial in the AKP's success. The party leadership was keen not to repeat the errors of the SP's predecessor, the RP, and its increasingly aggressive tone. The AKP was aware that this aggressive style, which brought rising tension between the Army and the party and ultimately to the closure of the RP by the Constitutional Court, was not well received in the Muslim community. The public image of the RP as an Islamic party was also challenged by the AKP, branding itself as a centre-conservative party committed to secular principles.

During the election campaign, religious concerns, including the headscarf issue, were put in the background in favour of economic and anti-corruption themes. Women candidates harbouring a modern look (not wearing a headscarf) were introduced and advanced. More important than the image the AKP created was the change in its understanding of the relationship between Islam and the state. The party leadership was keen not to run a religious agenda. The muddling of Islam with politics was seen as the main reason for stagnation in the relationship with broader sections of the Turkish electorate. During the election campaign, the AKP continuously reiterated its loyalty to the main principles of the secular system. This continued after the election as well. The leader of the AKP, Tayyip Erdoğan, in a post-election interview with Lally Weymouth (2002) of *The Washington Post* indicated this commitment clearly:

Weymouth: *In the West, some fear that your party is a threat to the secular state. Is this so?*

Erdoğan: Our party sees secularism as an important segment of democracy. Secularism establishes the administrative structure of this country.

Weymouth: *People in the West admire Turkey as a secular, democratic, Muslim country. They are worried that your party is really an Islamic party that will change the nation's character.*

Erdoğan: Our political party is not Islamic. It is not based on religion. A political party cannot be Islamist. It cannot be for Islam. These are inaccurate terminologies. Islam is a religion, and a party is just a political institution.

AKP's story illustrates the different modes Islam can go through in its relationship with the state and politics, depending on the circumstances. The years of uncertainty about how to deal with the Kemalist secular regime during the MSP, the RP, the FP and the SP leadership (mainly under Professor Necmettin Erbakan) appear to be over. The clearest and the most important sign of this came in January 2004 when the AKP declared itself as a conservative democratic party following an international conference in Istanbul. In his speech at the conference, the Prime Minister, Tayyip Erdoğan, said that the AKP's predecessors (referring to the tradition of the RP, the FP and the SP) were acting as a 'political community' on the basis of a certain ideology and appealing only to supporters of that ideology.

Erdoğan described this as dangerous politics of polarisation and drew a clear line between religion and politics. He asserted that establishing a party in the name of religion would be an injustice to religion and reiterated that the solution to this problem is to maintain a secular system. Secularism, Erdoğan continued, provides an essential tool to regulate the balance between religion and politics by keeping the state neutral towards, and at an equal distance from, all faiths and religions.[4] One week later, Erdoğan repeated his views to a different audience within a different context. Attending a business conference in Saudi Arabia, Erdoğan said: 'I do not find the idea of an Islamic common market to be a good one. Whatever happens, we will not base relations on ethnic and religious roots. Polarisation will emerge if we start to establish institutions as such'.[5]

Acknowledgement by the AKP of the most fundamental secular principle, the separation of religious and political affairs, is of primary importance in enhancement of democratic aspirations in Turkey. This is a clear paradigm shift in Islamic politics responding to present conditions. Comparing the differences between the SP and the AKP party programmes, Atacan (2003) draws attention to this shift in Islamic politics. She asserts that with the AKP breaking away from the long running *Milli Görüş* – National View tradition of the MSP, Islam has lost its backbone role in Turkish politics. Muzaffer Türköne (2002), analysing the 2002 general elections, opines that the reason behind the AKP's clear break from a politics oriented to Islam is its determination to escape from the pressures of the Kemalist elite and the state. According to Türköne, the AKP leadership found a once and for all solution, that is, the social, political and economic rights of Muslims could only be protected under a Western universal law system based on the protection of individual rights. It is hard not to see, in this, a parallel between Islam's response to Turkey's secular status quo and the reaction of Christianity to the Roman rule as interpreted by Gellner.

The most important consequence of this paradigm shift by the AKP is that it has created a climate for dialogue between once extremely alienated sections of Turkish society. Interestingly, the closest ally of the Muslims appears to be the liberal left. The Q study findings will testify to this reality quite strongly. On issues such as the role of the Army in politics, the perception of the headscarf issue as a human rights problem, the anti-state sentiment and anti-Kemalism, Islamic and Left discourses display strong similarities which herald a new kind of alliance in Turkish politics. Examples of this affinity are not widespread yet, but some close cooperation between the left and Islamic groups can be discerned in various forums and platforms such as among organisations dealing with human rights issues. This is certainly not a coincidence, given that the nature of this cooperation is based on acknowledgement of individual rights. The crucial point for both sides is that the notion of individual rights is a new concept demanding substantial review of the traditional way of defining the character of their politics. Their movement into a

---

4    In *Turkish Daily News* 12 January 2004 p 1.
5    In *Turkish Daily News* 20 January 2004 p 1.

new political terrain, as a result, has broadened the political scope of both sides leading to a new level of interaction, thus understanding between them.

However, it is imperative to indicate that the shift in the AKP's democratic paradigm sits on the background of strong nationalist tendencies that their anti-democratic, authoritarian nature swiftly surfaces following any controversial event with national significance – most prominently the Kurdish issue as well as discussions with the European Union and Cyprus. These nationalist tendencies will be discussed in detail later. For now, I would like to emphasise that particularly in the last decade, the traditional boundaries of nationalism expanded to such a degree that it now encompasses through an ever-larger spectrum ranging from extreme-right wing the MHP to Türkiye Komunist Partisi (TKP) – The Communist Party of Turkey. Within this spectrum unprecedented alliances between old foes of Turkish politics have become commonplace, such as emergence of a Kemalist left-wing group, called Ulusalcılar who openly supports direct or indirect army intervention into the political sphere and boldly collaborates with the MHP. The AKP's democratic credentials have consistently been tested by various nationalist arguments accusing the AKP leadership of being too soft on the issues indicated above. Among these, the crux of the matter has always been the Kurdish issue to which the AKP's response has been increasingly authoritarian in style, particularly in light of escalation of clashes between the Turkish Army and the Partiya Karkerên Kurdistan (PKK)[6] – Kurdistan Workers' Party since 2007. In this sense the AKP have begun mimicking other nationalist discourses who selectively define issues of human rights with respect to what this means for state security. The AKP's ossilation between its democratic commitments and the authoritarian rhetoric that its leadership has been developing exemplifies the kind of pressure Turkish nationalism can exert on democratic politics. However, as I will argue it is also possible that the divisive nature of these nationalist tendencies prevalent within the formal political sphere could be softened through a dialogic process oriented to understanding among ordinary citizens.

---

6 An outlawed Kurdish guerrilla organisation which has been fighting against the Turkish state since 1984.

# Chapter 4
# The Q Study

The Q study in Turkey, based on Q methodology, was conducted in the light of developments traced in Chapter 2. The study aimed to identify the kinds and characteristics of discourses available in the Turkish public sphere in relation to Islam, democracy and secularism. It was administered in Turkey during the November 2002 election campaign. Q methodology is a powerful tool to analyse existing subjective viewpoints and their relationship about any topic at hand. In the case of Turkey, the aim of using Q methodology was to pinpoint the possible instances of dialogue or cooperation between Islamic and secular groups. From the perspective of social learning the importance of those moments are invaluable since they indicate important clues about options to reconcile differences between conflicting views. The Q study can also be designed in a way that allows deliberation to play an important role. The aim of this chapter, therefore, is to explain what Q methodology is and the conduct of the Q study in Turkey.

## General Background

Q methodology was developed by British physicist/psychologist William Stephenson during the 1930s and afterwards as a technique to examine human subjectivity (Stephenson 1935, 1953, 1985). Stephenson's main interest was to measure and correlate different subjective viewpoints of individuals on any matter of personal or social importance and map out a typology of these perspectives, providing a point of convergence and/or disjunctions in relation to each other. The task of Q methodology is to provide a systematic examination of personal experiences to show how those personal views can be communicated to others with differing views. It is this focus on subjective frameworks that makes Q methodology not only a powerful tool to analyse situations in which personal attitudes show different ways of perceiving a matter of concern but also as a participatory exercise (Brown 1980, 1993, Block 1961).

Q methodology is distinguished from other statistical techniques such as those used in R methodology because of its concern with patterns of subjective perspectives among individuals as a result of its recognition of the communicability of personal references. R methodology refers to 'a selected population of n individuals each of whom has been measured in m tests. Q methodology by contrast refers to a population of n different tests (or essays, pictures, traits or other measurable material), each of which is measured or scaled by m individuals' (Brown 1980: 9). Q methodology, instead of abstracting those individual traits, works to understand the states of mind revealing how individuals with different views observe the topic in question. The result of this is more an in-depth analysis of small but well-selected samples rather than a large – n statistical analysis seeking to generalise the findings to a larger population, as in the case of R methodology.

An important difference between the two in relation to the role participants play in the process of measurement (Brown 1980). In the former R case, participants are passive in that they are measured as the object of the study, whereas in the latter case they are active in that they, as subjects of the study, evaluate the data themselves from their own standpoint. It is through this self-referential character of Q that its methodology can establish similar and differing views in any given topic available to personal examination. This is done through assessment of patterns of subjective perspectives among individuals. In the case of R, assessment uses objective variables rather than individual characteristics, such as professional status and gender. R methodology studies the relationship between these variables. It can also correlate opinions, yet does so in isolation from one another. Its real strength is being able to abstract characteristics from individuals to reach generalisations.

The difference between R and Q methods can also be described as a distinction between the methods of expression and impression. According to McKeown and Thomas, methods of expression measure the traits from an external point of view in that 'the respondent's own point of view on the matter is of little theoretical interest and technical significance' (1988: 23). In other words, the investigator holds interest neither in what kind of meanings respondents assign to questions, nor in the intentions of respondents when they answer the questions. With methods of impression under the Q method, on the other hand, the respondents' subjective views gain prime importance. When assigning scores to the items, the internal frame of reference of each subject is embedded in their responses. In this sense, Q methodology fully engages with the respondents' own logic and their personal experiences. This reveals itself also in the fact that Q methodologically does not ascribe any *a priori* meaning to the items in question. Meanings are created during the process of responses, which contrasts with R techniques in which both variables and traits in question are constructed by the researcher's frame of reference (McKeown and Thomas 1988). In short, by emphasising the importance of subjectivity, Q methodology proceeds in a naturalistic way in the sense that the research is 'less contaminated by the scientist's intrusions' (Brown 1993: 14).

The differences between the Q and R methods highlighted above indicate that Q methodology has affinity with some other research techniques such as grounded theory and feminist methodology. Q's capacity in extensively incorporating research subjects into the research project therefore enabling development of reflexivity and locally situated understanding also strongly resonates with feminist methodology. Due to these qualities Billard (1999) considers Q methodology as a valuable feminist methodology. As will be discussed in the context of the Turkish study, subjects' direct involvement in the process of creating statements through a free expression of views in discussion groups and of sorting these statements to reflect their personal (subjective) views certainly enables participants to speak for themselves. The fact that the aim of Q researchers is to detach themselves from the process until the interpretation of participants' responses, that is, researchers in no ways privileges their status in the process also resonates well with grounded theory. Founded by Glaser (1967), grounded theory shapes the research to find its theory from the data collected in the field. Grounded theory does not test a hypothesis; it stresses the discovery of theory from the research situation. This is similar to Q methodology in the sense that findings of Q are always indigenous to participants by way of participating the research from the very first moments without any *a priori* assumptions.

Within this framework, the Turkish Q study was conducted to explore the kind and number of discourses present in Turkey in relation to Islam, secularism and democracy in October 2002. The term 'discourse' is chosen for two specific reasons. The first is to define the meaning that people attribute to the domain in question, that is, revealing how people perceive the relationship between Islam, democracy and secularism in their daily engagement with those issues. In this sense, following Dryzek (2000), a 'discourse' is seen as an active part of the political process, capable of changing the course of political development. Therefore, the meaning that people attribute to Islam, democracy and secularism will not only show what they understand from those concepts, but also demonstrate what they can do with them in their own terms. This is also the main reason for choosing Q methodology as the principal research medium for this study. The capacity of Q methodology to work through the subjective values, judgments and preferences of individuals and create a typological map of those subjective frameworks makes it an effective methodology for comparing discourses.

The second reason is to observe whether, and to what extent, deliberative concepts such as understanding each other through dialogue or mutual respect are embedded within their discourses. Turkey is a divided society along lines related to Islam, democracy and secularism. There has been societal segmentation between religious and secular forces. By analysing the types of discourses through Q methodology, the study will provide an understanding of the points of convergence and divergence in relation to what kind of understanding different groups have about the conditions of deliberation. When people define their positions through discourses they do this in relation to the social context they are in, thus offering sometimes implicit, sometimes explicit, ways of interacting with others in their encounters. Therefore, developing an account of discourses can provide important clues for the available resources of deliberation among contesting groups at a given time.

## Technique and Method

The idea that Q methodology is a naturalistic study of human subjectivity conditions the logic of any study in which it is used. This is best understood by looking at the techniques of administering a Q study, particularly at the process of Q-sampling and Q-sorting. A Q-sample is a collection of statements related to the topic in question, to be ranked by subjects in the process of Q-sorting. There is no universal fixed formula to construct Q-samples as they can be developed in various ways from subjects' own oral or written contributions to letters to the editor or television and radio talk shows, depending on the approach researchers adopt.[1] It is, however, important to emphasise again that as a general rule the role of the researcher conducting a Q study is no more than an organiser who makes sure that the process runs appropriately whatever approach is taken.

In the Q study conducted in Turkey, the Q-sample was drawn from three discussion groups whose participants freely debated Islam, democracy and secularism. Participants in those discussion groups were different from those who later took part in assessment of the Q-sample. The idea behind forming three discussion groups was, first, to have separate discussions in Islamist and secularist groups so that ideas could flow without feeling the pressure of an opposition, then to have the discussion in a mixed group to see what the reactions are in a potentially more defensive position. The format of discussion in all groups was designed with characteristics of a social learning oriented deliberative practice in mind. Participants were provided with a fully free discussion environment. They were able to express themselves freely on any issue. Approximate discussion time for each group was two hours, though in the last group it took almost three hours to finalise the debate. Discussions were not constrained at any stage.

The first group consisted exclusively of nine secular minded people from various backgrounds. The second group was attended only by people who defined themselves as practising Muslims. (They indeed stopped discussion during the praying time.) The third group was a mixed group, attended by more than twenty people from both secular and Islamic backgrounds. More than two hundred statements were drawn from the discussion groups. Except in matters of grammar, statements were not edited. Sixty-four statements were selected for the Q-sample.

*Designing the Q-set*

In the next stage, a set of statements are selected to be used by participants. The main concern in designing a Q-sample is to include as broad a representation of different views as possible. Usually around 40-60 statements are used. As the final shaping of a Q-sample will involve selection and rejection of statements, a fair distribution of available views becomes important to avoid a bias of some kind. The usual practice is a factorial classification of statements breaking down the topic into some sub categories reflecting alternative views. This resembles representing a large set of statements in miniature, 'in a way analogous to that in which person populations are miniaturised through survey sampling' (Brown 1980: 187). In the selection of statements for each cell, if a certain degree of

---

1   For some examples: Thomas and Sigelman 1984, Thomas 1979, Baas 1979.

heterogeneity is achieved by choosing relatively different statements, this would produce a desirable level of comprehensiveness in the Q-sample as a whole. As Brown states, 'by selecting the most unalike statements from those which are alike in kind serves to minimise the constraining effects of the design and tends to produce a sample of stimuli more nearly approximating the complexity of the phenomenon under investigation' (1980: 189).

In the Q study in Turkey, in order to achieve the desired level of comprehensiveness, statements were chosen with the help of a 4X4 matrix divided between two sets of elements (see Appendix 2).[2] The first four elements chosen for the matrix are:

1. Ontology – the acknowledgement of a set of entities in the political system, such as the state, religion, social classes, civil society, individuals;
2. Agency – who actually has, or is expected to have, the capacity to act;
3. Motives – underlines the intentions behind actions, which can be related to a wide range of issues from self-interest to well-being;
4. Natural and unnatural political relationships – relationships between different entities, such as conflict and hierarchal structure between Islamic and secular forces, competition or harmony.

The second four elements based on Toulmin's typology are:

1. Definitive statements that define the meaning of the issue at hand;
2. Designative statements that attribute some empirical existence or nonexistence to the issue;
3. Evaluative statements that are concerned with determining the worth of the issue;
4. Advocative statements that argue for or against the matter.

At the next stage, these eight elements are combined within a 4X4 matrix providing a structure to categorise the statements. Available statements were assessed and divided according to the cell where they fit. A final selection was made to choose only four statements for each cell, providing 4x16=64 statements to form the final Q-sample.

**Table 4.1    Statement matrix**

|  | Ontology | Agency | Motives | Relationships |
|---|---|---|---|---|
| Definitive |  |  |  |  |
| Designative |  |  |  |  |
| Evaluative |  |  |  |  |
| Advocative |  |  |  |  |

---

2   The structure of the matrix is borrowed from Dryzek and Holmes (2002).

In the matrix, for instance, statement 2 (*Kemalism and secularism cannot be separated from each other. Separating them will mean the end of secularism. If you are secular you are also Kemalist, or vice versa*) belongs to the 'Definitive-Ontology' category since, first, it defines a situation and, second, both Kemalism and secularism are given an ontological emphasis. Statement 7 (*The Army is the guarantor of democracy and secularism*) falls into the 'Definitive-Agency' category since while the Army is clearly given an agency role, the overall meaning of the statement defines a position. A good example of the 'Designative-Motives' category is statement 27 (*The important thing is to start from somewhere. If people could start showing respect and tolerance to each other, this would force the state to do the same*). Here the motives of respect and tolerance are designated for a better outcome. Statement 61 (*We should trust our people whether they are Kurds, Turks, Laz, Alevi, whether they wear a scarf or not. The more divisions are created in the name of state protection, the more divided we become. This is the real danger*) refers to a relationship between different ethnic and religious groups and advocates a certain position; it was categorised in 'Advocative-Relationships'.

## Selecting Subjects (P-set)

The completion of the Q-sample signals the next step, that is, subject selection, or P-set as known in Q literature. Selecting subjects is a topic where the difference between Q and R techniques becomes very perceptible. In contrast to the large number of subjects R methodology requires, Q operates with only a small number of participants. The reason for this contrast is that the research orientations of the two differ substantially. In Q studies the subjects are treated as variables rather than sample elements like a set of items as in the case of R studies (Brown 1980). In other words, the purpose of the Q methodology is to study individual perspectives intensively from their own point of reference. According to McKeown and Thomas, 'the major concern of Q methodology is not with how many people believe such-and-such, but with why and how they believe what they do' (1988: 45). All that is required for Q studies is a sufficient number of subjects in order to establish different patterns (factors) and to compare one factor with another. Q is only interested in numbers of subjects up to a point where all such patterns are captured. Adding more subjects beyond this point does not produce any new information.

The nature of Q studies also brings the law of diminishing returns into play quickly since 'the number of *independent* assessments of value preferences … is apt to be limited' [emphasis in original] (Brown 1980: 194). That is to say that once a point of view is established there is no need to confirm it with the rest of the entire population. None of this is to suggest that Q methodology does not have to pay attention to the design of P-sets. As a general rule, people are chosen with the expectation that they might help to define a factor. A certain level of comprehensiveness, as in the case of designing Q-samples, can be expected from designing P-sets since the basis of a P-set selection is really variety across subjects.

In order to ensure that variety of views are reflected in the study, as many different kinds of people as possible should be interviewed.

In the Turkish study a total of 33 subjects, who did not attend the previous discussion groups, were chosen to assess the Q-sample (see Appendix 1). Even though Q methodology does not, as discussed in the previous section, assume that all existing social characteristics in the population are included, special attention was paid to obtaining a comprehensive sample reflecting variety in terms of subjects' social, cultural and religious background. Most of the subjects were chosen from the capital city, Ankara, because its cosmopolitan structure provided a good representation of secular and Islamic groups for the Q study. With more than four million residents, approximately half of whom migrated from various rural towns, Ankara offers the kind of variety sought by Q methodology. Subjects were randomly selected from specific neighbourhoods with secular and Islamic orientations to reflect a meaningful distribution of attitudes related to the topic of investigation.

The formation of the P-sample targeted a balanced representation of religious and political affiliations, education, gender, age, and occupation and rural/urban background. A breakdown of the table in Appendix 1 shows a certain level of variety in the social and political characteristics of the subjects. In terms of gender distribution, the P-set consisted of eighteen women and fifteen men.

The category 'religion' sought to identify how subjects defined their position in relation to Islam and secularism. Thirteen subjects identified themselves as secular, eleven as Muslim, eight as secular/Muslim and one as secular/Alevi. The key here was to express the position to which priority was given without necessarily excluding the other. In this sense, subjects who defined themselves as Muslim clearly put Islamic values ahead of secular and democratic values. Subjects in this category all belong to the dominant Sunni sect. Similarly, subjects who defined themselves as secular clearly sided with secular values. On the other hand, subjects, who had a strong religious background but still showed a clear loyalty to the secular system defined themselves as secular/Muslim. The only representative of the Islamic Alevi sect defined herself as secular. This is in line with the Alevi tradition which has always supported the secular Kemalist regime.

The political affiliations of subjects also show that the level of comprehensibility targeted in the study is achieved in the P-sample. One subject describes his/her political affiliation as non-political, five as Islamic, one as socialist, eleven as social democrat, six as left, two as conservative, two as feminist, two as centre right. This distribution quite accurately reflects the types found in the Turkish political sphere.

The first priority in the occupation category was to represent different income levels. In order to achieve this, subjects, with a range of income levels, were selected. Occupations extended from being unemployed to working in the manufacturing sector. A second consideration was to maintain the same level of diversity in the types of occupations. Choosing subjects from different occupational backgrounds including housewives and retirees has provided the study with the desired level of variation.

In terms of educational background, the same level of attention was given to obtaining variety. Subjects in the P-sample have a diverse range of educational backgrounds, some having completed only primary school, others post-graduate study.

The final category, 'Rural/Urban', also aimed at a balanced representation. The number of subjects from urban and rural background was sixteen and ten respectively. Seven subjects with urban/rural background were brought up in rural areas and then migrated to urban locations. They are still marked by the culture of their rural background yet have also adapted to urban conditions successfully.

*Evaluation of Statements by Participants (Q-sorting)*

Q-sorting is the process of gathering data whereby subjects rank order the statements according to their own personal point of view under some specific instructions given by the researcher. In the case of Turkey, before starting the sorting process, the purpose of the study was explained to participants who were assured that all information gathered, including the post Q-sorting interviews, would remain anonymous. They were also asked to rank the statements on a purely individual basis, that is, without feeling under pressure to reflect the position of their political affiliations in their responses.

The statements were presented as a deck of cards. Each card had a separate statement. As a first step, subjects were asked to read through the statements in order to obtain a general sense of the topic under investigation and then to sort them into three piles: agree, disagree, and remainder. The last pile may include statements about which subjects are either unsure or indifferent. After the initial breakdown of the statements, subjects were asked to proceed with a more detailed sorting procedure with a distribution from -6 (most disagree) to +6 (most agree).

At this stage, subjects were asked to read the statements in the agreed pile one more time and select the two most agreed statements. Upon selection, these statements were placed in +6 cells. The order of the statements with the same value does not constitute a problem; any statement with the same value can go to any cell with the same value. Subjects were then asked to go back to the 'disagree' pile and select the two statements with which they most disagreed and place them in the -6 cells. After completing this, subjects were asked to return to the 'agree' pile and select the three statements they most agreed with from the remainder of the pile, to place them in the +5 cells. Upon completion subjects returned to the 'disagree' pile and repeated the same process to fill the -5 cells. The process was repeated back and forth until all 64 statements were exhausted.

When the sorting process was completed all statements were spread out in a clearly visible view ranging from 'most disagree' to 'most agree'. Here, subjects were given one more chance to reassess the sorting and make changes to ensure the distribution adequately reflected their views. After completing the final assessment by subjects, the final result of the sorting process was recorded for later use in the factor analysis.

All subjects were very responsive to the instructions although it was a taxing mental commitment to finish evaluating 64 statements. While the average completion time of Q-sorting was around one hour, in some instances it lasted more than one and a half hour during which it was sometimes a challenge to maintain the focus of subjects on Q-sorting. All subjects eventually completed their Q-sorting successfully.

*Follow-up Interviews*

Follow-up interviews are common practice in Q studies. In this Q study, follow-up interviews were used to examine further subjects' attitudes towards dialogue based on mutual understanding. Special attention was paid to understanding under what conditions and what kind of framework subjects felt more comfortable to practice dialogue, particularly in relation to its location within the public sphere. During the interviews subjects were asked to clarify:

1. If they indeed believe that a dialogue is possible at all between secular and Islamic groups.
2. How they envisage that this dialogue could best occur, that is, what kind of conditions are ideal for achieving the dialogue.
3. What they think about the influence of the media in development of mutual understanding, particularly in light of current programming practices, such as discussion forums open to public, expert panels on controversial issues, etc.

The findings of the interviews were significant in that they have provided important supplementary data to clarify what was found using the factor analysis.

# Chapter 5
# Discourse Analysis

Following completion of follow-up interviews, factors were extracted from the Q-sorts using the statistical package PQ Method (version 2.06). The Q-sorts were correlated and subjected to centroid factor analysis and Varimax rotation, which produced four main factors. Factors produced in the process can be summarised in a narrative based on how a hypothetical individual loading 100 percent on the factor would sort the original 64 statements.

1. Kemalist Discourse
2. Nationalist Discourse
3. Liberal Left Discourse
4. Islamic Discourse

In what follows each factors will be analysed in three steps. First, the general characteristics of each discourse will be introduced. This is a brief depiction based on the information provided by the Q findings, showing how the Q study defines each discourse in relation to the concourse. It is not uncommon that the Q analysis could have produced results quite inconsistent with preconceptions. Hence, outlining the general characteristics of each discourse will also show if the outcomes of the Q analysis are any different from common perceptions.

Second, a historical account tracing the roots and development of each discourse in the Turkish public sphere as well as displaying the complex relationship between them will be presented. The term, 'Turkish public sphere', is employed in a broad sense in regard to its time frame. It will reflect developments not only within the Turkish Republic but also in the late Ottoman period. The aim is to probe the genesis of current political tendencies of modern Turkey in order to show that today's discourses in the Turkish public sphere share a more complex relationship than it is generally appreciated. Investigating the common ground these discourses share is imperative to gain further insights into the dynamics of interaction between discourses, which will in turn underscore the role of deliberation oriented to mutual understanding and social learning.

Parenthetically, the Q study in Turkey displayed a remarkable accuracy in picking up the clusters of opinions in the Turkish public sphere. It is not so uncommon that factor analysis produces factors without a clear link to coherent histories. The most likely reason for the accuracy of this study is that the topic in question, the relationship of Islam, democracy and secularism, has constantly been on the public agenda in Turkey during the last decade. It may well be that very few members of the Turkish public have not developed a position on these issues.

The fact that each factor in this study accompanies an important strand in Turkish political history is not a coincidence. It is a sign that the Turkish public is highly polarised. This is an important advantage for analysis of the findings since, as will be seen, Q results and historical stories run together in a generally complementary fashion.

The third step will involve actual interpretation of discourses. As there is no simple formula to interpret factors in Q studies, interpretation is mainly determined by the researcher's preferred approach to exploring meaning behind factors. This is not to suggest that interpretation is arbitrary. Quite the contrary, the process of interpretation is a matter of careful examination of how statements appear in relation to each other.

In this study, statements are analysed in groups according to the score line they belong to, between +6 and -6, reflecting the way subjects constructed their Q-sorts. The reason behind this method is that the way the statements were selected by participants in the Q study reflects the meaning of their subjective positions in relation to the concourse, which in return shapes the overall meaning of each factor. This is important because, as will be seen, the nature of the relationship between discourses can only be detected properly through examination of how each discourse groups its responses relative to others. This is partially imposed by the fact that the concourse, Islam, democracy and secularism, covers a large area and responses of discourses to individual statements signal specific references to certain aspect of the concourse. Hence, identifying the points of convergence and divergence between discourses requires careful examination of how the statements in each score are related to each other.

## Factor 1: Kemalist Discourse (KD)

*General Characteristics*

According to the Q study findings, the Kemalist Discourse (KD) displays a strong commitment to the Kemalist tradition. It fully adheres to the principles of a Kemalist state advocating a strong separation between religious and political affairs. For the KD, this is the single most important aspect of a secular society, which needs to be maintained in order to comply fully with the conditions of modernity. Kemalism and secularism are seen as mutually inclusive. Kemalism also distinguishes itself from the Army's hardline Kemalism in that while it supports the Army in general terms, it does not feel so comfortable with the dominant role it plays in daily politics. It advocates a system based on supremacy of law as the regulator of societal harmony. Compared to its conservative counterpart the Nationalist Discourse (ND), the KD favours a more balanced state and citizenship relationship. The KD appears to favour a non-antagonistic style in dealing with the Islamic population, appreciating the role of dialogue and mutual understanding in resolving differences. It is equally suspicious of Islamic claims that demand a share from the tightly protected Turkish public sphere. This suspicion mainly stems from belief that Islamic rule exerts pressure on individual rights and freedom. The KD looks at the headscarf issue from this angle and concludes that, as a religious symbol, scarfs should not be allowed in public institutions. In other words, the KD does not conceive the headscarf problem as a matter of individual freedom. Not allowing university admission to female students with the headscarf does not constitute undemocratic behaviour for the KD. With this the KD places the protection of secularism ahead of democratic principles, which causes an apparent internal tension in its defence of individual rights. The inconsistency displayed by the KD – on the one hand defending individual rights as a general rule of democratic governance and on the other making exceptions for religious practice – appears to be one of the main challenges that the KD faces.

## Historical Origins of the Kemalist Discourse

The origin of Turkey's current political discourses goes back to introduction of some key Western concepts when, in the 19th century, the Ottoman administration finally admitted that the traditional system was no longer capable of handling the problems linked to the growing modernity of Europe. The seven hundred year old empire that ruled half of Europe, the Middle East and North Africa was losing the battle against the new industrial forces of Europe, which were forcibly pushing their ways into the old structure of their archenemy, the Ottoman regime. In order to counter this assault Ottomans instituted a series of reforms called *Tanzimat*.

From the *Tanzimat* reforms until demise of the Ottomans, politics were mainly shaped by a juggling act aimed at preservation of traditional values which were intrinsically non-Western both culturally and religiously, and incorporation of Western ideals into the traditional system with the hope that a remedy could be found to a prolonged period of deep stagnation. The forces in this juggling act were quite diverse. They ranged from the increasingly desperate heads of Ottoman administration, including the Sultan himself, to some intellectuals as well as military personnel of the day who had been introduced to Western ideas.

The roots of today's main political discourses in Turkey lie at the heart of this juggling act between the forces of tradition and modernity. A proper understanding of this reform process is essential in order to appreciate the historical trajectory of each discourse revealed by the Q study and the possibilities that the current circumstances of Turkey offer for establishing dialogue between these discourses. Within this framework, in order to link Kemalism with the ideas that had an impact on its development, it is first necessary to look at the beginning of the reform period starting with *Tanzimat* in the mid-19th century. As will be seen, the political tendencies that emerged during this period had a fundamental impact on the final stages of the Ottoman regime and the Kemalist forces of the new Turkish republic.

*Early Ottoman Reforms*   Introduction of Western concepts during the 19th century represents a point of departure for the development of Kemalism. This is not so much because Kemalism was directly affected by the ideas behind those reforms, but because introduction of the reforms triggered an irreversible trend among Ottoman intelligentsia towards looking to the West and its ideals with a considerable degree of respect.

Following a series of military defeats against Western powers from the end of the 18th century onwards, the Ottomans started envisaging reforms from a purely military point of view. Confident of still being an imperial power, the Ottoman administration was not willing to concede that those defeats were also signs of a losing battle against a technologically superior civilisation. By the early 19th century the Ottoman state was resigned to the fact that the Ottoman Empire was far behind the West in terms of scientific and technological developments.

As a result, the 1839 *Tanzimat* reforms were announced. These reforms, which persisted until 1876, represented a fundamental shift from the traditional line of the Ottoman state (Karpat 1972, 2001, Findley 1980). They introduced a Western notion of common citizenship and political culture. According to Karpat, the reforms of the *Tanzimat* era forced a redefinition of the notions of state, community, freedom and faith since the political culture they created 'inadvertently moved toward giving political expression to the individual's primordial identities within the nation-state' (2001: 9). Traditionally the Ottoman state used to categorise its population on the basis of religious affiliations first and then according to whether people were part of the administrative system (one that governs) or not (one that is governed). The *Tanzimat* reforms represent a clear step away from this traditional line by advocating the vision of a secular nation and overcoming ethnic and religious differences. That is why the official text of the *Tanzimat* reforms (*Gülhane Hatt-ı Hümayunu*) is considered as the Magna Carta of Ottomans (Somel 2001) even though it still carried a traditional substance in terms of authoritarian tone and loyalty to the religious code (*Shari'ah*).

It might sound ironic, but the emphasis on individual rights was thought to be a remedy for growing dissent among different nationalities in the Empire, mainly affected by the nationalist sentiment arising from the French Revolution of 1789. The important point is that instead of developing a reactionary denial of Western values, Ottomans turned their face to the West. Even though this move had not been planned as a long term project, particularly in the formative stages, and mostly remained a spontaneous reaction to the problems of the day, its impact was permanent and continuing, eventually to shape the ideas of the Young Turks, Mustafa Kemal Atatürk and the leadership of the young Turkish Republic (Koçak 2001, Mardin 1991). It represented a historical moment. That is when the Islamic foundations of the Ottoman regime were for the first time challenged by secular notions derived from the West.

The groups who defended the principles of *Tanzimat* were mainly civil bureaucrats and members of the Army. This is usually linked to the fact that Ottoman capitalism was not sufficiently mature to have its own bourgeoisie to carry the flag of progress as had happened in many parts of Europe. The Army's involvement was normal since it was the first to be exposed to Western development. As a result, members of the Army and bureaucracy took the lead in opposing the old structure of the Ottoman state. Their opposition was limited since their aim was to protect the state rather than overthrowing or radically changing it. They remained in an awkward position in which they protected the *status quo* on one hand and defended changes on the other hand. Due to their close connection with the West, they could see the positive impact of Western style reforms; yet they were equally committed to protection of the state and Islam (Çetinsaya 2001a). Their support for change was not organised until 1865. That year, a group of young bureaucrats formed a secret organisation called the 'Young Ottomans'.

*Young Ottomans and Sultan Abdulhamid* Mardin, in *The Genesis of Young Ottoman Thought* (1962), analyses this period of reform from the point of view of the Young Ottomans. He argues that Young Ottomans' liberal views, seeking to establish an autonomous legal zone independent from the Sultan, should be considered as the genesis of liberal thought in the Ottoman regime. The Young Ottomans' influence had not only affected the Ottoman administration, but also shaped the thinking of the later opposition movements such as the Young Turks.

In 1876 the first Ottoman constitution (*Kanun-i Esasi*) was announced as a result of the Young Ottomans. This was followed by establishment of the first Western style parliament under Ottoman rule a year later. This period, called *I. Meşrutiyet* (Constitutional Monarchy), was an attempt to institutionalise the idea of individual rights in a more binding fashion. Those rights were first articulated in *Gülhane Hatt-ı Hümayunu*, but not necessarily put into the practice. According to Somel (2001), however, with *Kanun-i Esasi* not only were they constitutionally grounded, but also linked to the idea of a common citizenship. Item 8 of *Kanun-i Esasi* defined an Ottoman as someone living under Ottoman rule regardless of religious or ethnic origin (Somel 2001: 105). Under this broad definition of an Ottoman citizen, some basic rights such as freedom of religious practice and freedom of education became visible features of the new constitutional arrangements. In this sense, *Kanun-i Esasi* was trying to achieve a balance between the Islamic character of the Ottoman state and the secular features of the liberal reforms. As such, it was the promotion of a new policy called Ottomanism, an attempt to redefine the state to ensure the allegiance of all people living within the boundaries of the Empire irrespective of religious and ethnic affiliation (Davison 1977, Karpat 1982, Kayalı 1997).

*I. Meşrutiyet* did not last long. After less than a year, Sultan Abdulhamit banned the Parliament until the establishment of *2nd Meşrutiyet* in 1908. Sultan Abdulhamid ruled the period between the 1st and 2nd *Meşrutiyet* with absolute authority. This was a controversial period, represented by the Young Turks and the leadership of the new Turkish republic as a regime of oppression (*istibdat*). Mardin (1991), however, argues that Sultan Abdulhamid was more than a mere oppressor. It was true that after banning the Parliament Sultan Abdulhamid viciously pursued the opposition, demanding a return to the Constitutional regime. The threat of complete disintegration of the Empire led Abdulhamid to pursue a strictly controlled regime which closely monitored any opposition. However, even though the regime was strictly authoritarian, during his time Sultan Abdulhamid maintained many of the liberal reforms which started with *Tanzimat*. He was particularly keen to develop a modern education system, reforming much of the old religion-based schooling and developing a secular public education system. Ironically, Mardin (1962) argues that when in opposition the Young Turks gained most of their ideas from the secular education system that Abdulhamid initiated and mainly grew out of this period. Abdulhamid also incoorparated many of the Young Ottomans' liberal thoughts into his agenda (Koloğlu 2001). In Deringil's words, during this period, 'although the state spoke the political language of Islam, it was in fact implementing the concrete policy of a rational secular programme' (2002: 5).[1]

The dilemma of the Abdulhamid period can be linked to the same dilemma that had marred the Young Ottoman movement previously: what is to be done to save the Ottoman regime? In this sense, Abdulhamid was a pragmatist and used almost whatever was available to this end. For instance, he not only used Western ideas and technology; he used Islam as well. He directed the existing Islamic tendencies into an idea of 'Panislamism' which he used as a catalyst to protect the unity of the Empire (Karpat 2001, Mardin 1991).

The tension between the traditional and the modern, the challenge of Western liberalism, had a continuous impact on the political choices made not only by the Ottoman administration, but also by opposition groups such as the Young Turks. The Young Turks' opposition brought this tension to a different level. The Young Turks was a common name given to various opposition groups that flourished during the reign of Sultan Abdulhamid. They had a diverse range of opinions about the future of the Ottoman Empire. They usually appeared in agreement on the reestablishment of *Kanun-i Esasi* and the constitutional regime (Somel 2001). The Young Turk organisation, *Ittahat ve Terakki* (IT) – Unity and Progress, had a strong influence on Kemalism.

*İttihat ve Terakki (IT)*    IT's roots go back to the Young Ottomans. According to Aydın (2001) there were two main stages in development of the IT. Those stages represent a clear rupture in that a different path was followed in order to achieve what seems to be the common aim, ending the absolutist regime of Sultan Abdulhamid. At the initial stage, called The First IT, the influence of Young Ottomans was clearly visible. Following Sultan Abdulhamit's suspension of *Kanun-i Esasi* and the Parliament, the Young Ottomans continued their activities in Europe.

Influenced by their writings, in 1889 young students of a military medical college in Istanbul formed an illegal organisation, *İttihad-i Osmani* – Ottoman Unity, which, in 1895, became *Osmanlı İttihat ve Terakki Cemiyeti* – Association

---

1    Also see Mortimer 1982, Kasaba 1988.

of Ottoman Unity and Progress. Intellectual roots of the first IT's were largely affected by the Young Ottomans' Ottomanist vision and the principles of the French Revolution of 1789. Its statute indicated that all its members were absolutely equal irrespective of ethnic and religious background, and had total freedom of opinion and expression. They were seeking freedom not for a specific group but for the entire Ottoman community. The diverse ethnic background of its founding members was a sign of commitment to egalitarianism (Aydın 2001). Along this line, IT argued for the rights of minorities such as Armenians and non-Islamic groups; it cooperated with various ethnic organisations fighting against the Abdulhamid regime. Supporting these groups against Sultan Abdulhamid sometimes led to serious divisions between more conservative and liberal sections of the organisations. In one case, for instance, pro-Islamic Mizancı Murat left the organisation and returned to Istanbul to apologise to Sultan Abdulhamid. Nevertheless the leadership of the first IT remained reasonably intact until differences between the liberal and the pro-state wings of the organisation became apparent. Disagreement between the pro-statist Ahmet Rıza and anti-statist Prince Sabahattin brought a break-up of the organisation. Two separate groups were formed. This was the end of the first IT (Temo 1987).

The second IT differed substantially from the first. Its leadership had a completely different background. It was mainly composed of military personnel and some junior bureaucrats unhappy about the Abdulhamid regime. Aydın (2001) defines the second IT as a paramilitary group with little of the intellectual quality of the first IT. They mainly carried on using the name IT to show their loyalty to the idea of a constitutional regime, thus indicating that they were part of the *Meşrutiyet* tradition. Their aim was simple: to assassinate Sultan Abdulhamid. This military activism, coupled with a belief that the Army was the chief protector of the state, was the main characteristic of the second IT. Its influence extended to today's modern Turkish political culture.

The second IT also differed from the first in terms of its intellectual allegiance. The abstract, intellectual endeavours of the first IT had mainly been influenced by French and Anglo-Saxon traditions. The second IT was more influenced by the pragmatic and action-oriented German state tradition. This German tradition influenced Ottoman officers, particularly the founding members of the second IT. However, the most important difference of the second IT was a shift from the Ottomanism of the first IT to Turkish nationalism. For the second IT reformation of the Ottoman Empire could only be achieved through an emphasis on Turkishness. This approach, coupled with the strong state ideal of the Germanic tradition, had a permanent impact on Kemalism. Even though Ottomanism gradually slipped away from the second IT platform, Islamism in conjunction with Turkish nationalism always kept a presence (Ünüvar 2001). This is the root of *Milli Görüş* – National View – used as the intellectual basis of the Islamist political movements created after 1970. The thin intellectual background of the second IT affected both Kemalists and Islamic politics. Understanding this connection helps to explain the conditions of reconciliation in contemporary Turkey better.

The Second IT came to an end with Ottoman defeat in the First World War and the beginning of a new era with proclamation of the Turkish Republic. Under the leadership of Mustafa Kemal Atatürk, Turkey joined the list of young nations.

*The Principles of Six Arrows*    Mustafa Kemal was not directly involved with the IT regime but his ideas were influenced particularly by the strong secular tendency within its ranks. Not a systematic thinker, he had strong views on what social development should entail under the circumstances of the young Turkish republic. His ideas, expressed in different times and occasions, were presented as Kemalism for the first time in 1935, during the fourth congress of the Cumhuriyetçi Halk Partisi (CHP) – Republican People's Party, founded by Atatürk himself. The CHP remained the only political party in Turkey until 1950 when a multiparty system was put in place (Köker 2000). Ataturk's ideas were categorised into six main principles, symbolised as 'Six Arrows' – populism, republicanism, statism, secularism, reformism and nationalism. The importance of those principles comes from the fact that Turkey's current wavering between secularism and Islam largely rests on interplay between the modern core of these principles and the traditional norms representing a different set of values. In this sense, the principles of the 'Six Arrows' represent a synthesis between the remnants of the previous regime and the specific needs of the new regime.

While statism, reformism, nationalism and secularism appeared as a continuation of the second IT policies, the 'Six Arrows' concepts of populism and republicanism appeared to be new. Republicanism was a natural consequence of historical circumstances. With the collapse of the Ottoman Empire, priority shifted from protecting the Ottoman state and Empire to building a nation-state. The new Turkish Republic in this sense represented the ideal solution since it both advocated a constitutional regime and a new national identity fostered around the notion of Turkishness. Both nationalism and populism were used in building a sense of solidarity in the newly-formed republic. Following collapse of the multi-lingual Ottoman Empire, focusing on nationalism was easier than it had been before. The concept of 'one nation and one language' became the catalyst for the new Republic (Parla 1993).

Populism underlined commitment to the role of the public in a republican sense. According to Köker (2000), it was also used to legitimise one party rule by linking the idea of a classless society to the need for only one party, the Cumhuriyet Halk Fırkası – later became the CHP. In this sense, reforms instigated in the new Turkish Republic – particularly between 1913-1918 – and made under the leadership of Mustafa Kemal, were a continuation of the second IT reforms. These reforms aimed at creating a secular and modern society. Not unlike the second IT, the Kemalist regime used its power to impose an absolute authority on society (Lewis 1968, Zürcher 1993). Its reforms, thus, were implemented largely on the basis of this authority. For instance, as part of the secularisation process, the Kemalist regime banned all religious organisations in 1925. This was immediately followed by introduction of western-style dress codes; the traditional fez was replaced by the European hat. The strong reaction of the public to these rather drastic reforms was silenced heavy-handedly through military courts.

These secular reforms coexisted with acknowledgement that Islam was an important part of national identity. Contrary to the common belief, Kemalism tried to position secular reforms without antagonising traditional religious values. Mustafa Kemal personally did not disavow the religion, but he did oppose the religious elite's practice of religion in political terms. Instead, Kemalism tried to use religion and made it part of a nation building agenda by controlling it (Köker 2000, Türköne 2002). That is the main reason for creation of an office of religious affairs that took full responsibility for overseeing any religious activity within the republic. In this sense the process of secularisation went hand in hand with new arrangements for religion. Turkish politics in a way were shaped by responses to this state controlled religious activity by secular and Islamic sections of Turkey. The tension between Islamic and secular groups has always been related to the state's approach to religion.

In short, the crucial moments in development of Kemalism can be detected through the challenge that the previous Ottoman administration faced in order to counter the ultimate collapse of the empire. Mustafa Kemal witnessed the worst moments of this period, which helped him to form his own vision of modern Turkey. He adopted the strong state and the Army tradition of the Ottoman period as the leading forces of the modernisation process, blending them with the notion of Turkishness on one hand and in terms of formal western-style institutions on the other. In this framework, particularly in the early years of the republic, the idea of secularism always superseded democratic ideals, that is, a democratic state was not necessarily seen as the best option for protection of the secular state.

The tension that Kemalism created between secularism and democracy remains a major dilemma for Turkish politics, exposed clearly in the standoff between the Islamic-leaning AKP Government and contemporary Kemalists. Kemalism in its pure form is now mainly represented by Atatürk's party, the CHP, and some civic associations such as the Kemalist Thought Association. The Army also claims to be guardian of Kemalist principles. The KD, as a discourse of the Turkish public sphere, does not correspond to the position of any Kemalist organisations. It reflects a broader approach to Kemalism among the population existing at a personal level with ordinary citizens. Yet, as the factor analysis below will show, it still carries the burden of tension between secularism and democracy.

*Factor Interpretation*

Exploring meaning behind factors – discourses in this case – requires thorough examination of how statements relate to each other. This relationship should not only be looked at from the perspective of statements within the same score in the Q-sort, but also of statements grouped in different scores in the Q-sort. For example, a careful interpretation of the most prominent issues for each discourse necessitates taking into account +6 (most agree) and -6 (most disagree) scores with equal force. In order to realise this balance, scores are investigated in order according to their ranking: after starting with a +6 score, a -6 score is then examined to complete a full picture of the most prominent issues for each discourse. The same process is repeated for +5 and -5 scores. Switching between + and - scores will not only depict a better picture of the salient issues to which discourses subscribe, it also, and perhaps more importantly, will reveal some inconsistencies that discourses display in their attitudes towards Islam, democracy and secularism. In other words, instead of a linear analysis along the + score first, then - score later, shifting between + and - score will provide better checks and balances.

The basis of the most contentious issue between Muslims and seculars, the role of the religion in the public sphere, immediately surfaces as the most prominent issue for the KD (17). The idea that religion is a purely private matter and should remain within the private sphere has been the single most important line of the Kemalist tradition. In recent years the most forceful manifestation of this matter from the point view of the KD has been the scarf issue. Muslim women wearing the headscarf in public institutions such as universities have become a major concern for Kemalists who believe this is a breach of secular principles.

On these lines, statement (45) also indicates that, for the KD, the relationship between modern development and religion is not settled because the fundamental basis, upon which Turkey has built itself as a modern country, has recognised more substantial individual rights than any other Islamic country. The claim that Muslims are not allowed to practice their religion in Turkey is simply unwarranted. However, it is noteworthy that the statement (45) singles out the scarf issue as a problem in relation to the practice of religion in general. This could be indicative of contradictions existing within the KD about the headscarf saga, signalling a possibility that the KD might be willing to revisit the issue.

However, the KD strongly opposes arguments that secularism is atheism (3) and people are less corrupt under a *Shari'ah* regime (19). The rejection of these statements complements the tone that the KD set in the +6 score. One of the issues raised continuously by the secular subjects during the follow-up interviews was their frustration at being called anti-Islamic or atheist. But during the interviews, almost all subjects of the Kemalist and Nationalist discourses indicated that they have some form of religious belief. This is surely another way of saying that secular people have actually more in common with Muslims than is usually believed. What makes this even more interesting, as will be seen in the section on the factor analysis of the Islamic discourse (ID), is that the ID also disagrees with the statement (3). Muslims do not commonly believe that 'secularism is atheism'. Similarly, the ID, like the KD, does not agree with the suggestion that Islamic rule could create a less corrupt society (19). This is surely expected from the KD because of its commitment to the division between religious and public rule, yet it appears quite surprising for the ID.

The ID's position on these issues is dealt with more in interpretation of its Q-sort. At this stage it is important to underline that the Q study has already identified some important misunderstandings between seculars and Muslims, thereby paving the way for a possible reconciliation of their respective perspectives.

**Table 5.1    The KD statements and rankings (6 most agree, -6 most disagree)**

| | | |
|---|---|---|
| 17 | The purpose of religion will be defeated when it is carried over to the public arena. Beliefs are personal matters, thus they should be kept within the individual sphere. | 6 |
| 45 | To claim that Muslims in Turkey are not allowed to practise their religion is a totally unfair statement. If we do not count the scarf problem in public institutions, there has been no obstacle to Muslims practicing their religion. | 6 |
| 34 | Secularism is the undeniable foundation of religious pluralism and the most important norm for societal peace. We must hold on to it. | 5 |
| 38 | If Turkey has today become more modern than any other Islamic countries, it is mainly because law and education have been laicised by being separated from the influence of religion. | 5 |
| 53 | I support our President who defends the supremacy of law. We can only solve our democratic problems by creating a real system of law in our country. | 5 |
| 6 | The problem with Islamic law in relation to democracy is that Islamic communities exert social pressure on individuals. This conflicts with the democratic notion of individual freedom and rights. | 4 |
| 13 | Some remarks made by Islamic leaders contributed to increasing the tension between Islamists and Kemalists. An example of this is Mr Erbakan's remark suggesting that one day the deans, who do not allow students with headscarf into the universities, will be forced to salute those students. | 4 |
| 54 | The state is not supposed to carry a religious identity. Its task should only be to govern people. It should not question its people on the basis of their religious identities. | 4 |
| 58 | The fundamental condition is respect for others. If we achieve this at the grassroots level, then we can solve the problems created and imposed from above. | 4 |
| 18 | Democracy cannot be realised before economic equality is achieved. | 3 |
| 42 | The solution is mutual understanding. Groups, who oppose each other, should try to understand each other. | 3 |
| 57 | We have no other choice to solve our problems, but dialogue. However, we have to be careful of the tone of the dialogue, which should favour a rational, non-antagonistic style that respects others. | 3 |
| 59 | We have to find out what is common among us rather than focusing on differences. For instance, we have to emphasise the importance of education at the universities instead of arguing about the scarf controversy. | 3 |
| 60 | In a secular society everybody should abide by the law. If the law bans wearing the scarf in public institutions, the rule should be respected. | 3 |

**Table 5.1 continued        The KD statements and rankings (6 most agree, -6 most disagree)**

| | | |
|---|---|---|
| 4 | About one thousand female students have been refused entry to the University of Marmara because they dress themselves according to their religious belief. This shows that there is a serious problem with freedom of belief and education in Turkey. | -3 |
| 36 | Mustafa Kemal Atatürk is a very important personality who could only be respected. The Kemalism label unfortunately has been stuck on him and is being unfairly used against Muslims. Kemalism has now become a metaphysical concept with a religious-like content. Like democracy, its meaning has been abused and changed. | -3 |
| 44 | I am trying to survive economically to be able to feed my children. The debate between Islam and secularism does not interest me. | -3 |
| 46 | The secularists in Turkey claim that women who wear the scarf cannot be secular. This is not a democratic attitude. | -3 |
| 63 | If a law breaches a basic individual right it can be disobeyed. | -3 |
| 10 | The differences between us are too deep. We cannot reconcile them by talking. This system will remain as it is in the future. | -4 |
| 24 | The Qur'an does not praise a particular political system. Islam can fit into any system as long as it is fair. For instance, Islam could fit into a monarchy if the King were fair. | -4 |
| 30 | The reason behind the reaction to Kemalists is their antagonistic attitude towards Islamic people. The problem can be solved easily if they tried to understand Muslim people rather than attacking and dehumanising them. | -4 |
| 50 | We have to produce our own model of democracy. The cultural values of eastern countries are different from those in the west. Eastern countries should not be governed by an American model of democracy. | -4 |
| 1 | Today's oppressive attitudes against Muslims in the name of secularism are rooted in Kemalist ideology. | -5 |
| 20 | If everybody tries to live according to Islamic rule, a just system can come into existence. | -5 |
| 49 | In a Muslim society, the framework for freedom has to be determined according to Islamic values. | -5 |
| 3 | Secularism is atheism. | -6 |
| 19 | People are less corrupt under *Shari'ah* regime because it induces the fear of God. | -6 |

Secularism, the core principle of Kemalism, continues to dominate the KD's agenda. This time it is also seen as an essential tool for establishing societal peace and religious pluralism (34). It reiterates that separation of religious affairs is necessary to achieve a move towards modernity (38). The emphasis on education helps to explain the Kemalists' uncompromising attitude towards female students with the headscarf at universities. It also attributes a role to law as the main intermediary in resolving conflicts (53-38). Indeed, the role of the law has been emphasised most strongly in the KD compared to other discourses. This is also where the KD distinguishes itself from the other Kemalist discourse, ND, which relies more on the influence of the Army for maintaining social order. However, as will become clear soon, the KD's emphasis on law is not necessarily tied to the basic democratic principle of freedom of expression since it does not conceive wearing the headscarf as freedom of expression in the public sphere.

The KD's dilemma is closely linked to understanding of the public/private divide, which appears to be a confusing issue for the KD, as well as the ND. The KD tend to discriminate individual rights according to its strict secular criteria, that is, whether those rights are acceptable in the public sphere or not, thus leaning more to protection of existing secular system rather than establishing a democratic order.

Not surprisingly, the KD rejects the application of any religious rule for the maintenance of a just order (20). This is consistent with the position indicated in previous scores. However, on this the KD goes one step further by declaring Islamic values incompatible with individual freedom (49). Reinforcing this, the KD disagrees with the idea that a just society under Islamic rule is achievable (20). By rejecting these statements the KD clarifies the line it drew between secular and religious interpretations of a public order. The KD follows a consistent pattern advocating civil law and rejecting the influence of religion on the public issues. Yet, as already shown, what constitutes a public right is strongly tied to its strict secular criteria. The defence of Kemalism branded as a source of Muslim oppression is an expected reaction given the level of dedication to Kemalism shown in the KD (1).

After the initial step of laying out its position in relation to secularism, the KD starts to qualify what a liberal society entails. Individual freedom and rights emerge as fundamental democratic values in the critique of Islamic law (6). However, religious rights are also acknowledged as individual rights (54), indicating possible discontent with the state's interference with the practice of religion. The liberal secular discourse does not intend to dichotomise the relationship between Islam and secularism. This is supported further with approval of statement (58) calling for respect between conflicting groups. In the suggestion that the problems are 'created and imposed from above', dissatisfaction with the state, as a potential source of problems, appears again. This also points to support for grassroots initiatives to achieve reconciliation as an alternative to state-oriented initiatives. Statement (13) further qualifies the KD's positive attitude towards respect. It suggests a calm style of dialogue in order to keep the tension between the conflicting sides at minimum.

The KD continues to defend Kemalism against the idea that it has been a source of friction between seculars and Muslims (30). Meanwhile, the KD indicates discontent with pessimistic attitudes foreseeing no hope, along with a belief that differences can be resolved through dialogue (10). This, together with support for respect for others as a fundamental condition (58), indicates that the KD takes a substantial step towards reconciling differences with Muslims. Mutual respect and dialogue are key aspects of this and provide the essential ingredients of a deliberative framework.

The KD also defends a universal model of democracy based on western liberal values, applicable to different cultural systems, with core principles that do not need amending (50). The rejection of statement (24), suggesting the Qur'an can fit into any political system, may perhaps be linked to this universalistic approach since it might imply that fitting in the system suggested in the Qur'an might have ended up tampering with the core values of democracy.

The emphasis on dialogue reaches its peak in the +3 score. Three statements (57, 59, 42) emphasise the role of dialogue and mutual understanding. The need for rational dialogue, raised earlier (13), comes up again in statement (57), but more elaborately qualified. What the KD demands is a rational, non-antagonistic style to achieve productive dialogue focused on establishing a common ground between Muslims and seculars. The style of the secular leader, Mr Özden, is rejected as strongly as that of Mr Erbakan, the Islamic leader.

Focusing on what is common rather than on what is different is, together with mutual understanding, seen as the key for the successes (59, 42). However, the KD again emphasises the role of law as a regulatory force, thus suggesting that challenges to the system should be dealt with through existing rules and regulations. In relation to the scarf issue, for instance, it seems that the KD is suggesting obeying the law, first, and then discussing it (60). Economic equality is also perceived as an imperative to the success of democracy (18).

The KD's strong reaction against a non-political and pessimistic stand comes to the fore again (44). The importance earlier ascribed to economic equality does not grant a right to avoid political and social responsibilities to the economically disadvantaged. Thus, an awareness of the issues and a willingness to take part in debates are also marked as necessary for establishment of dialogue between conflicting sides. On the other hand, the KD rejects the statement arguing that refusing headscarf wearing-students entry to universities indicates a problem with freedom of belief and education in Turkey (4). The meaning of secularism for the KD as separation of religious and public affairs is also emphasised again as the scarf is seen as a religious symbol. Statement (46) appears to be a confirmation of this position since the KD does not conceive the scarf as part of the democratic struggle in Turkey. Being democratic means to act according to the rule of law, hence disobeying a law even if it breaches a fundamental right is not acceptable (63).

Statement (36) reinforces the KD's strong dedication to Kemalism. The claim that Kemalism itself has been turned into a kind of religion is commonly raised by Muslims in their argument with seculars. The KD's reaction to this is naturally consistent with its Kemalist stand.

*Overview*

The factor analysis displays clearly that the KD is strongly committed to the principle of Kemalism as explained in the earlier section on the historical origins of Kemalism. The KD favours a forceful separation of public and religious affairs. On the other hand, the KD appears to be committed to a system of law based on protection of individual rights. In this respect, the KD displays a liberal tendency in its conception of democratic politics. But the headscarf issue appears to be a testing point for the KD's self-proclaimed democratic attitude in the sense that it deals with the problem in an essentially uncompromising fashion. In fact, the scarf represents a peculiar dilemma for the KD. As the factor analysis reveals, the KD adamantly avoids seeing that the headscarf issue constitutes an individual rights problem. This inconsistency is one of the points that represents a potential challenge for the KD.

The KD's dilemma appears to be a consequence of the KD's understanding of the public/private divide. The KD tends to discriminate between individual rights according to its strict secular criteria, that is, if those rights cannot pass the secular criteria, then they have to be confined to the private sphere. As a result, the KD leans more to protection of the secular system rather than establishing a democratic order.

The important point, in relation to establishing dialogue with Muslims, is that no matter how much the KD talks in favour of the supremacy of law, the greater the inconsistency in how it relates secularism to democracy, the more it will be open to the charge that it represents an undemocratic position in relation to Islam, democracy and secularism. Similarly, the KD displays willingness for dialogue oriented to finding common points between different perspectives, yet again it falls victim to its discriminatory tendency towards religious practice and symbols.

What makes the KD's defence of Kemalist principles promising from a democratic perspective is its critical attitude towards some institutions such as the Army which claim to be flag-bearers of Kemalism. In other words, the KD does not offer unqualified support to the Army, which is not seen as above the law when it comes to maintaining the secular system. The KD shows some characteristics that are not representative of official, hard-line Kemalism. In the background section I referred to the close link between the Army and the Kemalist elite. Yet the commitment to the Army among non-elites does not match the commitment of elites to the Army. The KD distinguishes itself from a pro-Army approach. It does not dismiss the Army, as in the case of Liberal Left and Islamic discourses, yet does not approve its intervening in the political process either. In a similar manner, the KD displays signs of discontent about the heavy-handed treatment of the state towards groups that one way or another represent dissenting views. As will be seen, this represents a potential point of agreement with the Liberal Left and the Islamic discourses.

In relation to Islamic groups, the main problem for the KD appears to be trust. The KD does not believe that Islamic values can coexist with democratic principles; hence it prefers to keep them completely out of the public sphere. It perceives the idea that religious practice, as it is defended by Islamic groups in Turkey, is nothing but a deceitful act aimed at occupying the secular public system. As mentioned in analysis of the relationship between Islam and the state, this is the main reason that there is currently no clear sign of cooperation or dialogue between the Islamic and Kemalist sections of the political spectrum in formal politics in Turkey.

The Q study findings display some possible avenues for developing a better mutual understanding. In the case of the KD, it seems certain that sooner or later the KD will have to revisit the idea of democracy and secularism in relation to individual rights. The key will be whether the idea of individual rights will consistently be defended by Islamic groups, thus showing their commitment to democratic principles, and gaining the trust of the KD.

The dynamics of Turkish politics are creating a different basis for people who want to follow a more moderate line. The paradigm shift that occurred in Islamic discourse, that is, that Islam does not constitute the backbone of their politics any more, has been playing an important role in softening the lines in left and Islamic politics. Hence, a discursive interaction between members of both Islamic and Kemalist groups to resolve their differences seems a viable option.

This is an appropriate point at which to return to the role of the social learning model of deliberation in divided societies. The nature of disagreements between the major discourses and their representatives within the Turkish public sphere first require settlement of basic differences between those groups. This requires establishment of discursive practices oriented to mutual understanding between the members of opposing sides. This is, and should be, the task of deliberative processes acting towards mutual understanding and learning rather than decision-making.

## Factor 2: Nationalist Discourse (ND)

*General Characteristics*

The findings of the Q study indicate that, just like the KD, the ND subscribes to the main principles of a Kemalist state. It differs from the KD in its strong leaning towards Islamic values and support for the Army. The ND is only one of the four discourses identified in the Q study that continually fluctuates between secular and Islamic values.

One way of describing the ND's dual character is that it is culturally Islamic but politically secular and authoritarian. It also represents a large section of the community, composed of people who are both dedicated Muslims and supporters of the secular regime. As the next part on the historical origins of the ND will show, nationalism is an important concept in the Turkish Republic, cutting across a variety of political entities in a broad spectrum including the left. Yet the type of nationalist discourse that emerges from the Q study findings is mainly related to the conservative sections of the Turkish society, mostly associated with a rural background, even though they pursue a city life in metropolitan areas.

The dual character of the ND manifests itself most clearly in its approach to the scarf issue. Unlike the KD, for instance, the ND conceives the scarf problem unambigiously as an individual rights issue. The Q findings show that the ND is not comfortable at all with the way that women wearing the headscarf have been treated. Yet, its reaction immediately turns to rebuttal if it threatens the stability of the state or national unity. In this sense the ND is very suspicious of any reactionary move against the state or the Army, as they, in the ND's eye, are essential to the cohesiveness of society. In other words, issues relating to individual rights are usually subordinated to the supremacy of the state. The next part, on the historical origins of the ND, will illuminate the roots of the ND's dual character.

Finding a consistent way to deal with the different value systems is a major challenge for the ND. But its ambiguous position has some advantages. For instance, as in the KD, the notions of dialogue and common understanding are significant elements of the ND's agenda. With its emphasis on dialogue, the ND could in fact play a positive role in bridging the gap between seculars and Muslims. Even though it is not clear how supporters of the ND will react to the process of dialogue if the state or the Army are strongly criticised, the ND could, by being able to play a bridging role between the secular and Islamic sections of society, make an important contribution to the process of dialogue pending a reconsideration of its authoritarian tendencies in favour of a more democratic approach.

## Historical Origins of the Nationalist Discourse

The conditions leading to the emergence of modern Turkey following collapse of the Ottoman Empire were outlined in the section on Kemalism. One of the critical moments in this period was the surfacing of Turkish nationalism under the second IT. The roots of today's nationalistic discourse in modern Turkey go back to this period. Today's nationalism has a broader meaning. It covers a broad spectrum of people with conservative religious and political tendencies, all linked to Turkishness in varying degrees defining their relationship with the process of nation-building. Bora describes Turkish nationalism as 'a series of discourses and a vast lexis' (2003: 436). Nationalism in this sense influences not only conservative sections of Turkish society but also large sections of the left.

For instance, even though the ultra-nationalist MHP is considered as 'the nationalists' in the public eye, it occupies only a small place within the whole spectrum. Reference to nationalism in this section do not relate specifically to political formations or organisations but more broadly to a cultural process. In this respect, nationalist discourse departs from a strong emphasis on being a Muslim and a Turk. It is also secular to the degree that it fully respects Kemalist principles.

The difference between early nationalism, which existed at the time of the Ottoman rule, and contemporary nationalism, is best observed by examining how issues between Islam, Turkishness and secularism are polarised. The nationalism of the IT wavered between Turkishness and Islam. For a modern nationalist in Turkey, the dilemma would be how to find a balance between secularism and Islam. Since nationalism carries different meanings for different groups, it is essential that the characteristics of different types of nationalism in Turkey are established. In this section, I will identify three types of nationalism in Turkey to reveal their commonalities as well as their differences. The three types of nationalism are:

1. Kemalist nationalism
2. Conservative nationalism
3. Left nationalism

*1. Kemalist Nationalism*

The nature of the link between Kemalism and nationalism can easily be discerned by observing the development of nationalism. The Kemalist version of Turkey's history presents establishment of the Republic as a complete break with the past. Historians rightly debate the validity of this claim. Akman (2002), for instance, maintains that the strong state tradition in the Ottoman period played an important role in formation of Turkish nationalism under the Turkish Republic.[2] Mustafa Kemal belongs to the second IT generation; his regime discernibly carried the footmarks of the second IT, one of which was nationalism. The IT's nationalism developed as a reaction to growing ethnic divisions within the Ottoman Empire. The reforms of *Tanzimat and I. Meşrutiyet* which emphasised Ottomanism were carried out to counter this trend, but did not prove to be sufficient. Disintegration of the Ottoman Empire continued. Pan-Turkism was the solution offered by the second IT. However, the IT's attempt to revive the Ottoman Empire on the basis of Turkish nationalism was doomed to fail since it alienated not only non-Islamic groups but also ethnic minorities such as Arabs, who, with the exception of a few opposition groups, were initially largely loyal to the Ottoman state. The situation changed with disintegration of the Ottoman Empire at the end of the First World War. What remained made it easy for Mustafa Kemal to foster a national identity based on the idea of a homeland (*misak-i milli*) and Turkish nationalism.

Nationalism in this sense was imposed from above through creation of a nation in the context of a modernisation project. For the Kemalist regime, nationalism was the means to achieve a modern Turkey. In this sense it was tied not so much to ethnicity but to creation of a modern Turkey in a western mould. This particular strain of nationalism is one of the main differences between the Kemalist regime and IT. While IT favoured a synthesis between Turkism and Islam, the Kemalist regime chose secularism and Turkish nationalism as foundations (Köker 2000).

---

2  Also see Mardin 1991, Karpat 2001.

In fact, Kemalists used Turkish nationalism in conjunction with populism. Where ethnic and cultural sameness in conjunction with the unity of homeland were emphasised through nationalism, populism provided the catalyst for conveying the message of modernity to the population (Karaömerlioğlu 2001).

Belge (2001) draws attention to another difference between Kemalist nationalism and the IT's nationalism. He asserts that Mustafa Kemal always rejected the IT's elitist use of nationalism and always tied his nationalism to the legitimacy of his regime. He tried to instigate a legitimate regime by establishing institutions acting only with the power of law. Kemalist nationalism incorporated its nationalism in the creation of a legal order. Belge defines Mustafa Kemal's commitment to the legitimacy of the regime on the basis of legal norms as one of the most important contributions to the new republic. As shown above, the KD displayed the same interest in the supremacy of law, even though it was inconsistent. Kemalist nationalism's link to the idea of a legal regime is equally inconsistent since, from a nationalistic point of view, the unity of state and homeland represents the most important principle. It is through this principle that all nationalist tendencies are connected to each other. Kemalist nationalism thereby acts as a common denominator between different types of nationalisms of Turkey.

## 2. Conservative Nationalism

Conservative nationalism differs from its Kemalist form mainly because of its emphasis on the ethnic and religious origins of Turkish nationalism. Both share the same strong commitment to the state and to the Army in the name of national unity. This kind of nationalism has been referred to as populist nationalism since it exploits a popular notion of Turkishness which appears to be a strong but not clearly defined part of the Turkish psyche (Bora and Canefe 2002).

Emergence of conservative nationalism can be traced back to the decade from 1950 to 1960, which signified the end of the single party rule. During this period Demokrat Parti (DP) – Democrat Party emerged as the first opposition party against the ruling CHP and governed the Turkish Republic for ten years after winning multiparty elections. The DP linked nationalism to traditional values, particularly to Islam, for the purpose of legitimising its opposition to the Kemalist regime. The DP's use of nationalism was mainly an opposition-building exercise, which substantially differed from the purpose of nation building as in the case of Kemalist nationalism.

Emergence of conservative nationalism during the DP period paved the way for development of more radical nationalist tendencies. Responding to the challenges of the day, those tendencies managed to overpower the role Kemalist nationalism played. From the Cold War era to the 2002 general elections, conservative nationalism subscribed to much of the mainstream political agenda. These tendencies within conservative nationalism will be examined under three main headings: anti-communism; ethnic nationalism based on an anti-Kurdish sentiment; and Islamic nationalism.

*Anti-Communist Tendencies during the Cold War Era*   Towards the end of the DP Government, the nationalist discourse took another turn with the increasing importance of the Cold War. This time its emphasis was more on patriotism supported by anti-communist, racist and conservative themes. This change in nationalist discourse represents a major break from the populist nationalism of the 1950s. With emphasis on themes such as anti-communism and the superiority of Turkishness, the nationalism of the late 1950s became a basis for right wing conservative politics and eventually led to formation of the ultra-nationalist MHP in the 1960s (Bora and Canefe 2002). With the MHP, nationalism in Turkey entered upon an era of conflict-driven discourses.

The anti-communist character of the MHP was strongly tied to protection of Turkish identity which relentlessly attacked the members of left organisations, accusing them of treachery. Ironically, members of the CHP, the party Mustafa Kemal Atatürk founded, were also among the MHP's targets. For the MHP, the CHP's populist discourse was dangerous enough since its reference point was people rather than Turkishness. 'The people's government', a common term used by the CHP, was, for instance, seen as an example of communist terminology by the MHP. The MHP's anti-communist nationalism was always a potent force since its terminology characterised much of conservative politics during 1960s and 1970s. For instance, the most popular conservative party of this period, Adalet Partisi (AP) – Justice Party, which claimed to inherit the tradition of the DP after the 1960 military coup and ruled Turkey for a decade, was largely affected by the MHP's anti-communist discourse. Today's conservative nationalism in Turkey is still influenced by this anti-communist, anti-left sentiment.

The anti-communist phobia eventually influenced the Army as well. The anti-imperialist nationalist discourse of the Army, which endorsed the main principles of Kemalism during the 1960 coup, changed to follow conservative nationalistic tendencies. The 1971 and 1980 coups were clearly driven by an anti-communist agenda. In 1980, the generals did not hesitate to abandon even some of Mustafa Kemal's heritage such as Turk Dil Kurumu – The Institution of Turkish Language, seen as leaning too much towards a left discourse. Also abandoned were items of the 1960 Constitution regarded as threatening the unity of the nation and the state (Atacan 2003). This is one of the main reasons that the KD's support for the Army is not as unconditional as the support of the nationalists. The Q study findings clearly confirm this. The Kemalist discourse approaches the role of the Army in political affairs with caution.

*Emergence of Ethnic Tendencies*   Conservative nationalism reached its peak during the war against the Kurds in East Turkey. During and since the 1990s, the Turkish public sphere was marked by the rise of Turkish nationalism to its highest level, this time accompanied by a strong ethnic, racist tendency based on the idea that everybody who lived within the boundaries of Turkey was essentially a Turk. Threatened by the strong nationalist sentiment existing among the Kurdish population, conservative nationalism replaced its paradigm of anti-communism with ethnicity. The Kemalist notion of unity of the state and homeland was still at work but remained mainly in the background.

MHP's populist approach to nationalism successfully capitalised on strong anti-Kurdish sentiment of the Turkish public. Following the capture of Abdullah Öcalan, the leader of the PKK, the MHP attracted 20 percent of the general vote in the 1999 general elections and became the second largest party in parliament. Support for the MHP fell back to its normal level after 2001, as the Kurdish question gradually disappeared from the public agenda.

Nevertheless, during the war with Kurdish rebels the MHP's ethnic nationalism affected the whole political spectrum. Expansion of the MHP also represented a new stage in development of nationalism in terms of its grassroots support in Turkey. MHP's sizable grassroots support among the rural and urban population, from 1970 to 1980, was based on an anti-communist, anti-leftist stand, and jumped to a record level when the Kurdish issue became a real problem. During that time, the MHP also adopted an anti-intellectual populist discourse contrasting the national identity of ordinary people with the so-called elitist culture of the bureaucracy, which was identified as leftist. Conservative nationalism still carries this anti-intellectual sentiment in Turkey.

*Islamic Aspects*   An equally important dimension of the nationalist discourse was its proximity to Islam. First for the DP and then for the AP and the MHP, Islam was always considered a fundamental part of the national identity and linked to the anti-communist struggle by representatives of conservative politics such as the MHP and the AP. The anti-communist struggle was also a fight against the infidel. The Islamic tone of this nationalist reaction was echoed clearly in the war cry 'Allah is the greatest!' used when members of leftist organisations were attacked.

The anarchic conditions of the period prior to the 1980 coup helped to strengthen the link between Islam and Turkish nationalism. Atacan (2000) maintains that the formal ideology behind the 1980 coup was the synthesis of Islam and Turkish nationalism. The roots of the synthesis between Islam and Turkish nationalism go back to the *Aydınlar Ocağı* – The House of Intellectuals established in 1970. The synthesis asserts that Islam and Turkish nationalism are mutually inclusive, thus cannot be treated separately. Anything threatening this unity is considered as dangerous. Hence, communist or socialist ideologies were seen as harmful for the future of Turkey. The synthesis was also critical of Kemalism, particularly in its definition of secularism. According to the head of *Aydınlar Ocağı*, Professor Nevzat Yalçıntaş, secularism, as defined by the principles of 'Six Arrows', was turned into an ideological source of oppression against the freedom of religious practice. A consequence of this for Yalçıntaş would be the weakening of national identity which could lead to diminution of nationalism within the state culture.

Atacan (2000) argues that the Army adopted this synthesis to counter the strong socialist tendencies among the public and to use it as a means to overcome social and political divisions. She also draws attention to the interesting fact that while the Army supported some groups in line with this strategy, the generals disregarded Islamic groups which did not display an immediate interest in Turkish nationalism. Those that were supported by the Army were committed to nationalist ideas as much as to Islam, thus reflecting the spirit of the synthesis between Islam and Turkish nationalism.

The synthesis between Islam and Turkish nationalism by *Aydınlar Ocağı* had a profound impact on Turkey's political culture. Following the first general elections after the 1980 coup, Anavatan Partisi ANAP – Motherland Party Government continued to follow the path of Turkish-Islam synthesis. The result was a flourishing of Turkish nationalism and Islam that filled the vacuum created by forcing the left from political sphere. A direct consequence of this was rapid expansion of the ultra nationalist MHP's and the Islamist Refah Partisi (RP) – Welfare Party's grassroots. The period between 1980 and the early 1990s was also marked by the rise of Islamic rhetoric within the MHP. Can (2002) argues that the main reason for this Islamic influence in the MHP grassroots was the military regime's relatively tough stand towards the MHP notwithstanding that it had fought to protect the state. Resentment of the treatment MHP members suffered by the hands of the Army is best illustrated in this statement: 'We are the only party whose ideas are in power, yet its members are in jail' (quoted in Bora and Canefe 2002). As a reaction to this 'unfair treatment', some sought refuge within Islam, which affected the overall balance in the party. As a result of this leaning towards Islamic politics, the MHP, for the 1991 general elections, formed a coalition with two other Islamic parties, which was introduced as 'the believers are united' (Can 2002: 678).

Islamic influence in the nationalist discourse of the MHP did not last long. The population's growing reaction to the Kurdish separatist movement provided a golden opportunity for the MHP to return to its ethnicity-based nationalism. In 1992, party members who put Islamic values ahead of Turkish values were forced to leave the party. Later they formed their own party, Büyük Birlik Partisi (BBP) – Grand Unity Party, which still exists notwithstanding lack of electoral success.

With the elimination of Islamic influence from its ranks, the MHP reiterated its loyalty to the state, this time by emphasising secular values. In 1998, when the Army withdrew its support from Islam and started pursuing a tough line, the MHP clearly sided with the Army. The most crucial moment in this support appeared to be when the MHP supported the Army's position during the headscarf controversy. The Islamic vote almost completely deserted the MHP in the 2002 elections. This shift in the Islamic vote also affected the traditional Islamic line represented by Saadet Partisi (SP) – Felicity Party. The newly-established AKP was the choice of the Islamic votes. In this sense, the shift in the Islamic vote marks a turning point in Islam's relationship with nationalism, indicating an end to a longstanding alliance within the ranks of conservative politics. The analysis of the Islamic Discourse below will testify to this important development in Turkish politics.

## 3. The Left Nationalism

Some sections of the Turkish left have been characterised by strong nationalist tendencies. The left and nationalism both had to tackle the same problem, that is, fighting against the invasion of western powers and rebuilding a nation, particularly in the early days of the Republic after the First World War. This created a nationalistic tendency in the left which still endures. Other, more subtle reasons for this were the new Soviet regime's support for national struggles against imperial powers. Gaining the support of newly-emerging nation-states was crucial for the Soviet regime in order to counter the pressure from hostile capitalist nations.

Kemalism possibly played a more substantial role in development of the left in Turkey. The crossovers between the left, ethnic nationalism and Kemalism explain why in today's political climate some left parties in Turkey do not hesitate to ally themselves with their arch enemy, 'the Fascist' MHP, to fight against the new forms of 'colonialism' such as the European Union. Concepts such as the National Democratic Revolution, linked to a strong anti-imperialist sentiment, and Galief's idea of nationalist fighters as the only real revolutionaries are crucial to understanding this relationship.

The strong anti-imperialist sentiment, coupled with the patriotic arousal that it created, played a crucial role in development of left nationalism. Aydın (2002) links development of nationalism in the Turkish left to a strategic move instigated by the new Soviet regime. He argues that the Soviet regime was forced to find allies in order to survive the increasing isolation following defeat of the German revolution in 1919. Those allies, according to Lenin's formulation, were the emerging forces of anti-imperialist, nationalist movements, fighting against the old colonial rulers. Lenin grouped nationalism into two categories: oppressive and oppressed nation's nationalism. He allied himself with the latter. For Lenin, the oppressed nation's nationalism represented a progressive moment in history since this nationalism was first anti-imperialist and, secondly, helping to develop the conditions of socialism by defending an independent national economy. The Soviet regime categorised the oppressed nation's nationalism under the term, 'the National Democratic Revolution' (NDR), and supported the national struggles if they fitted into the NDR category. Turkey's independent struggle was one of them. Consequently the term, 'NDR', became a key concept for the emerging forces of Turkish left in Turkey.

Another important influence on the Turkish left during the early days of the Republic came from a Marxist nationalist, Sultan Galief. Galief formulated a theory on the basis of the struggle of the Central Asian Turks against the Old Russian colonialism. He defined those nationalist movements as the real revolutionary forces and criticised the Soviet regime for continuing to oppress their struggle. He called for a unity of Turks in Central Asia and Siberia to oppose Soviet colonialism. The Soviet regime branded Galief's nationalism first, as revisionist, then as counter-revolutionary. The Turkish left, however, quickly picked up these major themes (Aydın 2002).

The ideological foundations of the NDR in Turkey were first established by Türkiye Komunist Partisi (TKP) – The Communist Party of Turkey. What was crucial here was that the focus on nation as the driving force of the revolution eventually undermined the class-based formulation of the revolution. 'Class' as the subject of history was replaced by the 'nation'. As a result, concepts such as national independence, national economic development and national unity were used as guiding principles of anti-imperialist struggle (Aydın 2002). The Kemalist regime was already using these concepts successfully. Besides, the Soviet regime supported the Independence War and later the Kemalist regime almost unconditionally. This created a strong link between the left and Kemalism, a link which still persists. From the perspective of left nationalism, the most interesting crossover between the left and the nationalist discourse is currently being realised in some coalitions formed between the main representative of the NDR tradition, İşçi Partisi (IP) – Workers Party, and the ultra nationalist party, the MHP. For the IP the anti-imperialist struggle today, as during the Independence War, is the main objective. For this, the IP calls for re-implementation of Kemalist principles, as described in the Six Arrows, and supports the Army as the protector of national unity and the secular regime against the ethnic separatist and Islamic threats. IP's nationalism reaches such a degree that its leftism almost disappears behind its nationalist discourse. These themes will be further considered in analysis of the left tradition in Turkey.

The analysis has so far shown that there are various overlaps between the Kemalist, the Nationalist and the leftist discourses in terms of links with nationalism. Nationalism runs through all discourses in Turkey, including Islamic discourse. The only exception to this overwhelming influence can be seen in the socialist left, which differentiated itself from the left nationalism during fragmentation of the left in the late 1960s and 1970s. The determining factor in the link to nationalism appears to be affinity with Islam. In the case of the ND, for instance, its attraction to Islam plays a crucial role in its dual character, which continuously fluctuates between secular and Islamic values. The factor interpretation below will clearly display this tendency in the case of the ND.

*Factor Interpretation*

The ND immediately points to education as the main reason for tension between Muslims and seculars, and then offers a solution to the problem (43). The ND's approach is substantially different from that of its liberal counterpart, the KD, whose first step was immediately to assert the meaning of secularism and defend it. The ND instead emphasises commonalities in the community, which are important to preserve the unity of the Turkish social fabric (59). In other words, the ND does not immediately define the relationship in secular and Islamic terms, as in the case of the KD. The emphasis on social unity comes first and maintains its presence throughout sorting.

Consistent with emphasis on the commonality in the +6 score, the support for focusing on common issues rather than differences appears again in rejection of the idea that differences cannot be reconciled (10). The ND brings the idea of dialogue to the fore notably earlier than its counterpart, the KD. This indicates a stronger desire to solve problems through dialogue. The ND, just as the KD, disapproves of the inherent pessimism and apolitical stand inherent in statement (10).

The ND's reaction to statement (3) is as strong as the KD's, possibly for different reasons, however. It is most likely that those holding an ND oppose the statement since the claim, 'secularism is atheism', violates their desire for unity. In other words, subjects defending the ND react to a possible secularism/atheism divide, whereas in the KD it is simply a matter of defending seculars against an unwarranted claim.

The statements scoring +5 are indicative of major differences between the KD and the ND. The ND defines the scarf issue as a human rights problem and expects the secular regime to deal with it positively without completely dismissing the importance of it (47-54). Given that (47) scored only -2 by the KD, a major breaking point between the two secular discourses emerges.

Statement (32) represents another strong point of divergence. The KD disagrees (-1) with the ND's firm belief (+5) that the tension between Islamic and secular people is easing and that mutual understanding is the key to this development. The disagreement is not about the role mutual understanding plays, but about the ND's belief that the tension between the two sides is easing. The ND's proximity to the Muslim population is possibly the most likely reason behind its less antagonistic approach to the headscarf issue.

On the issue of the state's neutrality towards religious practices (54), though, the ND's score (+5) is similar to the KD's (+4). The ND's line, however, appears to be more consistent than the KD's since the ND does not treat religious rights and the headscarf as separate issues, which is what happens in the KD. In other words, unlike the KD, the ND advocates that the right to wear the headscarf in public institutions should be treated as a basic individual right.

Contrary to statements categorised with a +5 score, those categorised with a -5 score indicate that there are points of convergence between the KD and the ND. The ND, together with the KD, rejects the idea that religious values can neither be the basis of a framework for freedom nor for a less corrupt society (19-49).

The idea that Kemalism is a source of oppression against Muslims is rejected (1), confirming the ND's commitment to Kemalism. The two discourses, therefore, join each other in their opposition to reinforcement of religious values forming the rules of governance and in defence of Kemalism.

Statements categorised in the +4 score are indicative of divergences between the ND and the KD. The biggest margin of disagreement between the two discourses surfaces in relation to a model of democracy. The ND endorses a shift from the core Western values towards a framework determined more by local values (50). This move is sharply rejected by the KD (-4). However, the ND's emphasis on local values is consistent with its endorsement of the use of scarf and of the freedom of

**Table 5.2    The ND statements and rankings (6 most agree, -6 most disagree)**

| | | |
|---|---|---|
| 59 | We have to find out what is common among us rather than focusing on differences. For instance, we have to emphasise the importance of education at the universities instead of arguing about the scarf controversy. | 6 |
| 43 | The lack of education is the main reason why we are having such problems between secular and Islamic people. People do not like reading and investigating. They believe in whatever they hear. | 6 |
| 54 | The state is not supposed to carry a religious identity. Its task should only be to govern people. It should not question its people on the basis of their religious identities. | 5 |
| 32 | Recently, Islamic and secular people have been softening their attitudes. It shows that we can solve our problems better when we try to understand each other. | 5 |
| 47 | My wife has been refused to be issued a health card only because she wears a scarf. This is against basic human rights and secularism. | 5 |
| 17 | The purpose of religion will be defeated when it is carried over to the public arena. Beliefs are personal matters, thus they should be kept within the individual sphere. | 4 |
| 7 | The army is the guarantor of democracy and secularism. | 4 |
| 25 | Whether I cover myself with a scarf or not should not be anyone else's business. This is what I understand from secularism. Everybody should pay respect to different beliefs. | 4 |
| 50 | We have to produce our own model of democracy. The cultural values of eastern countries are different from those in the west. Eastern countries should not be governed by an American model of democracy. | 4 |
| 34 | Secularism is the undeniable foundation of religious pluralism and the most important norm for societal peace. We must hold on to it. | 3 |
| 42 | The solution is mutual understanding. Groups, who oppose each other, should try to understand each other. | 3 |
| 2 | Kemalism and secularism cannot be separated from each other. Separating them will mean the end of secularism. If you are secular you are also Kemalist, or vice versa. | 3 |
| 37 | In Turkey, more than 80 percent of Islamic people have a moderate line. They cannot be a threat to the secular regime. | 3 |
| 64 | The Islamists are only softening their lines because of the strong resistance shown against them by the Army and Kemalists. | 3 |
| 16 | Islam, as a system of law, cannot be compatible with democracy. The role and the place attributed to women by Islamic law, which denies women basic individual rights, is enough to prove this. | -3 |

**Table 5.2 continued** **The ND statements and rankings (6 most agree, -6 most disagree)**

| | | |
|---|---|---|
| 21 | Whether the state is secular or not should not be dealt with by the Constitution. The state should only act as a guarantor of the freedom of religious practice. There should not be a state institution to organise religious practice. | -3 |
| 62 | The state must trust its people. We are here for our country and the state. I served in the Army and fought against Kurdish separatists in the east. Today, the state considers me as a fundamentalist threat because my wife wears a scarf. | -3 |
| 36 | Mustafa Kemal Atatürk is a very important personality who could only be respected. The Kemalism label unfortunately has been stuck on him and is being unfairly used against Muslims. Kemalism has now become a metaphysical concept with a religious-like content. Like democracy, its meaning has been abused and changed. | -3 |
| 24 | The Qur'an does not praise a particular political system. Islam can fit into any system as long as it is fair. For instance, Islam could fit into a monarchy if the King were fair. | -3 |
| 33 | The military tradition has paralysed the self-reflective ability of our society. That is why we still have been governed by a mentality, which is out of date. | -4 |
| 39 | Notwithstanding the claim, our state is not a secular one. Forcing people to declare their religion on their identity cards or having compulsory religious lessons in schools are examples of this. | -4 |
| 44 | I am trying to survive economically to be able to feed my children. The debate between Islam and secularism does not interest me. | -4 |
| 20 | If everybody tries to live according to Islamic rule, a just system can come into existence. | -4 |
| 1 | Today's oppressive attitudes against Muslims in the name of secularism are rooted in Kemalist ideology. | -5 |
| 49 | In a Muslim society, the framework for freedom has to be determined according to Islamic values. | -5 |
| 19 | People are less corrupt under *Shari'ah* regime because it induces the fear of God. | -5 |
| 10 | The differences between us are too deep. We cannot reconcile them by talking. This system will remain as it is in the future. | -6 |
| 3 | Secularism is atheism. | -6 |

religious practice in that the ND wants to broaden the scope of the existing secular regime by underpinning of the importance of local practices. The endorsement of statement (25), arguing that wearing the headscarf is a private matter and therefore not subject to interference, is again consistent with this line.

A completely different point of divergence with the KD appears in the ND's solid support for the Army's role (7). This is one of the main points defining the ND as conservative. The ND is labelled as conservative, first, because it supports traditional values; second, because of its strong endorsement of the Army as an agent defending the secular system. In contrast, the KD supports the rule of law rather than intervention of the Army in politics.

The ND continues to oppose suggestions that religious rules can be the basis of a just system (20). The claim that apathy is partly linked with economic difficulties experienced is rejected by the ND (44), as it was by the KD (-3).

The main difference between the ND and the KD emerges one more time when the Army's role in democratic development is questioned. The ND's commitment to the Army as the guarantor of the secular system appears to be almost unreserved (33). The ND's unreserved support for the Army can be linked to its quest for social unity. The Army is seen as the only institution capable of maintaining social unity in a divided society.

Statement (39) also appears as a point of divergence between the ND and the KD (+1). The ND's support for the Army extends to the state, indicating support for a regime that centrally controls religious affairs.

The +3 score is indicative of major consensus points between the ND and other discourses. The role of mutual understanding in reconciling differences is supported by the ND (42), the KD (+3), the left liberal (+1) and the Islamic discourses (3).

The ND also moves to define its position in relation to secularism, stipulating that religious freedom can only be realised within a secular framework (34), though compared to the KD this move appears notably late. Affirming that Kemalism and secularism are inseparable also reinforces support for a secular framework (2). The simultaneous commitment to Kemalism and to secularism is where the ND and the KD break away from the liberal left and the Islamic discourses. The score obtained for statement (64) indicates a continued support for the role of the Army, this time by approving its tough stand against Islamic groups including Refah Partisi – Welfare Party (RP), which was the principal partner of the coalition government in 1998. Its support for statement (37), suggesting that a majority of Muslims do not constitute a fundamentalist threat the regime also displays a conciliatory attitude.

The ND's emphasis on a strong state emerges again with the expectation that the state should take an active stand in the organisation of religious practice (21). The ND's stand here is stronger than that of the KD (-1). The negation of the statement (62) is another example of the ND's pro-state attitude even if the matter is related to a statement on the scarf, previously supported. Consistently with its general commitment to Kemalism, the ND also rejects the claim that Kemalism has become a quasi-religious concept used against Muslims unfairly (36).

Another interesting major difference between the ND and the KD appears in statement (16) concerning compatibility of Islam and democracy. The ND's proximity to Islamic values prompts the rejection of the assertion that Islam cannot be compatible with democracy (16). This again leaves the ND at odds with the KD (+2).

*Overview*

As explained in the background section, nationalism is an overarching concept in the vocabulary of Turkish politics. It cuts deep into the conceptual framework of most political groups, from far right to a large section of the left. The ND, though, mainly represents the conservative sections of Turkish politics.

The Q study findings reveal that it carries the indicators of Kemalist and ethnic nationalism in that it subscribes to Kemalist principles with a strong emphasis on Turkishness. Yet, because of its strong leaning towards Islamic values, the ND clearly differs from the KD's Kemalist line. Unlike the KD, the ND perceives Islam as an essential part of Turkish identity. The ND's strong pro-state and pro-Army attitude also diverges from the KD's. Carrying the remnants of the Ottoman tradition of state supremacy and of the Army as the protector of the state, the ND subscribes to a rather authoritarian view of the state. Hence, the ND wavers between two different concepts, the secular state, on the one hand, and Islamic values with which it culturally associates itself, on the other. For the ND it is the unity of the state, which plays the most important role in its conceptual framework, rather than a system of law as with the KD. The ND, like the KD, is inconsistent when dealing with the scarf issue, for instance. Yet its inconsistency does not stem from a discriminatory attitude against the scarf, as in the KD. Unlike the KD, the ND frames the headscarf issue as an individual rights problem, yet its support for the scarf immediately drops when the state is challenged.

The ND's difference with the KD also surfaces in relation to the importance of local values. Unlike the KD's pro-Western attitude, the ND displays a more sympathetic approach to the values that reflect a local core. This is possibly one of the reasons that the ND does not subscribe to the idea of individual rights as much as the KD does. Unlike the KD, the ND does not represent the views of the Kemalist elite. In this sense it is closer to the periphery of the Turkish society than to its centre.

The ND has strong views about the cohesiveness of society and is willing to find common points between conflicting sides, which indicates openness for dialogue. The challenge for the ND will be how to reconcile its traditional cultural and religious views with its strong commitment to the state and the Army. It displays its discontent about the way the scarf issue has been handled by the state, yet stops short of condemning the state's action. It ultimately reverts to supporting the state.

It is important to recognise the ND's close connection with Islam makes it potentially very significant providing a bridge between secular and Islamic values. The ND's proximity to Islam would eventually force it to reconsider its unreserved commitment to the state's and the Army's actions. In other words, a paradigm shift towards a democratic politics based on individual rights within the Islamic camp sooner or later will put pressure on the ND to rephrase its democratic principles.

A similar development may also affect the KD. Yet the ND could have an advantage deriving from its ties with Islamic values; it would not need to establish trust with Islamic groups. The ND's problem will mainly be enhancement of its framework for a democratic polity. Effectiveness of this process will depend on how much a proper dialogue oriented to understanding and learning would be developed. In its dialogue with Muslims, if the ND is sincere in its concern about treatment of women with the headscarf, recognising it as a democratic issue about protection of individual rights, it would be forced to revisit the unqualified support that it accords to the state and the Army. That is, as long as the right framework for dialogue is provided, the democratic framework that Islamic groups have developed over the years would sooner or later influence the ND.

### Factor 3: The Liberal Left Discourse (LLD)

*General Characteristics*

The factor analysis findings indicate that the LLD represents a highly democratic secular position which does not subscribe to the Kemalist vision. What distinguishes the LLD from Kemalist and Nationalist discourses is strong emphasis on fundamental human rights. Unlike Kemalists, for instance, there is strong opposition to the role of the Army in politics and it is expected that the unity of the state will be founded upon basic individual rights. The diverse nature of Turkish society is not seen as a threat; instead, great weight is accorded to common ground. In this sense, the LLD has similarities with the Islamic discourse, particularly in its lack of sympathy for the Army and the state. The LLD also opposes the state's heavy-handed policy on the scarf issue.

A major difference between the LLD and other discourses appears to be that the LLD is less optimistic in the role that it attributes to dialogue in resolving differences. As the factor analysis will show, it does not have a great deal of support for dialogue compared to other discourses. The most likely reason for this is the LLD's historically unfriendly relationship with the other groups including Islamists and nationalists. Unlike the ND, for instance, the LLD does not have immediate rapport with either the ID or the KD. On the contrary, as will be explained below in discussion of the historical origins of the LLD, the relationship of the left particularly with conservative groups has always been difficult. Also, having always been prosecuted as the enemy of the state, the left understandably does not have many options but to maintain its emphasis on the rule of law. The LLD's commitment to the rule of law based on protection of individual rights does not carry any inconsistencies as in the case of the KD and the ND. It sincerely attends to the problems of Muslim women even though it does not subscribe to any religious assertions made by Muslims. It is in this sense that the LLD is closer to the Islamic discourse than two other secular discourses. In terms of the dichotomy that the KD and the ND create between secularism and democracy, democracy is subservient to secularism; for the LLD democracy takes precedence over secularism. This is one of the most important findings of the Q study in Turkey, which will be evaluated in Chapter 7.

*Historical Origins of the Liberal Left Discourse*

The emerging anti-establishment groups in the Ottoman regime followed development of socialism in Europe, particularly after the Paris Commune in 1871. The ideas of socialism attracted opposition groups such as the Young Ottomans who used them against the authoritarian ruling of Sultan Abdulhamid. Yet none of these groups had the correct class origin for the practice of socialist ideas. The Young Ottomans, for instance, were mainly young intellectuals from middle to upper classes which had certain links with the state. In other words, in the initial stages, socialism seemed more a romantic idea for the disillusioned, young intellectuals.

The first worker-based movements and organisations flourished during the *II. Meşrutiyet* period. Following reestablishment of *Kanun-i Esasi* in 1908, workers in different industries in several cities started a series of strikes. This was a new and surprising phenomenon for the Ottoman regime. The strikes spread quickly and the state resorted to excessive force to curb them. However, branding these strikes as socialist would be premature (Tuncay 2000). Even though the workers supported the move against the Sultan for reestablishment of the Constitution, *Kanun-i Esasi*, they were not motivated by class consciousness. The motives behind their reactions to foreign investors and their representatives were more characterised by nationalistic impulses (Akdere and Karadeniz 1996).

These initial reactions led to circulation of socialist ideas more among workers. Subsequently, in 1909, the first socialist association, the Socialist Workers Federation, was established in Selanik. This was immediately followed by establishment of *Osmanlı Sosyalist Fırkası* (OSF) – Ottoman Socialist Party and its publication *İştirak* – Participation in 1910. OSF's socialism was also affected by nationalist and Islamist tendencies. They conceived socialism from an Islamic perspective, arguing that Islam had a socialist essence. Meanwhile, they were critical of the IT Government for its failure to foster national unity. The demands of OSF were usually limited to establishment of a national economy with no specific reference to a socialist ideal (Akdere and Karadeniz 1996). Following collapse of the second *Meşrutiyet* in 1913, the IT government retreated from the democratic practice of *Meşrutiyet* and ruled the country with absolute authority. The autocratic style of the IT allowed no opposition. As a result the OSF and its paper, *İştirak,* were closed. Some members of the leadership were prosecuted and sentenced to death; others were exiled.

Collapse of the Ottoman Empire ended the IT regime. Exiled members of the OSF returned and established a new party, *Türkiye İşçi Çiftçi Sosyalist Fırkası* (TSF) – Workers' and Farmers' Socialist Party, in 1919. The TSF was more successful among workers. The party members organised several strikes which brought some gains for workers and helped to increase the popularity of the TSF. But there was not much change in the party's ideological platform. Islamic and nationalistic influences were still clearly visible. In the journal of the party, *İdrak* (Understanding), the links between socialism and Islam were kept alive (Akdere and Karadeniz 1996). Yet the TSF also had a short political life. Soon after the murder of its leader, who was becoming increasingly unpopular with the rank and file, the TSF was permanently banded in 1922.

But the end of the TSF was not the end of the socialist struggle in Turkey. While the TSF was active in Istanbul, Türkiye Komunist Partisi (TKP) – Communist Party of Turkey was organising outside Turkey, particularly in Baku, Azerbaijan, in 1920. The TKP has survived until today and has had a long-lasting impact on the Turkish left. What was interesting in the early days of the TKP was that Mustafa Kemal was monitoring it very closely. In a letter written to the founder of the TKP, Mustafa Suphi, Mustafa Kemal stated that the aim of Turkey's independence struggle was similar to the TKP's aim. He asked Mustafa Suphi, the founder of the TKP, to join the Great Assembly instead of following a separate agenda so that the national unity was not harmed (Tuncay 2000). It is widely held that Mustafa Kemal's approach to the TKP's leadership was motivated by pragmatic thinking, oriented to maintaining the support of the Soviet regime, rather than an expression of genuine interest in socialism. On other occasions he indicated that the idea of socialism would not match the Turkish cultural and moral values (Tuncay 2000). Mustafa Suphi and members of the central committee of the TKP were assassinated in 1921. Whether Mustafa Kemal played any role in the assassinations never been clarified. The crucial point is that even after the assassination of the first leaders of the TKP, the Soviet regime continued to support Mustafa Kemal and Turkey's national independence struggle because of its commitment to 'oppressed nation's nationalism'. This is possibly the key to understanding why the next leadership of the TKP was overwhelmingly pro-Mustafa Kemal. Şefik Hüsnü, for instance, the new leader of the TKP, regarded the Grand Turkish Assembly founded during the Independence War as a Soviet-kind of governing body. He believed that the Kemalist regime was trying to realise a national democratic revolution by developing a national economy in order to eliminate the feudal structures of the Ottoman period. The influence of the NDR on the theoretical formulations of the TKP is easy to discern. The TKP often subordinated key socialist concepts such as 'workers' and 'labour' to the nation and national interest. The TKP's sympathy towards Mustafa Kemal and the Independence War reached such a degree that the Kemalist state, through its overarching national character, was seen as the representative of the working class (Akdere and Karadeniz 1996).

Despite sympathy for the Kemalist leadership and Mustafa Kemal himself, the TKP was never able to gain their trust. In 1927, during a nation-wide campaign against the TKP, the Kemalist regime arrested most of TKP's leadership. In the following year a large number of members deserted the TKP and joined the Kemalist ranks (Aydın 2002). In a nutshell, the influence of nationalism and Kemalism on the TKP was so obvious that in many respects the TKP could be regarded as a leftist Kemalism. They were so much in favour of the Kemalist regime that the Comintern (the international peak body of communist parties) criticised them for carelessly supporting national interest ahead of the class interest of workers in Communist International's Fifth congress (Tuncay 2000).

Following the 1927 arrests, the left in Turkey entered a long period of ineffective opposition until the 1961 coup. During the one-party regime, dominated by the CHP, the socialist opposition was forced underground.

From the mid-1960s, following implementation of some democratic articles in the Constitution after the 1961 military coup, the Turkish left started becoming a vibrant component of Turkish political life. During this period the issue of the NDR was again brought onto the agenda of the left. The idea of nationalism continued to play a fundamental role in development of the left.

One of the most important of these groups was *Yön* (Direction). Also affected by the Chinese revolution, *Yön* adopted Mao's 'first democratic, then socialist revolution' principle and changed it to 'first Kemalism, then socialism' (Aydın 2002). *Yön*, in this sense, was the first group directly linking Kemalist principles with a democratic nationalist revolution to the extent that Kemalism was called national socialism. The nationalistic accent in the discourses of the left was also affected by other examples of anti-imperialist struggle such as Nehru's in India, Musaddık's in Iran and Nasser's in Egypt. The Army and the armed forces were increasingly favoured as potential coalition partners and quick, top-down revolutionary formulations became commonplace. For the *Yön*, for instance, the Army was the driving force of the anti-imperialist struggle.

After the mid-1960s a less nationalistic, more socialistic version of the NDR appeared within leftist ranks. Mihri Belli, a member of the newly-established Türkiye İşçi Partisi (TIP) – Turkish Workers Party, challenged both *Yön*'s analysis and the TIP leadership's 'mild socialist attitude' which was seeking a regime change mainly through parliamentary and constitutional means. Belli (1988), while recognising Kemalism as a positive step towards achievement of the NDR in Turkey, defined the culture of the Kemalist elite, including the state and the Army hierarchy, as 'petit bourgeois' and asserted that without the socialist leadership of the working class, imperialist forces would easily lure the petit bourgeoisie to their side. Thus, for Belli, cooperation between the revolutionary forces and the representatives of the petit bourgeois was essential in order to realise a revolution. Within this coalition, Belli also included representatives of the national capital as potential allies against the imperialist forces.

Belli's version of NDR became the main theoretical framework for most of the left factions which flourished between 1974 and 1980. With the exception of pro-Soviet factions, such as the TKP, the TIP and, later on, Türkiye Sosyalist İşçi Partisi (TSIP) – Socialist Worker's Party of Turkey, most of the factions subscribed to the idea of NDR though they differed in their interpretations of it. The idea of a national struggle remained a major theme among the left until its demise after the 1980 military coup. However, with Mihri Belli's influence, the left – with one major exception – managed to look at the idea of nationalism from a more class-based perspective. A group called *Aydınlık* distinguished itself from the rest of the left by increasingly focusing on nationalism and nationalist struggle rather than socialism. The nationalistic nature of *Aydınlık* was perhaps the main reason its members survived the 1980 coup with the least possible damage and resumed their political activities soon after. Today, İşçi Partisi (IP) – Workers Party carries the ideas of the *Aydınlık* tradition with a stronger accent on nationalism directly derived from Kemalism. The nationalism of the *Aydınlık* tradition is so strong that socialism is largely secondary. A good example of the level of its nationalism is its strongly anti-Kurdish position in favour of the Kemalist idea of *Misak-i Milli* (the unity of nation and homeland). IP's nationalism eventually was so strong that they did not hesitate to cooperate with the Left's arch enemy, the ultra nationalist, 'fascist' MHP. Cooperation between the IP and the MHP reached a new level when they recently joined ranks in an anti-European Union campaign and to fight against a solution to the Cyprus problem proposed by the United Nations. Aydın (2002) argues that the nationalistic character of *Aydınlık* and the IP has risen to such an extent that it is now acting with a mission to carry the socialist tradition in Turkey into the ranks of ethnic nationalism. Whatever this mission is, it is hard to dispute that today the IP represents the highest point of convergence between the Kemalist and the nationalistic discourses within the left. In this sense, it substantially differs from the Liberal Left Discourse which followed a different development path after the 1980 military coup.

The 1980 military coup represented a fundamental turning point for the left. The military regime's assault on the left was relentless. The Army's agenda was to eliminate the left opposition completely. Thousands were arrested, tortured and jailed. With the possible exception of *Aydınlık*, left organisations were completely crushed. From the mid-1980s some of these groups reformed associations and political parties and tried to revive their old grassroots. None of them was able to recover previous levels of support. The collapse of the Soviet regime in 1989 was the last nail in the coffin. In the eyes of ordinary people, the idea of socialism was dead and the left discourse had no alternative to offer than repeating the nostalgia that socialism would win one day.

Disabling the left eventually prompted the rise of a different discourse seeking an alternative approach to the definition of democratic politics by the traditional left. Dissatisfied by traditional class-based analysis, the new left discourse took a liberal turn by focusing on individual rights and freedom. The most apparent manifestation of this was rapid expansion of the İnsan Hakları Derneği (IHD) – Human Rights Association, formed in 1986 and supported by members of different left organisations which defended individual democratic rights. By 1996, the IHD had 58 branches in almost every major city in Turkey and more than 16,000 members (Plagemann 2001). The IHD's consistent defence of individual rights also attracted various community groups into the ranks of the organisation. These groups, such as feminists, gay and lesbian groups and environmentalists, traditionally did not have strong ties with the left in Turkey. The natural outcome of this growth for the IHD was continuous expansion of its discourse based on individual rights and freedom which is detected by the Q study. So far in Turkey, the Liberal Left discourse has remained outside mainstream politics in that its characteristics have not been represented fully in any political organisation. In this sense it remains a potential political force to be mobilised. With the liberal turn in Islamic politics, its influence in establishing a democratic polity in Turkey may be crucial.

*Factor Interpretation*

Mistrust towards the state and the Army emerges immediately in the LLD which points to a superficially-created conflict between seculars and Muslims, manipulated by the dominant groups in the state in order to maintain their status quo (48). The indication here is that the LLD, unlike ND, does not subscribe to an abstract notion of the state that citizens are expected to support unconditionally. Indeed, among four discourses, the LLD appears to be the most consistent in its critical approach towards the state and the Army.

Hostility towards the state is followed by the suggestion that existing divisions can be overcome by working on commonalities (59). The LLD's proximity to the ND (+6) is, in this case, noteworthy. Its emphasis has a different substance than that of ND. In the case of LLD, the emphasis on the commonality signifies building solidarity around those differences by first acknowledging them, then negotiating the common points, whereas ND underlines commonality primarily in reference to national unity, often ignoring existing cultural and ethnic differences.

The LLD's anti-state and anti-Army attitude is also linked to its stand on Kemalism. The LLD does not subscribe to the Kemalist line as the ND and the KD do. The LLD clearly disapproves of the idea that the Army should play a role in politics (7). With this, the LLD seems more in line with the Islamic discourse (ID) than the two secular discourses. However, the LLD also draws a line between the ID and itself by moving against the Islamic idea that religious values should play a role in determining the framework for freedom (49). In these most prominent score lines the LLD establishes its main priorities. It is clearly a secular theme but with substantial differences from the ND and the KD's. It wants to see a polity based on acknowledgement of basic individual rights with no interference from the Army or from religion.

In the +5 score, the LLD moves to define the scarf problem as a human rights issue (47). Again, this brings the LLD closer to the ND (+5). However, their reasons for defending the scarf appear to be different. The LLD is mainly concerned with human rights and sees its position as a sign of its commitment to recognition

**Table 5.3    The LLD statements and rankings (6 most agree, -6 most disagree)**

| 59 | We have to find out what is common among us rather than focusing on differences. For instance, we have to emphasise the importance of education at the universities instead of arguing about the scarf controversy. | 6 |
|---|---|---|
| 48 | The conflict between secular and Islamic people has been created superficially. The groups who are in control of the state have always created enemies in order to maintain their power. Yesterday it was communism, today fundamentalist Islam. | 6 |
| 47 | My wife has been refused to be issued a health card only because she wears a scarf. This is against basic human rights and secularism. | 5 |
| 61 | We should trust our people whether they are Kurds, Turks, Laz, Alevi, whether they wear a scarf or not. The more divisions are created in the name of state protection, the more divided we become. This is the real danger. | 5 |
| 40 | The fear of communism and fundamentalism has contributed to the inclusion of very undemocratic rules in the penal code (141, 142, 163) against them. If they were let develop freely, they would be able to reach new synthesises, thus avoid today's problems. | 5 |
| 54 | The state is not supposed to carry a religious identity. Its task should only be to govern people. It should not question its people on the basis of their religious identities. | 4 |
| 25 | Whether I cover myself with a scarf or not should not be anyone else's business. This is what I understand from secularism. Everybody should pay respect to different beliefs. | 4 |
| 33 | The military tradition has paralysed the self-reflective ability of our society. That is why we still have been governed by a mentality, which is out of date. | 4 |
| 39 | Notwithstanding the claim, our state is not a secular one. Forcing people to declare their religion on their identity cards or having compulsory religious lessons in schools are examples of this. | 4 |
| 17 | The purpose of religion will be defeated when it is carried over to the public arena. Beliefs are personal matters, thus they should be kept within the individual sphere. | 3 |
| 53 | I support our President who defends the supremacy of law. We can only solve our democratic problems by creating a real system of law in our country. | 3 |
| 6 | The problem with Islamic law in relation to democracy is that Islamic communities exert social pressure on individuals. This conflicts with the democratic notion of individual freedom and rights. | 3 |

**Table 5.3 continued**    **The LLD statements and rankings (6 most agree, -6 most disagree)**

| 21 | Whether the state is secular or not should not be dealt with by the Constitution. The state should only act as a guarantor of the freedom of religious practice. There should not be a state institution to organise religious practice. | 3 |
|---|---|---|
| 1 | Today's oppressive attitudes against Muslims in the name of secularism are rooted in Kemalist ideology. | 3 |
| 64 | The Islamists are only softening their lines because of the strong resistance shown against them by the Army and Kemalists. | -3 |
| 23 | One cannot claim to be a real Muslim if one does not interpret Qur'an in the light of today's living condition. | -3 |
| 41 | Quite a few female students, who had to take off their scarf to be admitted to universities, later became quite happy with their new look. May be this rule allowed them to do what they really want. | -3 |
| 10 | The differences between us are too deep. We cannot reconcile them by talking. This system will remain as it is in the future. | -3 |
| 3 | Secularism is atheism. | -3 |
| 15 | Islam can accommodate different groups including atheists. | -4 |
| 52 | Respect for individual rights, the fundamental principle of democracy and secularism, exists in Islam. | -4 |
| 51 | If the freedom of belief is overemphasised, Muslim people might be affected by the ideas that are dangerous for the secular regime. | -4 |
| 24 | The Qur'an does not praise a particular political system. Islam can fit into any system as long as it is fair. For instance, Islam could fit into a monarchy if the King were fair. | -4 |
| 60 | In a secular society everybody should abide by the law. If the law bans wearing the scarf in public institutions the rule should be respected. | -5 |
| 20 | If everybody tries to live according to Islamic rule, a just system can come into existence. | -5 |
| 19 | People are less corrupt under *Shari'ah* regime because it induces the fear of God. | -5 |
| 7 | The army is the guarantor of democracy and secularism. | -6 |
| 49 | In a Muslim society, the framework for freedom has to be determined according to Islamic values. | -6 |

of cultural differences. On the other hand, ND is motivated by its conservative, Islamic inclinations rather than by human rights. The different scores obtained for statement (61), suggesting that people must be trusted no matter what their backgrounds are, testify to this difference between the two discourses. Compared to the high score in the LLD, the ND scores a relatively low +2.

With statement (40), the LLD expands its critique of the state's undemocratic measures. This is consistent with its pro-human rights attitude since articles 141, 142 and 163 of the Turkish Criminal Code are related to freedom of expression. Indeed, the LLD is highly consistent on the issue of human rights compared to other discourses. Statement (40), for instance, receives (+2) both from the KD and the ID, and is simply rejected by the ND with a (-2) score.

The -5 score reinforces the LLD's negation of Islamic rule used as a framework for implementation of a just system. In this sense, the LLD makes its secular position very clear in that it disapproves the interference of religious rule with the rules of public life (19-20). The rule of law appears to be the most likely medium for the LLD in organising the public life. However, the LLD points to a controversial direction indicating that defying the law is also possible if it is against basic individual rights (60), thus again emphasising the importance of human rights ahead of other issues. Here, the LLD again moves away from the other secular discourses (the KD +3, the ND 0) towards the Islamic discourse, which scores a high (-6).

While statements in the +4 score category reinforce what has been said so far, with statements (39) and (25) the LLD expands its critique of the state, this time focusing on its credentials on secularism. It indicates that both compulsory religious lessons and the forceful treatment of the scarf problem run against the state's claim to secularism. In this sense, the LLD subscribes to a liberal secular line, advocating a freedom of religious practice immune from state intervention. Similarly, the LLD also agrees with statement (54), which expects the state not to interfere with citizens' religious practices. The LLD's liberalism here differs from the KD's liberal secular line since, unlike the KD, the LLD does not subscribe to the Kemalist state tradition. Consistently with this, the LLD also affirms that the military tradition has had a negative impact on the intellectual capacity of the society (33).

Yet, the LLD has also a critical attitude towards Islam. It does not support Islam as a political entity (24) and expresses doubt about the inclusive capacity of Islam in terms of both individual and minority rights (52-15). Indeed, among all discourses it is the LLD that finds Islam's argument on individual rights the least convincing. However, it still defends the freedom of religious practice (51) as part of its commitment to human rights more extensively than the two other secular discourses do, and nearly as much as the Islamic discourse.

The +3 score reaffirms that the LLD sees religious practice as a fundamental individual right that should not be interfered with by the state (21). This is in sharp contrast with other discourses including the ID. The support for religious practice is, however, qualified through the indication that it should remain within the private sphere since it is an individual matter (17). The perceived problem with Islamic law that it conflicts with democratic rights is also introduced to underline the importance of individual freedom (6).

The LLD brings the role of the law to attention as well. In line with the KD, it advocates the law as the main regulator of the social order (53).

The LLD's anti-Kemalist stand emerges most clearly in the +3 score. It agrees that in the secular camp Kemalism is the source of oppressive tendencies towards Muslims (1). The LLD's position is in sharp contrast with other secular discourses, the KD (-5) and the ND (-5). In fact, this time its reaction to Kemalism is even stronger than the ID's which also disagrees with the statement (-1).

An expected reaction to the claim that secular people are atheists (3) is followed by rejection of the claim that the differences are too deep to be reconciled through dialogue (10). Statement (10) emerges as one of the consensus points among discourses, presenting a high degree of willingness towards understanding each other; the KD (-4), the ND (-6) and the ID (-5).

The LLD takes a further step by refusing the suggestion that the Islamists have softened their lines due to the tough resistance shown by the Army and Kemalists (64). With this, the LDD again moves parallel to the ID (-4). The suggestion that female students became happy after they removed their headscarfs is rejected (41) by all discourses, yet again, the LLD's score (-3) positions it closer to the ID (-4).

*Overview*

Unlike the KD and the ND, the LLD has a coherent position in relation to Islam, democracy and secularism. It does not subscribe to Kemalist principles. Its conception of democratic politics is based on protection of fundamental individual rights. It is in this sense that the LLD consistently defends the right to religious freedom and conceives the scarf issue as a human rights problem.

In parallel to its commitment to individual rights, the LLD consistently argues against heavy-handed state practices as well as against the role of the Army in politics.

The LLD is committed to a secular system yet it defines secularism from a different perspective than that of the KD or the ND. Since, for the LLD, the basis for a democratic polity is establishment of individual rights, it does not pay much attention to the unity of the state. It supports attempts to reach a common framework between different groups and views of the Turkish public sphere, yet it does so to build solidarity between different groups rather than to secure the unity of the state. In other words, acknowledgement of differences comes first for the LLD. To this end democracy has priority over secularism.

Prioritising democracy over secularism is the main reason that the LLD stands closer to the Islamic Discourse than to other secular discourses, the KD and the ND. For the development of democratic politics in Turkey the proximity of the LLD to the ID is new and important. This issue is considered in Chapter 7. For the time being it suffices to say that this unusual alliance between the LLD and the ID could be the genesis of a new phase in Turkish politics. This is where the individual rights-based paradigm shift that occurred both in the left and Islamic groups represents a potential for a new form of cooperation between groups once considered at opposite poles of the political spectrum. A politics based on universal acceptance of individual rights rather than on class or religion constitutes the grounds of this new cooperation.

What makes the LLD's positive approach to religious freedom significant is that the LLD does not compromise the principle of religious freedom even though it is doubtful about the democratic credentials of Islam. Unlike the KD and the ND, the LLD does not let any fears hijack the fundamental principle of individual rights and performs consistently on the basis of this principle. The effects of this consistency are already discernible in the Turkish public sphere. New forms of alliances emerging between the left and Islamic groups point one more time to the importance of deliberation as social learning and understanding. An account of one of those alliances may be found in Chapter 6.

### Factor 4: The Islamic Discourse (ID)

*General Characteristics*

According to the Q study findings, the ID fully subscribes to Islamic values and expects them to play a role in public life. This is surely the major point of contention between the ID and secular discourses.

Naturally, it opposes many Kemalist ideas, particularly those related to secularism. Yet the ID bases its opposition to secularism on democratic points of view by emphasising the importance of freedom of religious practice. Hence, it defends the freedom of using the headscarf as part of a democratic practice. As in the case of the LLD, democratic principles have priority over secularism in the ID. Similarly, on the role of the Army and the state in dealing with religious matters, the ID shares the same sentiment with the LLD. In fact, on those issues the Q findings indicate a remarkable similarity between the ID and the LLD. The Q study findings also indicate that the ID, as with the KD and the ND, is in need of resolving the issue in relation to the public and private divide, that is, even though the ID argues for democratic values it is not clear how it would react if there were a conflict between democratic principles and some Islamic concepts.

Apart from its specifically Islamic aspects, what clearly distinguishes the ID from other discourses is its emphasis on the role of dialogue and mutual understanding. The Q findings show that all statements related to dialogue and mutual understanding are ranked very highly by the ID. Indeed, emphasis on these points is so distinctive that, in terms of prospects for democracy in Turkey, it could be described as the most important single finding of the Q study. The ID, as the factor analysis will show, consistently argues for reconciling differences through a process of rational dialogue and rebuffs suggestions that Islam and democracy are irreconcilable.

## Historical Origins of the Islamic Discourse

The background for the Kemalist discourse included an outline of how the process of modernisation developed under Ottoman rule in the 19th century. Following announcement of the first official reforms, *Tanzimat*, in 1839, the Ottoman culture in both social and political spheres went through an unstoppable change until collapse of the Empire after the First World War. Islam was at the centre of this remarkable transformation process. The roots of the Islamic Discourse in contemporary Turkey go back to the beginning of this reform process in Ottoman administration. After almost 1,300 years of supremacy, Islam, for the first time, had to negotiate the conditions of coexistence with a value system that is different because it is based on western ideas and ideals.

Introduction of western liberal principles to Ottoman administration prompted a reaction from some elements of the Ottoman elite. This reaction was the basis for establishment of Young Ottomans, who aimed at formulating an alternative plan for rescuing the Ottoman state. This plan initially sought to develop a notion of Ottomanism that could be espoused by both Muslims and non-Muslims living under the Ottoman regime. Young Otttomans' ideas were liberal in essence. Yet the increasing influence of western powers over the Ottoman regime, coupled with the successive gains of the non-Muslims in terms of social and economic rights, stirred an Islamic sentiment among the Young Ottomans even though they still maintained commitment to liberal values. From this moment, Islamic values became part of a political agenda to be called Islamism.

Islamism in this sense developed as a reaction of the Ottoman elite to western values introduced with *Tanzimat*. The purpose of this reaction was not by any means aimed at halting the modernisation process. In fact, as Türköne (2003) asserts, Islamism was represented a positive step towards change. It was seen not so much as a tool to resist transformation of the unwieldy Ottoman administration but as a catalyst to achieve accord with Ottoman values so that the change could in fact be sustained. In other words, development of Islamism was an attempt to accomplish a balance between traditional and modern ways of living in order to achieve a successful transformation of the state. In this sense it also represented a challenge to traditional, scriptural readings of Islam. For instance, with Islamism, a rational way of thinking based on individuals' reasoning capacity was introduced. The traditional ways of accepting God's word as a transcendental order was replaced by conscientious actions of individuals. In sum, Islamism represented a synthesis of traditional Islam and some key western concepts.

Türköne's observation is important for two main reasons. Firstly, it shows that the liberal roots of today's Islamic Discourse can be located in the Islamism of the 19th century. Secondly, with introduction of new concepts to traditional Islamic thinking, Islamism also opened the possibility of digesting other western concepts such as the ideas of nation-state and nationalism, which later dominated the political discourse. The interplay between Islamic, nationalist and later Kemalist discourses was more noteworthy than is usually now appreciated. This issue will be analysed in detail in the concluding chapter since it is fundamental to appreciating the conditions of dialogue in today's Turkey.

With the beginning of modernisation, Islam became part of the political discourse in the 19th century Ottoman regime. The Young Ottomans were constantly arguing that the failure of the Ottoman regime was mainly stemmed from erosion in Islamic values. This pro-Islamic stand was carefully crafted to gain the support of *ulema* (Islamic intellectuals) (Türköne 2003). Soon the idea of *ittihad-i İslam* (the unity of Islam) appeared in the political grammar. The *ittihad-i İslam* was seen as the solution for re-establishing the unity and authority of the Ottoman state. The Ottoman elite was not initially enthusiastic about *ittihad-i İslam* because it conflicted with the idea of Ottomanism. The idea of Ottomanism lost its appeal following the Ottoman defeat in the Russian War of 1878, when two-fifths of Ottoman land inhabited by one-fifth of the Empire's population (mainly non-Muslims) was lost. The Ottoman administration, under the rule of Abdulhamid the Second, then adopted a new policy to enhance the living conditions of the Muslim population instead of protecting the rights of non-Islamic minority groups. This was a clear policy shift towards *ittihad-i Islam* resulting in implementation of several big projects ranging from education to transport to strengthening solidarity among the Muslim communities of the Empire (Çetinsaya 2001b).

Sultan Abdulhamid's Islamism was mainly motivated by pragmatism. He was more interested in using Islam to combat the growing sense of nationalism and separatism among Muslim but non-Turkish ethnic groups, such as Albanians, Kurds and Arabs. He did not pay much attention to Pan Islamic ideals; his Islamism had a defensive character and was largely focused on restoring internal order (Alkan 2001). While doing this, Sultan Abdulhamid created a state-controlled Islam. During his reforms he managed to eliminate the influence of *ulema* by creating a western-type education system and reorganising the religious class under his control. Ironically, this is exactly what Mustafa Kemal later did in the Turkish Republic. The roots of statism in Kemalist principles can be readily discerned in the Ottoman tradition.

Sultan Abdulhamid also tried to incorporate Turkish nationalism into Islamism. The outcome was an Islam-Turkish synthesis in which Turkishness was subordinated to Islam in a complementary fashion. Sultan Abdulhamid's main concern to keep the Empire intact was reflected clearly in his pragmatic approach to Islam. The end of Abdulhamid regime also signalled the end of Islam's influence. Following the second *Meşrutiyet* in 1908, Turkish nationalism assumed the ascendancy. Alkan (2001) defines this period as the transformation of Islam-Turkish synthesis to Turkish-Islam synthesis. The rise of Turkish nationalism and western secularism were particularly prevalent during the *Ittihat Terakki* regime which lasted from 1911 till the end of the First World War, which brought a new era for Turkish Islam. The fate of Islam under the Turkish Republic has already been traversed in the account of the five stages of Islam and its relationship with the state in Turkey.

The crucial point in this background is the strong parallel between the Young Ottoman's and the AKP's appropriation of liberal ideas into their Islamic way of thinking. The difference is that while the Young Ottomans never managed to rule the country, the AKP is already in government and, indeed, serving a second term. What kind of difference this could make will be seen more clearly through the following analysis of the Islamic Discourse. The fact that attempts within the Islamic ranks to reconcile their traditional values with the realities of the modern world is not new may shed light on present conditions.

*Factor Interpretation*

Compared to other discourses, the ID makes the strongest plea for dialogue and recognition of different identities. The call for dialogue is qualified, carefully favouring a rational and conciliatory style (57). The antagonistic style of Mr Erbakan, who led the Islamic movement in Turkey from the early 1970s until he was banned from politics in 1998, is also dismissed, indicating a high level of self-critique among Muslims.

Willingness for dialogue is strongly supported by another call for acknowledging the ethnic and cultural realities of Turkey instead of conceiving them as a potential threat in the name of the unity of the state and the nation (61).

The ID's reaction to two major issues, the scarf and the Army's interference in politics, emerges strongly through the -6 sores attributed to statements (7) and (60). The ID questions the unreserved support given both to the Army and to law. The ID's strong reaction against statement (60), suggesting that if a law bans wearing the scarf in public institutions, people must be abide by it, expresses its discontent with the current situation. This does not necessarily suggest law is to be disobeyed, since the ID later on shows that it is not in favour of civil disobedience (63). It is more to do with the state's heavy handling of the scarf issue. Consistently with this, the ID also displays strong disapproval of the state's interference with religious affairs (54). Reaction to the state's paternalistic involvement with religion in fact appears to be a strong point of consensus between all discourses. It is in this sense that the ID points at the Qur'an's indifference towards political regimes as long as they are fair (24). From an Islamic perspective, this statement is important since it suggests that Islam and a secular regime can indeed coexist together. As shown previously, this claim has been one of the major arguments that Islamic scholars have been defending in favour of the relationship between Islam and democracy. It simply suggests that the Qur'an leaves the issue of how to govern their society to its followers. It does not offer a blueprint for any kind of political regime. Politics, in other words, is a worldly affair to be conducted by believers. Although the statement offers a positive approach to the relationship between Islam and democracy, it has not been evaluated positively by other discourses. One reason for this could be that the statement is perhaps understood differently by secular discourses. Clarifying this difference between the ID and others would possibly represent an important step towards reconciliation among all discourses.

**Table 5.4     The ID statements and rankings (6 most agree, -6 most disagree)**

| | | |
|---|---|---|
| 61 | We should trust our people whether they are Kurds, Turks, Laz, Alevi, whether they wear a scarf or not. The more divisions are created in the name of state protection, the more divided we become. This is the real danger. | 6 |
| 57 | We have no other choice to solve our problems, but dialog. However, we have to be careful of the tone of the dialogue, which should favour a rational, non-antagonistic style that respects others. | 6 |
| 54 | The state is not supposed to carry a religious identity. Its task should only be to govern people. It should not question its people on the basis of their religious identities. | 5 |
| 14 | The universities are important places where secular people and Islamists can close the existing gap between the two groups. When we do not allow female students wearing scarf into the universities we also throw them out of the modern world. By doing this we jeopardise the possibility of living together. | 5 |
| 24 | The Qur'an does not praise a particular political system. Islam can fit into any system as long as it is fair. For instance, Islam could fit into a monarchy if the King were fair. | 5 |
| 25 | Whether I cover myself with a scarf or not should not be anyone else's business. This is what I understand from secularism. Everybody should pay respect to different beliefs. | 4 |
| 58 | The fundamental condition is respect for others. If we achieve this at the grassroots level, then we can solve the problems created and imposed from above. | 4 |
| 15 | Islam can accommodate different groups including atheists. | 4 |
| 49 | In a Muslim society, the framework for freedom has to be determined according to Islamic values. | 4 |
| 59 | We have to find out what is common among us rather than focusing on differences. For instance, we have to emphasise the importance of education at the universities instead of arguing about the scarf controversy. | 3 |
| 48 | The conflict between secular and Islamic people has been created superficially. The groups who are in control of the state have always created enemies in order to maintain their power. Yesterday it was communism, today fundamentalist Islam. | 3 |
| 47 | My wife has been refused to be issued a health card only because she wears a scarf. This is against basic human rights and secularism. | 3 |
| 42 | The solution is mutual understanding. Groups, who oppose each other, should try to understand each other. | 3 |

**Table 5.4 continued**      **The ID statements and rankings (6 most agree, -6 most disagree)**

| | | |
|---|---|---|
| 4 | About one thousand female students have been refused entry to the University of Marmara because they dress themselves according to their religious belief. This shows that there is a serious problem with freedom of belief and education in Turkey. | 3 |
| 11 | In some religious cities, during the Ramadan people were beaten if they ate or drank in daytime. How can I be sure that Islamists will not do the same if they come to power? How can I trust them? | -3 |
| 9 | Islamists are not as tolerant towards atheists as atheists are towards Islamists. | -3 |
| 34 | Secularism is the undeniable foundation of religious pluralism and the most important norm for societal peace. We must hold on to it. | -3 |
| 13 | Some remarks made by Islamic leaders contributed to raising the tension between Islamists and Kemalists. An example of this is Mr Erbakan's remark suggesting that one day the deans', who do not allow students with scarf to the universities, will be forced to salute those students. | -3 |
| 44 | I am trying to survive economically to be able to feed my children. The debate between Islam and secularism does not interest me. | -3 |
| 16 | Islam, as a system of law, cannot be compatible with democracy. The role and the place attributed to women by Islamic law, which denies women basic individual rights, is enough to prove this. | -4 |
| 2 | Kemalism and secularism cannot be separated from each other. Separating them will mean the end of secularism. If you are secular you are also Kemalist, or vica versa. | -4 |
| 64 | The Islamists are only softening their lines because of the strong resistance shown against them by the Army and Kemalists. | -4 |
| 41 | Quite a few female students, who had to take off their scarf to be admitted to universities, later became quite happy with their new look. May be this rule allowed them to do what they really want. | -4 |
| 17 | The purpose of religion will be defeated when it is carried over to the public arena. Beliefs are personal matters. They should be kept within the individual sphere. | -5 |
| 10 | The differences between us are too deep. We cannot reconcile them by talking. This system will remain as it is in the future. | -5 |
| 51 | If the freedom of belief is overemphasised, Muslim people might be affected by the ideas that are dangerous for the secular regime. | -5 |
| 60 | In a secular society everybody should abide by the law. If the law bans wearing the scarf in public institutions, the rule should be respected. | -6 |
| 7 | The army is the guarantor of democracy and secularism. | -6 |

The headscarf issue remains the top priority, this time through the suggestion that allowing students to wear the scarf at university would enhance the chance of reconciliation (14). The ID acknowledges that modern university education is not only a medium allowing Muslim students to embrace modernity, but also a melting pot for different groups in society.

Along with other discourses, the ID affirms its strong opposition to the suggestion that reconciling existing differences in society is not achievable (10). Consistent with its call for dialogue, it remains committed to development of mutual understanding between the groups. It is in this respect that it also rejects limiting freedom of belief because too much of it could be dangerous for the secular regime (51).

The ID disagrees with one of secular discourses' main arguments that religious beliefs should remain within the private sphere since they are purely personal matters (17). This is one of the most important differences between the ID and other discourses, which shows that the ID perceives a public/private divide differently from others. The tension between the ID and others is fundamental, requiring both sides to clarify what they mean by 'public'.

The problem in relation to the public/private divide reappears, in this case showing the ID's tendency more clearly. The ID approves of applying religious rules in the conduct of public life (49). In conjunction with statement (17) above, the ID is now clearly at odds with secular discourses as well as with the secular idea itself. The strong disparity between the ID and others shows that it is a major issue and that it requires a certain effort to revamp the idea of public rule particularly from an Islamic point of view. When this is considered together with the way the KD and the ND envisage the public and private divide, it clearly points to one of the major issues to be resolved between the ID, on one hand, and the KD and the ND on the other. The LLD, with its consistent argument in favour of individual rights, remains outside this troubled zone.

The headscarf issue appears again (25), this time more clearly linked to secularism and individual rights. The ID, the LLD and the KD are clearly in agreement on this matter. Mutual respect is reemphasised in statement (58), which affirms that change should start from the grassroots. Similarly, skepticism about the treatment of minority groups under Islamic rules is not shared by the ID, which comfortably approves statement (15) indicating its belief that Islam is indeed tolerant towards different groups. Other discourses are clearly skeptical about this claim, indicating a major point of contention.

The ID deals with the issue of Kemalism first time in the -4 score. This is noteworthy given that the issue represents a major rift for the ID and is dealt with almost immediately by the KD. The ID opposes the idea that Kemalism and secularism are mutually inclusive, suggesting that one can be secular without necessarily being Kemalist (2).

The ID also rejects the suggestion that pressure from the Army and Kemalists has been the only reason Islamists softened their lines (64). On the basis of what has been said in the follow-up interviews, rejection here is more about representing the issue as the 'only' reason. Overall subjects adhering to the ID acknowledged that stiff resistance from the Army played a role in changing their attitude.

Islam's compatibility with democracy is defended on the basis that Islamic law does not deny basic individual rights to women (16), again a major contentious issue to be resolved. The suggestion that some female students became happy after they remove the headscarf to be able to continue their university education is also predictably rejected, but this time with some support from the other discourses (41).

The ID continues to represent the scarf issue as a major problem by linking it to basic individual rights. While statement (4) elaborates the issue as a problem of freedom of education and belief, statement (47) cast it directly as a breach of human rights.

On the other hand, strong support for dialogue and mutual understanding continues to surface. Statement (42) directly refers to mutual understanding as the solution to curb antagonistic tendencies among opposing groups. Statement (59) further supports this by suggesting focusing on commonalities rather than on differences in society. The headscarf issue is in this sense seen as an obstacle to achieving a common understanding. More importantly, with statement (48) the ID points to the source of the problem, indicating that it is easier to find a solution outside state power, thus reaffirming its support of a grassroots-based approach to solve the problem.

The -3 score mainly indicates scepticism of the ID about some secular claims. The claims that Islamists are less tolerant than atheists (9) and tension between secular and Islamic people has been created by provocative remarks of some Islamic leaders (13) are both believed to be unsubstantiated. The ID also rejects drawing up some general patterns on the basis of isolated incidences such as beating non-fasting people in some cities (11). The follow-up interviews indicated that attacks on non-fasting people during Ramadan are uncommon and cannot be used as an example of how Muslims could behave if they came to power. Representation of secularism as the foundation of societal peace is also questioned (34).

The exception is rejection of statement (44), which condones an indifferent attitude towards the debate between seculars and Islamists. The ID here displays the same attitude as other discourses.

*Overview*

The factor analysis clearly displays the ID's Islamic and anti-Kemalist position. The ID culturally submits itself to Islam and displays a strong anti-Kemalist disposition. Linked to its anti-Kemalism, the ID also exhibits an anti-Army and anti-state attitude.

The ID's reaction to the core institutions of the Kemalist regime represents a crucial step for the future of democratic practice in Turkey, because the ID resorts to a new strategy based on recognition of individual rights. For instance, the ID's main argument against Kemalism targets the way Kemalism defines secularism.

The ID questions the Kemalist claim of a mutually exclusive relationship between secularism and the freedom of religious practice. The strictly anti-religious standpoint of Kemalists represents an anti-democratic stand for the ID.

The ID's attempt to define religious freedom from the point of view of democratic rights is a fundamental step away from traditional Islamic politics, which was mainly preoccupied with defending Islamic values. The ID is now replacing the traditionally defensive strategy with an assertive one, advocating religious freedom within a broader framework of freedom. As part of this strategy, the ID favours recognition of different cultural and ethical identities and makes a strong plea for dialogue between different groups. In fact, the ID's position for reconciliation is the strongest among the discourses revealed by the Q study.

Some background to this change in Islamic politics is provided in section on Background to the Case of Turkey. The Q study confirmed this tendency within the discourses of the Turkish Muslim population. The ID's emphasis on individual rights signals a new opening for a democratic polity in Turkey. Proximity between the ID and the LLD and the genesis of a new form of cooperation between these groups has already been noted. The shift to an individual-rights based politics also brings the possibility of broadening this new form of cooperation to include larger sections of Turkey. The basis of this possibility is signaled in the findings of the Q study. The aim of the next chapter is to analyse the Q findings further in order to identify the possibilities of potential dialogue between the divided groups of the Turkish public sphere.

# Chapter 6

# Discourse Comparison

## Topic-based Analysis of Similarities and Differences

The factor interpretation in the previous chapter has revealed some important patterns between discourses. The information gathered could lead to mapping out possible ways of reaching understanding between the discourses by identifying both the points they share and those they disagree about. There are points of convergence between all four discourses, but also, and perhaps more importantly, between pairs of discourses. Thus there are similarities between the Liberal Left and the Islamic discourses as well as the Kemalist and the Nationalist discourses. A pair wise comparison of discourses provides a more flexible way of finding potential points upon which mutual understanding can be built. For instance, there are some striking similarities between the Liberal Left and the Islamic discourses which could only be revealed by looking at these two discourses closely. It is, therefore, the aim of this section that those converging and diverging points are clearly identified so that a better comprehension of how, under the specific conditions of the Turkish public sphere, a framework for mutual understanding could be developed. The comparison of discourses will be done by looking at their attitudes towards the topics that appeared in the statements and in Turkish politics most commonly, such as the scarf, secularism, Islam and democracy. A topic-based comparison will be followed by a discourse-based comparison revealing specific interactions more clearly.

### Dialogue for Mutual Understanding

Dialogue oriented to mutual understanding and respect for differences emerges as the main issue upon which an agreement between discourses seems to be possible. It appears that in general terms, all discourses agree about the benefits of dialogue and mutual understanding. Some individual differences emerge when the issue is discussed in more specific terms but they do not display a strong divergence.

Several statements stand out as strong consensus points between discourses. Statement (59) focuses on what is common between groups rather than on differences. It is therefore a strong indication of the tendency among the discourses to attempt to reach a common understanding about controversial issues. Even though the KD and the ID's support of statement 59 are slightly weaker than that of the ND and the LLD's (both scoring +6), statement (59) represents one of the major consensus points between all discourses. What makes this more meaningful is the commitment shown by all sides to mutual understanding as a solution to current problems between seculars and Muslims (42), though the LLD lags slightly

**Table 6.1    Dialogue for mutual understanding (6 most agree, -6 most disagree)**

|  | Statements | KD | ND | LLD | ID |
|---|---|---|---|---|---|
| 59 | We have to find out what is common among us rather than focusing on differences. For instance, we have to emphasise the importance of education at the universities instead of arguing about the scarf controversy. | 3 | 6 | 6 | 3 |
| 42 | The solution is mutual understanding. Groups who oppose each other should try to understand each other. | 3 | 3 | 1 | 3 |
| 10 | The differences between us are too deep. We cannot reconcile them by talking. This system will remain as it is in the future. | -4 | -6 | -3 | -5 |
| 27 | The important thing is to start from somewhere. If people could start showing respect and tolerance to each other, this would force the state to do the same. | 2 | 1 | -1 | 1 |
| 57 | We have no other means of solving our problems, but dialogue. However, we have to be careful of the tone of the dialogue, which should favour a rational, non-antagonistic style that respects others. | 3 | 1 | 1 | 6 |
| 30 | The reason behind the reaction to Kemalists is their antagonistic attitude towards Islamic people. The problem can be solved easily if they tried to understand Muslim people rather than attacking and dehumanising them. | -4 | -2 | -1 | 1 |

behind the others. This is indicative of its caution about dialogue. But it is more important that the opposite sides of the debate, that is, the ID representing Muslims, and the KD and the ND representing secular people, agree on the importance of mutual understanding. Consensus on statement (42), even if it excludes the LLD, is indicative of the role of mutual understanding in resolving conflict that all discourses agree about. The strong rejection of the view in statement (10) that reconciliation is not possible since differences are too deep further boosts support for dialogue and mutual understanding.

Levels of agreement vary according to the issue in question. For instance, the LLD's anti-state line seems to have a certain impact when it objects to statement (27). The LLD's indifference here is not so much to the idea of showing respect to each other, but to the suggestion that the state can be forced to do the same.

The LLD's reservations about dialogue also shows itself in other ways. In statement (57), the LLD seems not so enthusiastic with the view that there is no other choice but dialogue to resolve the problems. In a similar fashion, the KD's commitment to Kemalism singles itself out in statement (30). However, those differences do not emerge as sharp divisions between the discourses. The general pattern for dialogue and mutual understanding is therefore quite consistent between discourses, which all agree on the importance of dialogue as a major medium to resolve conflict. It is worth stressing that these points of convergence should also be treated with caution since they may change when the issue is discussed in more specific terms. For instance, after reading statement (59) one could readily ask, 'if everyone agrees that there should not be argument about the scarf, why is there so much argument about it?' The differences between discourses appear more clearly when their positions are tested in the context of specific cases. Overall support for dialogue and mutual understanding remains important since it becomes a binding force once it is used publicly, no matter how lightly it is treated. So, for instance, after committing themselves to statement (59), the KD and the ND would be forced to offer a good argument about why they support not allowing students to wear a headscarf at universities. This is related to consistency which is examined further in Chapter 8.

*The Scarf*

The headscarf emerges as one of the most controversial issues in the Q study. There is virtually no agreement. The only exception to that is related to the claim that some female students seemed quite content after they removed the headscarf (41), rejected in differing degrees by all discourses. Nevertheless, the scores of each statement reveal that consensus between individual discourses is always a possibility.

For instance, statement (25) falls short of a consensus between discourses, yet there is strong agreement in three discourses (the ID, the LLD and the ND) about the idea that secularism and religious practice (in the form of wearing the headscarf in public places) are not necessarily mutually exclusive. Only the KD does not agree with that. Statement (47) equally receives a similar type of consensus, since the ID, the LLD and the ND, but not the KD, support framing the scarf problem as a human rights issue. Statement (46) also shows a similar pattern, though with a less strong agreement than statement (47).

On the other hand, the issue of not allowing female students to wear the headscarf at university (4-14) points to a different collaboration between discourses. In both statements, the KD and the ND position themselves against the ID and the LLD. In other words, the line of thinking of the KD and the ND forms a consensus, which runs against that of the ID and the LLD. The LLD's neutral attitude seems closer to the ID's affirmative position than to its secular counterparts. Hence, even though there seems to be little consensus between the ID and the LLD's position, it is clearly distinguished from the other two discourses, putting the ID and the LLD in a closer proximity in their understanding of the issue. In this sense, the factor analysis reveals some essential differences about the meaning each discourse attributes to the issue. This is important since it allows interpreting some tendencies more determinately, since differences are interpreted more clearly.

**Table 6.2     The scarf (6 most agree, -6 most disagree)**

| | Statements | KD | ND | LLD | ID |
|---|---|---|---|---|---|
| 41 | Quite a few female students, who had to take off their headscarf to be admitted to universities, later became quite happy with their new look. May be this rule allowed them to do what they really want. | -1 | -1 | -3 | -4 |
| 25 | Whether I cover myself with a headscarf should not be anyone else's business. This is what I understand from secularism. Everybody should pay respect to different beliefs. | 0 | 4 | 4 | 4 |
| 47 | My wife has been refused to be issued a health card only because she wears a scarf. This is against basic human rights and secularism. | -2 | 5 | 5 | 3 |
| 46 | The secularists in Turkey claim that women who wear the scarf cannot be secular. This is not a democratic attitude. | -3 | 2 | 0 | 0 |
| 4 | About one thousand female students have been refused entry to the University of Marmara because they dress themselves according to their religious belief. This shows that there is a serious problem with freedom of belief and education in Turkey. | -3 | -1 | 0 | 3 |
| 14 | The universities are important places where secular people and Islamists can close the existing gap between the two groups. When we do not allow female students wearing scarf into the universities we also throw them out of the modern world. By doing this we jeopardise the possibility of living together. | -2 | -1 | 1 | 5 |

For instance, differences between the secular discourses appear to be quite striking. While the KD shows no signs of compromise, the ND and the LLD join with the ID by defining the issue in human rights terms. However, the ND retreats from this coalition and acts together with the KD when the issue is discussed at a more practical level, such as how to deal with the problem at the universities. In fact, the ND displays the most inconsistent attitude towards the scarf issue arising from its simultaneous allegiance to the conflicting values of Islamic and Kemalist ways of living. Whereas, as a secular discourse, the LLD, with the exception of statement (14), appears to be consistently in agreement with the ID on the scarf issue since it argues the problem from a human rights perspective but nothing else, flagging a possible alliance between the two.

*Islam*

The topic of Islam and its link to democracy portrays a different picture of relationship between discourses than the scarf issue. This time, the KD and the LLD react in a similar way particularly in relation to Islam's empathy with democracy in contrast to the ID's and the ND's more affirmative approach. The ND again wavers between secular and Islamic positions. On this issue it leans more comfortably to the ID since the statements on Islam are usually related to

**Table 6.3    Islam (6 most agree, -6 most disagree)**

| | Statements | KD | ND | LLD | ID |
|---|---|---|---|---|---|
| 49 | In a Muslim society, the framework for freedom has to be determined according to Islamic values. | -5 | -5 | -6 | 4 |
| 16 | Islam, as a system of law, cannot be compatible with democracy. The role and the place attributed to women by Islamic law, which denies women basic individual rights, is enough to prove this. | 2 | -3 | 1 | -4 |
| 9 | Islamists are not as tolerant towards atheists as atheists are towards Islamists. | 2 | -2 | 1 | -3 |
| 11 | In some religious cities, during the Ramadan people were beaten if they ate or drank in daytime. How can I be sure that Islamists will not do the same if they come to power? How can I trust them? | 0 | -1 | 2 | -3 |
| 15 | Islam can accommodate different groups including atheists. | -2 | 0 | -4 | 4 |
| 17 | The purpose of religion will be defeated when it is carried over to the public arena. Beliefs are personal matters. They should be kept within the individual sphere. | 6 | 4 | 3 | -5 |
| 6 | The problem with Islamic law in relation to democracy is that Islamic communities exert social pressure on individuals. This conflicts with the democratic notion of individual freedom and rights. | 4 | 1 | 3 | -2 |
| 37 | In Turkey, more than 80 percent of Islamic people have a moderate line. They cannot be a threat to the secular regime. | 1 | 3 | 1 | 1 |
| 19 | People are less corrupt under *Shari'ah* regime because it induces the fear of God. | -6 | -5 | -5 | -1 |
| 20 | If everybody tries to live according to Islamic rule, a just system can come into existence. | -5 | -4 | -5 | 0 |

some general remarks with no clear link to the state and/or to the public affairs. (Where this happens the ND again shifts into a pro-state position.) The KD and the LLD's objections mainly stem from skepticism that Islam is indeed compatible with democratic values. Nevertheless, all secular discourses come into a strong consensus against the suggestion that the framework for freedom in a Muslim society should be determined by Islamic values (49). This is the strongest level of consensus achieved among secular discourses. Against their reaction, the ID strongly agrees with the statement, pointing to one of the most contentious issues to be resolved between the sides.

On the other hand, statements (16, 9, 11) are clear indications of the polarisation between the ND and the ID, on the one hand, and the LLD and the KD, on the other. While the issue of Islam's compatibility with democratic values in relation to women's rights is affirmed by the ND and the ID, the KD and the LLD disagrees (16). The same pattern continues when it comes to trusting Muslims (11) and tolerating minority groups (9, 15), which are particularly deemed as satanic in Islam, though in (15) the ND remains neutral indicating that the issue of Islam accommodating non-Islamic groups is an uncertain one. The ND slightly shifts its position towards other secular discourses when it is suggested that Islam exerts social pressure on individuals (6). The secular discourses show a strong tendency to agree to the suggestion that religious affairs belong to the private sphere and should be kept outside the public sphere (17). This issue emerges as one of the strongest points of disagreement between the ID and secular discourses. The disagreement peaks when it is suggested that in an Islamic country Islamic values should be used to regulate public affairs (49). The consensus among the secular discourses reaches its highest point against the idea of using Islamic values in public affairs, confirming that the issue remains one of the most fundamental matters to be resolved between seculars and Muslims.

But some issues about Islam are also agreed on by the ID and the secular discourses. Most interestingly, all discourses have a shared understanding that most of Turkey's Muslim populations represent a moderate line, which does not pose a threat to the secular regime (37). This is indicative of the discontent among both seculars and Muslims about the firmness with which the state handles the fundamentalist threat. For seculars and Muslims, even if there is a real threat, it cannot be attributed to the entire Muslim population.

Another consensus point emerges in relation to the suggestion that Islamic law (*Shari'ah*) can reduce corruption since it induces the fear of God (19). Along with the secular discourses, the ID also tends to disagree with this statement. Even though the ID remains neutral, statement (20) also points to a similar tendency, indicating that creating a just society requires a common approach to public affairs.

Overall, statements referring to Islam indicate what needs to be done between secular and Islamic people. The most contentious issue to be resolved appears to be Islam's capacity to deal with individual rights as manifest in a traditional secular system. A constructive dialogue on this issue will most likely help to reduce the level of anxiety seculars display when dealing with Muslims.

## Kemalism and Secularism

One of the main arguments of the Kemalist tradition has been that Kemalism and secularism mutually require each other to the point that secularism would hold no meaning without Kemalism, and vice versa. This proposition is controversial and its legitimacy has been one of the main topics hotly disputed by both secular and Islamic groups. The Q-sort also indicates controversy surrounding this issue, shifting the ground around the discourses one more time. The ranking of the

**Table 6.4    Kemalism and secularism (6 most agree, -6 most disagree)**

|  | Statements | KD | ND | LLD | ID |
|---|---|---|---|---|---|
| 1 | Today's oppressive attitudes against Muslims in the name of secularism are rooted in Kemalist ideology. | -5 | -5 | 3 | -1 |
| 2 | Kemalism and secularism cannot be separated from each other. Separating them will mean the end of secularism. If you are secular, you are also Kemalist, or vice versa. | 2 | 3 | -2 | -4 |
| 64 | The Islamists are only softening their lines because of the strong resistance shown against them by the Army and Kemalists. | 1 | 3 | -3 | -4 |
| 36 | Mustafa Kemal Atatürk is a very important personality who could only be respected. However, the Kemalism label unfortunately has been stuck on him and is being unfairly used against Muslims. Kemalism has now become a metaphysical concept with a religious-like content. Like democracy, its meaning has been abused and changed. | -3 | -3 | 0 | 1 |
| 30 | The reason behind the reaction to Kemalists is their antagonistic attitude towards Islamic people. The problem can be solved easily if they tried to understand Muslim people rather than attacking and dehumanising them. | -4 | -2 | -1 | 1 |
| 45 | To claim that Muslims in Turkey are not allowed to practice their religion is a totally unfair statement. If we do not count the headscarf problem in public institutions there has been no obstacle for Muslims to practice their religion. | 6 | 1 | 1 | -2 |
| 38 | If Turkey has today become more modern than any other Islamic countries, it is mainly because law and education have been laicised by being separated from the influence of religion. | 5 | 2 | -1 | -1 |
| 3 | Secularism is atheism. | -6 | -6 | -3 | -2 |

statements related to Kemalism shows that the ID and the LLD again join ranks against the Kemalist line of the KD and the ND. Statement (2) emerges as a clear testimony to this difference. The ID and the LLD reject the idea that Kemalism and secularism are inseparable. Perhaps more strikingly, when the LLD points the finger at Kemalism as the source of oppressive behaviours against Muslims (1), its anti-Kemalism surpasses even that of the ID. The LLD and the ID anti-Kemalist line continue with joint rejection of the assertion that Kemalists and the Army's stiff resistance are the only reasons behind Islamic groups' softening attitudes (64).

On the other hand, both the KD and the ND display an almost identical reaction against the LLD and the ID's anti-Kemalism. In all statements related to Kemalism (1, 2, 36, 30, 64), they act in defence of Kemalism. However, this collaboration weakens when the issue shifts from Kemalism to secularism. Most notably in the ranking of statements (45) and (38), both related to the contribution of secularism to Turkey's more advanced social conditions compared to what happens in other Islamic countries. The ND, even though it agrees with the statements, clearly lags behind the KD's enthusiastic affirmation. Indeed, on secularism alone, the ND moves towards the ID and the LLD, indicating a more cautious approach to defining religious freedom in relation to secularism. The source of this shift can again be seen in ND's dual commitment to Islamic values and secularism.

In this controversial issue, there is one point agreed on by all discourses. Statement (3)'s suggestion, that secularism is atheism, is rejected by all discourses, though most strongly by the KD and the ND. The fact that the ID's and the LLD's disagreement with the suggestion is weaker than in other discourses is a reminder of the differences between discourses.

*Democracy*

There is only limited difference between discourses on the topic of democracy. Indeed, the statements related to democracy reveal some interesting points upon which all discourses agree. This suggests that the principles of democracy have a common meaning to all parties, reinforcing a shared attitude. For instance, all discourses disagree with the assertion that overemphasising freedom of belief can cause some Muslims to be swayed by fundamentalist arguments, and that it should thus be limited (51). A basic liberty, the freedom of belief, is acknowledged by all discourses even though the degree to which they support the idea differs. This shared sentiment is qualified further by agreeing on the principle that the law should be the only means for resolving problems in a democracy (53). In fact, the ID's agreement with this statement becomes more significant in the context of former President Sezer's intransigence on the headscarf.

More remarkably, what could potentially be a contentious issue turns out to be another consensus point. All discourses share the sentiment that the most important obstacle for democracy in Turkey is not Islam, but political parties that display corrupt, unethical political behaviour (8). Notably the KD and the ND rank this

**Table 6.5    Democracy (6 most agree, -6 most disagree)**

|  | Statements | KD | ND | LLD | ID |
|---|---|---|---|---|---|
| 51 | If the freedom of belief is overemphasised, Muslim people might be affected by ideas that are dangerous for the secular regime. | -2 | -2 | -4 | -5 |
| 53 | I support our President who defends the supremacy of law. We can only solve our democratic problems by creating a real system of law in our country. | 5 | 1 | 3 | 1 |
| 8 | Today, the biggest obstacle for democracy in Turkey is not Islam, but the political parties, which offer no solution to corruption. | 2 | 2 | 1 | 1 |
| 40 | The fear of communism and fundamentalism, has contributed to the inclusion of very undemocratic rules in the penal code (141, 142, 163) against them. If they were let develop freely, they would be able to reach new syntheses, thus avoiding today's problems. | 2 | -2 | 5 | 2 |
| 50 | We have to produce our own model of democracy. The cultural values of eastern countries are different from those in the west. Eastern countries should not be governed by an American model of democracy. | -4 | 4 | 2 | -1 |
| 52 | Respect for individual rights, the fundamental principle of democracy and secularism, exists in Islam. | 0 | -2 | -4 | 2 |

problem even higher than does the ID, indicating that they do not perceive Islam as the only impediment to establishing a democratic regime. The anti-corruption theme in fact played a major role in the election victory of the AKP in 2002. The AKP attracted a high percentage of votes from other major parties, testifying to this finding of the Q study.

Statement (40) points to another agreement between secular and Islamic discourses, with the exception of the ND. The ID, the LLD and the KD agree that suppression of freedom of belief by the state led to the current stalemate. Thus, these three discourses favour free circulation of ideas no matter what their content is. ND remains outside of this agreement, once again because of its strong pro-state leaning.

The proximity between secular and Islamic discourses takes a different shape when it comes to deciding what kind of democracy is needed (50). The ID and the KD join together in objecting to the idea that eastern countries are different from western countries, and thus should be governed according to their own model of democracy rather than a western model. On the other hand, the ND and the LLD defend the need for a localised version of democracy. What is most striking here is that the ID, by objecting to changing democratic values according to local standards, points to a commitment to democracy as a universally applicable system. What this implies is that the ID is ready to negotiate the rules of coexistence between Islam and a western democratic system. It supports its position by agreeing with another statement stipulating that the fundamental principle of democracy, respect for individual rights, exists in Islam (52). However, the secular discourses, particularly the LLD, disagree with this assertion, testifying that the issue still remains as one of the main gray areas waiting to be resolved.

*The State and the Army*

Similar to the discourses' response to what a democratic system should entail, there appears a strong agreement between all discourses about the role the state is expected to play. The support shown for statement (54) by all discourses is one of the strongest consensus points, emphasising that the task of the state should be to govern people irrespective of their religious background. The importance of neutrality in the practice of governing emerges as a shared concept by all discourses.

**Table 6.6     The state and the Army (6 most agree, -6 most disagree)**

| | Statements | KD | ND | LLD | ID |
|---|---|---|---|---|---|
| 54 | The state is not supposed to carry a religious identity. Its task should only be to govern people. It should not question its people on the basis of their religious identities. | 4 | 5 | 4 | 5 |
| 55 | For a state taking measures to help the practice of religious freedom should not be against secularism. Quite contrary, a secular system requires this. | 0 | 1 | -1 | 2 |
| 56 | The state should lead the reconciliation process. It should not treat some of its citizen as enemies. | 1 | 2 | 2 | 2 |
| 48 | The conflict between secular and Islamic people has been created superficially. The groups who are in control of the state have always created enemies in order to maintain their power. Yesterday it was communism, today it is fundamentalist Islam. | 0 | -1 | 6 | 3 |
| 7 | The Army is the guarantor of democracy and secularism. | 0 | 4 | -6 | -6 |
| 33 | The military tradition has paralysed the self-reflective ability of our society. That is why we still have been governed by a mentality, which is out of date. | 1 | -4 | 4 | 1 |

This is followed by another prerequisite that the state should take an active role in the process of reconciliation (56). Both secular and Islamic discourses share a strong discontent with the state's heavy-handed interventions in religious affairs. Expanding on these two points, the ID and the ND join to call the state to help religious practice instead of preventing it (55). Here, the religious pluralism and the freedom of religious practice are qualified as a prerequisite for a secular system. Against the ID and the ND's position, the KD remains neutral and the LLD expresses a low level of disagreement, denoting that they are also not far from agreeing with the others.

This generic approach to the state, however, changes, especially in the case of the ND, when the matter is related to some practical issues, particularly preservation of the unity of the state. The ND rejects the claim raised in statement (48) that the groups who control the state create the conflict between seculars and Muslims deliberately in order to keep the upper hand. The ID and the LLD also agree on the issue, the KD remains neutral. The LLD's opposition to the state peaks on this issue.

A similar attitude is displayed against the Army in statement (7). The ID and the LLD together reject in the strongest terms the suggestion that the Army is the guarantor of democracy and secularism in Turkey. The ND, on the other hand, happily accepts the suggestion, in line with its pro-Army leaning. The KD, however, consistent with its mild anti-statism, remains neutral. Similarly, the LLD strongly supports the claim made in statement (33) that the military tradition is one of the major reasons why society's critical thinking ability has not been developed. As expected, the KD and the ID join the LLD in support of the statement, while the ND, maintaining its loyalty to the Army, strongly opposes the idea.

*The Media*

All discourses converge in their negative opinion about the impact of the media. This is clear in their joint rejection of statement (5) which suggests that the media contributes to the process of mutual understanding among people. A similar statement (12) is also rebuffed by all discourses except the ND. This reaction towards media also emerged strongly during the follow-up interviews. Most of the subjects indicated that their discontent with the media basically related to commercial TV formats used particularly in discussion forums in which different sides usually engage in fruitless arguments focused not on understanding other parties, but simply on trying to assert their own points of view. The equation of media with commercial TV might be misleading but also seems quite normal given that it is overwhelmingly preferred by the Turkish people as the main medium for receiving information. Nevertheless, it also shows an awareness of what a rational argument should entail.

To conclude, the topic-based correlation of discourses provides useful insights not only into how and where an interaction is possible between discourses, but also into the circumstances under which this interaction could collapse. In other

**Table 6.7    The media (6 most agree, -6 most disagree)**

|  | Statements | KD | ND | LLD | ID |
|---|---|---|---|---|---|
| 5 | The state does not want people's consciousness to rise. Nevertheless, maybe thanks to the media, people from different backgrounds have started understanding each other better. | -2 | -1 | -2 | -2 |
| 12 | The debates in media, such as discussion forums on TV channels, are playing an important role in allowing people to understand each other. | -2 | 1 | -1 | -2 |

words, the topic-based correlation makes the points of convergence and divergence between discourses more discernible. The topics that each discourse reacts to in a certain way also point to areas in which an alternative way of looking at the issues at hand is possible. In the case of the KD, for instance, advocating the rule of law without necessarily acknowledging basic individual rights appears to be a weakness, which could be exploited easily unless the inconsistency of the argument is fixed. Perhaps more importantly, the correlation shows the points that each discourse could target to clarify more in order to avoid misunderstandings on several issues. The view of the secular discourses that Islam could not accommodate different groups including atheists represents a certain challenge to the ID. If the ID is sincere in its call for dialogue, it has to clarify what it means to be different in an Islamic setting. Similarly, it forces the ND to reconsider what it means to be Islamic and secular at the same time. The ND's double face makes it the least consistent of the discourses; this becomes more obvious when discourses are correlated through a topic-based analysis.

From a deliberative point of view, the issues that appear in the topic-based analysis offers a road map exploring possible avenues of establishing a healthy dialogue between conflicting sides. The possibilities that this map presents can be further explored through another type of analysis, this time based on comparison of discourses rather than topics. In this way the specificity of relationship between particular discourses can be put under further scrutiny providing additional evidence about how discourses relate to each other.

**Discourse-based Analysis of Similarities and Differences**

The topic-based comparison immediately above aimed at identifying the positions of each discourse in relation to the topics appearing in the statements. A discourse-based comparison focuses more on the interrelationship between discourses. Through a discourse-based comparison it is possible to develop a better understanding of how each discourse could relate to others in terms of overall similarities and differences. There are two correlations of particular interest. The first will look at the general relationship between secular discourses, that is, the KD, the ND and the LLD, on the one hand, and the ID on the other. The second will specifically investigate the relationship between the LLD and the ID in order to look closely at similarities that they display.

*Islamic versus Secular Discourses: Similarities*

In several statements, it is possible to find a certain degree of commonality between discourses. More interestingly, the ID appears to be backing the general sentiment displayed by secular discourses. For instance, the strong anti-Kemalist sentiment in (1) is rejected, as might be expected, by the KD and the ND; more importantly, the ID also disapproves. The ID's rejection is not as strong as that of others; nevertheless, it points to the possibility of dealing with the misunderstanding that Muslims are strictly anti-Kemalist. What makes the ID's support important is that it also falls close to the LLD affirmative position, providing an opportunity to be in touch with all secular discourses. A similar observation can be made in relation to statement (3). The ID, along with other discourses, rejects the claim that secularism is atheism. Again, the ID's objection is less strong than that of others; however, it possibly helps to ease the discomfort felt by secular discourses about the issue.

There is an almost perfect consensus between the ID and secular discourses in seeing the issue of the headscarf as a personal matter to be respected (25). Framing the scarf issue as a problem of individual rights has substantial support from the ID, the LLD and the ND. Only the KD remains neutral. Finding a common point on this most contentious issue is surely crucial for reconciling differences. It also shows the ID has a direction on how to formulate the issue best in order to gain a more common acceptance.

Another common point emerges in statement (27). It highlights mutual respect and tolerance of differences, initiated by a grassroots-based movement. The only opposition to the idea comes from the LLD, possibly owing to the reference to the state in the statement. Nonetheless, an affirmative approach on the key issues of mutual respect as well as a grassroots-based initiative provides plenty of scope to develop a common platform to act upon.

Statement (31) highlights another issue around which the ID and secular discourses converge. The ID is indifferent towards religious sects, paving the way for rectifying another point that has been mostly misunderstood, that is, that the ID does not necessarily recognise religious sects as an essential part of religious practice, implying that the private sphere is where religious activities should belong. This surely clears the way for a constructive dialogue between seculars and Muslims.

The possibility for dialogue increases further with the LLD and the KD's positive approach to the scarf issue. A consensus emerges in statements (46) and (47) between the ID and the LLD, and the ND. Even though the KD remains outside this consensus, the common understanding between the LLD and the ND represents a crucial moment in development of a strong base for dialogue.

**Table 6.8    Similarities between Islamic and secular discourses (6 most agree, -6 most disagree)**

|   | Statements | KD | ND | LLD | ID |
|---|---|---|---|---|---|
| 1 | Today's oppressive attitudes against Muslims in the name of secularism are rooted in Kemalist ideology. | -5 | -5 | 3 | -1 |
| 3 | Secularism is atheism. | -6 | -6 | -3 | -2 |
| 25 | Whether I cover myself with a headscarf should not be anyone else's business. This is what I understand from secularism. Everybody should pay respect to different beliefs. | 0 | 4 | 4 | 4 |
| 27 | The important thing is to start from somewhere. If people could start showing respect and tolerance to each other, this would force the state to do the same. | 2 | 1 | -1 | 1 |
| 31 | I do not see anything wrong with religious sects. People should be able to get together if they believe in the same thing. Everybody, religious people, atheists etc., should be able to live together in peace within the same nation. | -1 | -1 | -2 | 0 |
| 46 | The secularists in Turkey claim that women who wear headscarf cannot be secular. This is not a democratic attitude. | -3 | 2 | 0 | 0 |
| 47 | My wife has been refused a health card only because she wears a headscarf. This is against basic human rights and secularism. | -2 | 5 | 5 | 3 |
| 8 | Today, the biggest obstacle for democracy in Turkey is not Islam, but the political parties, which offer no solution to corruption. | 2 | 2 | 1 | 1 |
| 10 | The differences between us are too deep. We cannot reconcile them by talking. This system will remain as it is in the future. | -4 | -6 | -3 | -5 |
| 44 | I am trying to survive economically to be able to feed my children. The debate between Islam and secularism does not interest me. | -3 | -4 | -2 | -3 |

Statement (47) sends the strongest signal by linking the scarf issue with a breach of human rights and secularism. Notably, the LLD and the ND's reactions here are stronger than the ID.

Another interesting agreement between discourses emerges in statement (8) which identifies corrupt political parties rather than Islam as the real obstacle to democracy. Interestingly, the KD and the ND support the statement more strongly than the LLD and the ID. This could possibly be linked to the LLD's and the ID's more suspicious approach to the state in that they see corruption endemic not only within political parties but in the political system as a whole, including the state apparatus.

Statements (10) and (44) together display a strong agreement between secular and Islamic discourses that apathy and pessimism are not acceptable. This commitment towards working for reconciliation shared by all discourses suggests an important opportunity for democratic endeavour in Turkey.

*Islamic versus Secular Discourses: Differences*

The differences between the secular discourses reveal important clues about how to establish a more successful dialogue between discourses. The KD, the ND and the LLD all agree on general statements about secularism yet their different treatment of some issues such as the scarf, the Army, the state and Islam provide avenues for narrowing the gap between Muslims and seculars.

The major differences between the ID and the secular discourses mostly revolve around issues related to Islam's political interpretations, particularly its compatibility with democracy. The ID's affirmative approach to those issues is mostly challenged by a high level of skepticism in secular discourses. The biggest margin of difference appears in relation to statements (17) and (49). Statement (17) suggests that religion is a personal matter, and thus should be kept within the private sphere. The strong opposition to this statement by the ID testifies to a major difference between Islamic and secular interpretations of the public and private divide. The issue appears to be difficult, but might be solved more easily than it looks, pending an agreement on the scarf issue, since the scarf is seen as the symbol of Islam's invasion of the public sphere in many secular arguments.

Statement (49) is again related to the public/private divide, this time endorsing implementation of Islamic values in the public framework. Similarly, statement (20) argues that a just system can be created if everybody lives according to Islamic rule. All secular discourses predictably oppose these statements strongly, though the difference appears to be more rigorous in statement (20). The opposing role is reversed when, for instance, Islam's compatibility with democratic values is questioned in (6) and (16). Those issues are possibly the most critical in the sense that they touch upon the heart of the matter. Resolving them will be very difficult.

It is interesting to note that differences become less severe when practical matters dominate the agenda, such as the headscarf problem at university (4, 14), the role of economic equality (18), or the difference of Turkey's secular regime in terms of modern rights and conditions compared to other Islamic countries (45, 38). The practical implications of these issues in daily life render them relatively easy to compare. Hence they represent a good starting point for a dialogue aimed at mutual understanding.

**Table 6.9      Differences between Islamic and secular discourses (6 most agree, -6 most disagree)**

|  | Statements | KD | ND | LLD | ID |
|---|---|---|---|---|---|
| 17 | The purpose of religion will be defeated when it is carried over to the public arena. Beliefs are personal matters. They should be kept within the individual sphere. | 6 | 4 | 3 | -5 |
| 49 | In a Muslim society, the framework for freedom has to be determined according to Islamic values. | -5 | -5 | -6 | 4 |
| 20 | If everybody tries to live according to Islamic rule, a just system can come into existence. | -5 | -4 | -5 | 0 |
| 6 | The problem with Islamic law in relation to democracy is that Islamic communities exert social pressure on individuals. This conflicts with the democratic notion of individual freedom and rights. | 4 | 1 | 3 | -2 |
| 16 | Islam, as a system of law, cannot be compatible with democracy. The role and the place attributed to women by Islamic law, which denies women basic individual rights, is enough to prove this. | 2 | -3 | 1 | -4 |
| 4 | About one thousand female students have been refused entry to the University of Marmara because they dress themselves according to their religious belief. This shows that there is a serious problem with freedom of belief and education in Turkey. | -3 | -1 | 0 | 3 |
| 14 | The universities are important places where secular people and Islamists can close the existing gap between the two groups. When we do not allow female students wearing headscarf into the universities we also throw them out of the modern world. By doing this we jeopardise the possibility of living together. | -2 | -1 | 1 | 5 |
| 45 | To claim that Muslims in Turkey are not allowed to practice their religion is a totally unfair statement. If we do not count the scarf problem in public institutions there has been no obstacle for Muslims to practice their religion. | 6 | 1 | 1 | -2 |
| 38 | If Turkey has today become more modern than any other Islamic countries, it is mainly because law and education have been laicised by being separated from the influence of religion. | 5 | 2 | -1 | -1 |

**Overview**

A topic-based analysis of discourses provides a distinctive depiction of both the discourses themselves and the subjects of Islam, democracy and secularism. The importance of this lies in the fact that it points to a direction where understanding differences, and perhaps settling them, becomes more likely. The assumption is straightforward; once a presumed difference is denied, it immediately opens a possibility for establishing a dialogue to rectify misconceptions, thus leading to better understanding among the parties involved. For instance, the state's interference with religious affairs is strongly opposed by all discourses in favour of a more liberal approach. This reaction is quite expected in the case of the ID and the LLD, but not in that of other secular discourses, particularly the ND, which has displayed a strong statist attitude as revealed in the study. Resentment about the state's heavy handedness thus denotes a moment that can be captured as a starting point towards mutual understanding. Other encouraging signs appear when consensus is reached on the view that the main obstacle for democracy in Turkey is not Islam, and the belief that the majority of Turkey's Muslim population are not fundamentalist and, as a consequence, a serious threat to the secular regime.

Reconciling differences emerges as a major priority common to all discourses. In terms of commitment to reconciliation, differences between the discourses do not display a great level of divergence. The high level of support for mutual understanding only slightly decreases when the future prediction for the success of reconciling differences is evaluated. Here, the ID and the ND carry higher hopes for a positive change in the future. All discourses agree with the self-critical line that in reality, Turkish people's tolerance usually applies to their inner circles. Broadening this self-serving attitude will be necessary if a positive outcome towards reconciling differences is to be achieved. Factor analysis also revealed that good intentions towards dialogue seem conditional, particularly in the case of the KD and the ND. This inconsistency is the most likely reason that the tendency towards dialogue is not always reflected in Turkish politics, particularly at the formal level of engagement between parties. It is through a topic-based analysis that those inconsistencies along with the possible ways of resolving them can be identified.

A topic and discourse-based analysis of the Q findings also displays important clues about the nature of the relationship between different views. Areas of agreement and disagreement become discernible for further elaborations. Furthermore, the Q analysis also identifies changes in attitudes when ideas are tested in real life contexts. For instance, respect for individual rights as a general idea has appeared to be of prime importance for all discourses. Yet, when these rights were tested in real life conditions, the result displayed major differences between discourses. For example, for both the Kemalist and the Nationalist discourses the importance of respecting individual rights withered away when the scarf issue appeared on the agenda.

The inconsistencies exhibited in application of these generic ideas in specific cases mainly stem from preconceptions about each other that create a circle of mistrust between conflicting parties. In the case of the headscarf issue, for instance, the headscarf is seen as a sign of Islam's political ambition to dominate the public sphere with anti-secular values and symbols, particularly by the Kemalist discourse. For the Islamic discourse, the headscarf symbolises a democratic right necessary for the practice of religious freedom. The issue here seems in deadlock unless the parties clarify what they mean by secularism and individual rights. This is precisely where deliberation oriented to social learning and understanding can play a significant role by simply revealing potential areas of common interest. My main argument, it will be recalled, is that the chance of turning these common areas into practical, workable arrangements between parties has only a limited chance within the confines of decision-making oriented deliberative settings. What makes social learning oriented deliberation vital is not only its virtue in turning possibilities of agreement into workable arrangements, but also its capacity to reveal possible changes in attitudes of participants during their discursive engagement, hence further reinforcing mutual understanding and social learning. This point will be further evaluated in the next chapter through a case study.

# Chapter 7
# Prospects for New Forms of Cooperation

The previous chapter considered possible points of convergence and divergence between the main discourses of Turkish politics. The background exposition of each discourse suggested that these discourses share a more common milieu than is usually appreciated. In terms of the framework sketched in the first section as the social learning model of deliberation, these common points constitute the setting for a prospective dialogue between the discourses of Turkey. Further elaboration of these commonalities will show why the social learning stage of deliberation plays an important role in consolidation of different views.

The Q study has also picked up the signs of paradigm change that has occurred in both the left and Islamic discourses during the last two decades. Analysis of the dynamics of this shift would provide further understanding of why deliberation as social learning and understanding could play a crucial role within a socially and culturally divided country such as Turkey. A recapitulation of similarities between the Islamic and Liberal Left discourses as revealed in the Q study findings will lay the ground for the rest of this chapter, showing how the possibility of an unprecedented alliance between Islamic and leftist forces emerges in line with the Q findings. This will lead to an account of the development of the notion of individual rights both in the Left and the Islamic groups, focusing on two human rights associations: İnsan Hakları Derneği (IHD) – Human Rights Association from the Left and Mazlum-Der – The Association of Human Rights and Solidarity for Oppressed People, an Islamic group. An examination of a women's organisation, Barış İçin Sürekli Kadın Platformu (BSKP) – Women's Platform for Peace, will illustrate how the emergence of an individual-rights based politics helped to form an alliance among a diverse political and cultural representation of groups from various backgrounds.

## Similarities Between Islamic and Liberal Left Discourses

The factor analysis revealed some important similarities between the ID and the LLD. The level of proximity between these two discourses is such as to suggest emergence of an important phase for democratic practice in Turkey. This relationship between the ID and the LLD should be monitored more closely. This would not only provide a better picture of the current and future interactions between the two discourses, but also would suggest how to expand the boundaries of this new cooperation in the broader community, particularly into other secular sections of Turkish society. The following table shows the closeness of these two discourses in their understanding of a democratic framework based on a system of rights.

**Table 7.1     Similarities between the ID and the LLD (6 most agree, -6 most disagree)**

| | Statements | LLD | ID |
|---|---|---|---|
| 1 | Today's oppressive attitudes against Muslims in the name of secularism are rooted in Kemalist ideology. | 3 | -1 |
| 2 | Kemalism and secularism cannot be separated from each other. Separating them will mean the end of secularism. If you are secular, you are also Kemalist, or vice versa. | -2 | -4 |
| 7 | The Army is the guarantor of democracy and secularism. | -6 | -6 |
| 10 | The differences between us are too deep. We cannot reconcile them by talking. This system will remain as it is in the future. | -3 | -5 |
| 25 | Whether I cover myself with a headscarf should not be anyone else's business. This is what I understand from secularism. Everybody should pay respect to different beliefs. | 4 | 4 |
| 41 | Quite a few female students, who had to take off their scarf to be admitted to universities, later became quite happy with their new look. May be this rule allowed them to do what they really want. | -3 | -4 |
| 48 | The conflict between secular and Islamic people has been created superficially. The groups who are in control of the state have always created enemies in order to maintain their power. Yesterday it was communism, today it is fundamentalist Islam. | 6 | 3 |
| 60 | In a secular society everybody should abide by the law. If the law bans wearing the scarf in public institutions the rule should be respected. | -5 | -6 |
| 61 | We should trust our people whether they are Kurds, Turks, Laz, Alevi, whether they wear a scarf or not. The more divisions are created in the name of state protection, the more divided we become. This is the real danger. | 5 | 6 |
| 64 | The Islamists are only softening their lines because of the strong resistance shown against them by the Army and Kemalists. | -3 | -4 |
| 59 | We have to find out what is common among us rather than focusing on differences. For instance, we have to emphasise the importance of education at the universities instead of arguing about the headscarf controversy. | 6 | 3 |
| 51 | If the freedom of belief is overemphasised, Muslim people might be affected by the ideas that are dangerous for the secular regime. | -4 | -5 |
| 47 | My wife has been refused a health card only because she wears a headscarf. This is against basic human rights and secularism. | 5 | 3 |

The table shows substantial similarities between the ID and the LLD. Both define individual rights as the main paradigm for their democratic framework. They both consider the headscarf matter as a human rights issue irrespective of its impact on the state (25, 41, 47). Interestingly, though, the LLD feels even stronger than the ID when the issue is clearly tied to another aspect of individual rights, such as health, as in the case of (1).

Consequently, both agree that if the law does not conform with human rights standards it does not warrant the respect of citizens (60). This is a quite remarkable result from an Islamic point of view since it simply puts Muslims into the same anti-establishment category as the LLD. Although an anti-establishment sentiment can be easily associated with the left in general, it is a new element for the Islamic population particularly when it is brought to the fore with a clear emphasis on human rights. Agreement about a common framework based on individual rights has fundamental implications for democratic practice in Turkey. It provides the basis for new forms of cooperation between the LLD and the ID.

It is equally important that both discourses and their corresponding formations in the social strata have gone through a significant learning process. Initially, this process was mainly internal in that it occurred with almost no interaction between Islamic and left groups. What was learned mostly remained within their own sphere. This shift occurred first among leftist, then Islamic, groups, creating a real opportunity for them to gather around the same platform for the first time in the history of the Turkish Republic. This interaction, in turn, helped to expand the scope of learning significantly. There will be more about this in the next two sections.

LLD's and ID's anti-establishment tendency brought a hostile attitude to the state. This is one of the main reasons both the LLD and the ID have similar views about the role of the state and the Army in democratic practice in Turkey. They strongly disagree with the suggestion that the Army is the guarantor of democracy and secularism (7). They also agree that the state's anti-democratic measures, manipulated by existing power holders, are the main source of conflict between seculars and Muslims (48). Both discourses are clearly anti-Kemalist (1, 2), though interestingly the LLD's reaction to Kemalism surpasses the ID's (1). These issues clearly separate them from the KD and the ND.

Another important similarity between the LLD and the ID comes to the fore when they agree that the current system is bound to change and dialogue could be an important tool in mediating the change (10). Even though the LLD in general is sceptical about the concept of dialogue, it still throws its support behind this statement. When this is considered with the LLD's very strong endorsement of the idea that conflict between secular and Islamic people is superficially created and provoked by some groups within the state rather than by ordinary people (48), then establishing a ground for possible cooperation between leftists and Islamists appears to be within reach. A positive approach to people's empowerment also underlines their suspicion about the kind of politics that promotes a state-centred framework (61).

It is not difficult to conclude that the LLD and the ID display some similar characteristics in relation to their understanding of a democratic polity. Both of them consistently defend the primacy of individual rights as the normative base for a democratic framework. It is this commitment to a system of rights that makes their reaction to the state and the Army meaningful. In this sense, the LLD and the ID positions are clearly distinguished from those of KD and the ND since the latter do not consider secularism as the main paradigm for establishment of a democratic regime.

The focus here is mainly on similarities between the two discourses, LLD and ID, in order to make a future projection about the basis of what is currently happening between them. I discussed their differences in detail in relevant sections previously. For instance, the Q findings showed a sharp contrast between the LLD and the ID about the role of Islamic values in determining societal norms (49). Similarly, the LLD is not convinced that respect for individual rights exist in Islam (52). But it is not these differences that determine the possibility of cooperation between leftist and Islamic groups. The differences will possibly affect the scope of their interaction. Yet, it is, and has been, the similarities that play a decisive role in any form of cooperation between the two. The issue will then be linked to the role of social learning in those settings since the scope can also be expanded under the conditions of social learning. The next two sections will show how this process is already at work in some real life cases.

## Development of Individual Rights in Islamic and Left Groups

Starting within the left in the late 1980s, then within the Islamic discourse from mid-1990s onwards, a politics of basic individual rights rather than of class or Islam-based politics has become the main paradigm in some segments of the leftist and Islamic groups. For the future of democracy in Turkey, this shift was one of the most significant steps in the Turkish politics. It helped the AKP to win the 2002 general elections with one of the biggest majorities in the history of the Turkish Parliament, after breaking from the ranks of the SP, the flag-bearer of the tradition of political Islam in Turkey since 1970.

The idea of individual rights ironically owes its existence to the interventions of the Turkish Army in politics. Before 1980, the issue of human rights was generally limited to discussing torture cases in leftist groups (Plagemann 2001). Following the 1980 coup, first within the left, and then within Islamic movements, the notion of individual rights appeared in the political discourse as offering the possibility of protection against the state and the Army's relentless assaults.

The IHD was established, in 1986, by some left-wing intellectuals and members of various left-wing organisations. Most of the founding members belonged to left groups with a traditional class-based understanding of the world, but the IHD adopted a different approach to define its place on the political spectrum. The IHD's constitution identified working for the defence of basic individual rights and freedom as IHD's primary task (Article 2). The IHD's individual rights platform provided a viable basis for those who wanted to develop alternative politics. The IHD soon gathered a pool of leftists disgruntled with the traditional left politics (Plagemann 2001).

The IHD grew steadily. By 1996, membership was more than 16,000. There were 58 branches throughout Turkey. Initial focus on human rights abuses in prisons, particularly torture, widened following an increase in the level and the kind of support received. Its agenda broadened to embrace various social issues including the rights of workers, minority groups, women, and the environment. A good example of IHD's shift into a paradigm beyond class is the Declaration of Pedestrian Rights issued on the World Environment Day in 1990. This was completely new terrain for left politics, and brought a further expansion of the IHD by attracting support from feminists, homosexuals and environmentalists.

The paradigm shift within the left was soon echoed within Islamic groups as well. Members of different Islamic groups ill-treated by the 1980 military regime formed their own human rights association, Mazlum-Der, in 1991. Mazlum-Der initially focused on human rights abuses inflicted on Islamic people but it soon adopted a more neutral approach and dealt with all sorts of human rights abuses including those related to the Kurdish problem, workers' rights, and even the rights of patients ill-treated in hospitals (Plagemann 2001).

For the first time Islamic discourse was opening itself to a new conceptual terrain. Mazlum-Der's formulation of human rights was by no means a cut and paste approach. Extensive discussions on the relevance of individual rights to Islam and vice versa were held during the early stages of Mazlum-Der. The founding president, Mehmet Pamak, for instance, argues that the western notion of human rights does not reflect a universal notion of human rights because of its origin in a power struggle between different ethnic, regional and national powers which produced a pragmatic view of human rights. It was mainly applicable to Europeans. In the rest of the world it was mainly used to gain advantages for colonial regimes. Contrary to the western notions of human rights, Islam is capable of offering a real universal human rights approach based not on any national, ethnic or class based interests but on universal veneration of individual life (Plagemann 2001).

The founders of Mazlum-Der tried to cushion the impact of the introduction of a western notion of individual rights on Islamic thought by distancing themselves from the representatives of a more western approach. They argued, for instance, that the IHD's human rights defence was limited to defending leftist people and was thus not worthy of their cooperation. But this initial interpretation was short-lived. From 1995 onwards, Mazlum-Der adopted a more common interpretation of human rights as formulated in international treaties. It subscribed to a universal understanding of human rights and even defended resolutions in international treaties enforcing unrestricted application of human rights.[1]

---

1   www.mazlumder.org.tr/tanitim.htm [accessed 20 January 2003].

This was a fundamentally important turning point in several respects. Firstly, it signalled the end of an initial reactionary period and opened the possibility of dialogue with other human rights associations both at national and international level, such as the IHD, Amnesty International and Human Rights Watch. A special commission was established to coordinate relations with other organisations. By 2003, Mazlum-Der managed to establish direct links not only with more than 35 international human rights organisations, but also within the United Nations and the European Union.[2]

Secondly, as a result of this dialogue, traditionally conservative Islamic discourse started evolving commonalities with arguments of the newly developed LLD on nationalism, secularism and religious freedom. This reinforced the dialogue, which became cooperation on those common issues. Following the Army crack down on RP's Islamist politics on 28 February 1998, the IHD joined Mazlum-Der in condemning actions against women wearing the headscarf, thus advocating freedom of religious practice and opposing the state's disciplinary measures on the issue. Another left wing civil rights association, Sivil Haklar Girişimi (SHG) – Civil Rights Initiative, supported the right of attending parliamentary sessions wearing a scarf after a female member of Parliament was expelled from the chamber when she refused to remove her's. On another occasion, the IHD and Mazlum-Der joined in defending the publishing rights of an Armenian newspaper, *Agos*.[3]

Yüksel Mutlu, a member of the executive committee of the IHD, explains how this process of cooperation has developed:

> In its seventeen-year-old history, the IHD has come a long way to reflect the concerns of a diverse spectrum of views. Our initial left-leaning agenda has become more overarching by emphasising the universal characteristics of individual human rights. It is mainly for this reason that nowadays the IHD is capable of dealing with the problems of a variety of groups who are traditionally not aligned with the left. What played an important role in this development is that the notion of individual rights has recently become a common theme within the discourses of Islamic groups. When they formulate their problems with reference to individual rights, instead of some Islamic concepts, it has become much easier for us to cooperate with them (2003).

At the beginning of this cooperation, members of the IHD also went through a learning process. As Mutlu says:

> I would like to stress that this has also been an important experience for us. The debate on the scarf issue particularly has been a challenging one. Initially, a large number of our members did not consider this problem as our problem. They argued that the Islamic human rights association, Mazlum-Der, was already

---

2    www.mazlumder.org.tr/tanitim.htm [accessed 20 January 2003].
3    www.ihd.org.tr/eindex.html [accessed 25 January 2003].

dealing with it, so there was no need for us to devote our time and energy. They simply could not associate themselves with the problem. There were historical facts behind this reaction. In the past the left was never on good terms with Islamic groups. In fact both the left and Islamic groups always considered themselves as being on opposite sides of the political spectrum. Some of our members put it blatantly by saying, 'when the state was torturing us, what they did for us, nothing. So, why should we support them now?' To tell you the truth, even I was feeling pretty much the same way. We were simply communists in the eyes of any Islamic group. Yet things have changed specifically with the 28 February ultimatum of the Army by which Islamic groups also became a target of the state. In 1998 and 1999 more than 30,000 female students wearing a scarf were not allowed admission to the universities. We could not remain neutral about this kind of state oppression (2003).

These examples of cooperation between Mazlum-Der and other human rights organisations were also reflected in the dialogue between the left and the Islamic scholars. The issue of individual rights in Islam, with specific reference to constitutional rights, was extensively discussed in different forums, most notably in Abant meetings between secular and Islamic scholars (Gündem 1998).

It was critical from the point of view of the deliberative framework that these interactions between secular and Islamic groups naturally enhanced the understanding of each other's position. Traditionally, the left and the Islamic groups are considered as being on opposite sides of the political spectrum. While the left claimed to be representing development and progress, Islamic groups confined themselves to the dynamics of right-wing politics. This started with the support of the DP at the beginning of the multiparty regime in 1946. Until the 1980 military coup, Islamic groups flirted not only with right-wing and conservative groups but also with ultra-nationalistic groups such as the MHP. Historically, the relationship between the left and Islamic groups has been antagonistic. Paradigm shifts in both Islamic and Leftist ranks created the opportunity to embark upon a process of understanding. The IHD and Mazlum-Der cooperation has been exemplary in this sense. This cooperation has later fashioned establishment of the BSKP, in which a more organic relationship between the members of Islamic, leftist and some other secular groups has been realised.

Established as an anti-war alliance between different women's organisations, BSKP has attracted various groups from an unusually wide range of backgrounds. Zeliha Şalcı, a member of the executive committee of BSKP, explained that when they formed the platform at the beginning of 2001 they were not so sure what kind of support they would receive from other organisations. They were quite surprised when a large number of women's organisations from various backgrounds, including feminists, Kemalists, Kurds, gays and transsexuals, and Muslims, were interested in joining the platform. As Şalcı (2003) explains:

> This was a new experience for us. Even though in the past we supported each
> other in different activities this was the first time we got together under the
> umbrella of the same organisation. I think for all of us it has been a great learning
> experience even though it has not always run smoothly and we encountered
> some serious problems between several groups (2003).

While the emergence of some problems within the platform were expected, such as
tension between Kemalist and Muslim women, some took them by surprise such as
the conflict between feminists and leftists. The problem existing between Kemalist
and Muslim women was familiar. The Kemalists pursued a tough line in relation
to Muslim women, sometimes completely ignoring their presence in meetings. In
Şalcı's words, 'They [Kemalists] were very self-righteous and simply refused to
communicate with Muslim women' (2003). Another problem surfaced between
feminists and leftists. According to feminists the culture of left-wing groups was
very masculine. Feminists were not very comfortable with Muslim women either,
even though the Muslim women were part of an organisation known as Islamic
feminists.

These divisions within the BSKP were a reflection of existing problems within
the Turkish public sphere at large as shown by the Q study findings. What is crucial
in the case of BSKP, though, is that it has provided a forum within which to find
a way for reconciling those differences. The outcome has not been completely
successful, since the reluctance of Kemalists and feminists to develop a dialogue
with others eventually led to withdrawal of both groups from the BSKP. The
remaining groups have managed to build a successful cooperation around the aims
of the platform. Şalcı regrets that they were unable to resolve their differences with
Kemalists and feminists.

> This was in a way the unsuccessful side of our story. Yet, the ones who remained
> showed a remarkable persistence for establishing a dialogue with each other.
> These were leftists, Muslims, Kurds, gays and transsexuals. However, I must
> single out Muslim women for their effort to create a common platform with the
> rest. They tried so hard that they finally convinced everybody of their sincerity. I
> sometimes question myself about whether we have made a mistake by allowing
> other groups to treat Muslim women so negatively. But, I suppose, in a way this
> is how things developed. Everybody needed some time to get know the other
> and establish confidence. Those who could not believe in that left early. Yet now
> we act together a lot more comfortably than we did initially. For instance, just
> today we submitted a petition to the French Embassy to protest against the recent
> decision of the French Government prohibiting female students from wearing a
> headscarf in schools (2003).

Behind the success of this process there is one more parameter – the process of
building solidarity through social learning governed by a common principle upon
which all parties agree. In other words, coordination of participants' dialogic

action requires a central principle that holds the process together by acting as the backbone of participants' interaction. As Şalcı indicates, in the case of the BSKP, this principle was individual rights and freedom, which provided the main medium for the groups' cooperation with one another.

> What is important for us here is that we no longer classify people on the basis of their cultural, political, religious or ethnic background. Our point of reference is individual rights and freedom. Some left groups are vehemently opposed to this anti-class approach. For Kemalists, it was only good as long as it did not facilitate the rise of Islamic claims. Yet we insisted that the idea of individual rights cannot, and should not, be superseded by any cultural, religious or class-based idea. It is through our loyalty to this principle that we have managed today to build a new form of cooperation between groups that have never been considered as part of a left alliance before. What we have achieved in our anti-war platform in a short period of time is almost impossible to realize within the mainstream political parties or institutions (2003).

Şalcı's observation is crucial to the point that the members' experience within the BSKP has been a process of learning and understanding of each other's position. According to Şalcı, once the initial concerns and prejudices were eased and a sense of trust established, the groups were able to function better during moments of decision-making. If Şalcı's observation is also correct for the Muslim women as the most marginalised group in the BSKP, then the experience of the WFPF appears to be a good example for the role that the binary deliberation model could play in deliberative practice.

Hidayet Tuksal of Başkent Kadın Platformu (BKP) – Capital Women's Platform provides an insight into the reaction of Muslim women. Apart from her active role in management of the BKP, Hidayet Tuksal is a renowned Islamic scholar particularly known for her work on the role of women in Islam. She maintains that the recent discussions about democracy within Islamic groups have helped them to understand democratic principles better. As a result of these discussions, Tuksal tells:

> There has been a sharp increase in the number of women participating in the meetings we have organised. This is important because almost in every meeting we discuss issues related to democratic rights of women. Formulating our problems around some democratic rights not only increased our self-understanding but also our perception about other groups that are not Islamic. I consider this interaction very important because it helps us to define things from women's perspective. The perception of women in the Islamic community is strongly tied to some religious references which are very difficult to challenge and change (2003).

Tuksal indicates that apart from internal discussions, the BSKP's cooperation with other women's organisations has certainly played a crucial role in learning how to move beyond traditional perspectives and understand better the nature of problems that are specific to their gender. Tuksal asserts that the Muslim women's participation in the BSKP also constitutes a good example of this learning experience. Parallel to Şalcı's statement, Tuksal reiterates that it has not been an easy process for Muslim women, since they encountered some stiff resistance, particularly from Kemalist women:

> As you know the BSKP was organised by members of IHD, but later supported by various women's organisations including Kemalists, feminists, transsexuals and gays. At the beginning there was a sense of not knowing what to do with us. Kemalist women, for instance, simply did not want to listen to what we said. It was very discouraging. We were more willing to communicate because we voluntarily joined the group. So we insisted, stayed and in time our interaction with others affected their perception about us. I think that when they heard about our problems directly from us they understood our position better. I must say that being a woman has always played an important role in this process. We were able to establish an empathy with the groups who were willing to listen to us (2003).

Making themselves accepted was only one side of the coin for Muslim women. They also had to resolve their own issues towards some groups within the BSKP. Tuksal indicates that Muslim women's relationship with gay and transsexual groups was a challenge and it took them a while to feel empathy towards them. As explained before, homosexuality is a tough issue for Islamic culture and certainly represents a major challenge for Muslims who aspire to respond to the demands of mutual accommodation within culturally diverse settings such as Turkish society. As Tuksal explains:

> From our point of view, gay and lesbian rights are the most intricate issue since the Qur'an explicitly prohibits homosexual relations. So some of us were scared even to shake hands with them, thinking that it would be a sinful act. I personally feel no problem with cooperating with these groups. For me, it is important that we do not limit ourselves by some scriptural reading of religious texts. Yet it is not easy to convince Muslims of this. It took some time to persuade our friends to communicate with these groups. However, when the dialogue started, things became much easier. We realized that some of these women (gays and transsexuals) had strong religious convictions. They identified themselves as Muslims. For us this was a big step in understanding and establishing empathy with them. Today, I believe, we are much more relaxed in working with these groups. Just recently our group donated some money to support one of their members to attend a conference in Europe. And in general I can say that our relations with friends from the IHD, who were mainly lefties, as well as with gays and transsexuals, has now reached a certain level of maturity. I think we can comfortably say that we now understand each other better (2003).

Muslim women's story in the BSKP testifies to the vital role that social learning plays in deliberative processes. Tuksal's reference to empathy is particularly important since it underlines a critical dimension in deliberative activity towards building trust. If democratic culture is conceived as the catalyst of solidarity in any given society, then establishing empathy between parties that are involved in deliberation becomes an essential part of building solidarity. The social learning phase of deliberation offers the natural venue for this vital process. As proposed in the binary deliberation model, the level of achievement reached in this phase of deliberation will be reflected in the quality of decisions made during the decision-making phase of deliberation.

Firstly, it is essential that groups who are traditionally considered as being in opposite camps should be given opportunity to meet together in order to understand their differences or similarities clearly, which would provide a new breathing space for different groups to reflect upon their problems in the public sphere. Secondly, through their interaction, groups would be able to find out how to reconcile their differences as long as they were able to abide by the principle that governs their interaction.

Two things are crucial here. The future of the process is dependent on the practice of social learning within those civic organisations like the BSKP. Platforms or alliances like the BSKP are the real domains for this kind of interaction between groups, since they provide the opportunity to practise the social learning and decision-making aspects of deliberation together. They are oriented to a practical task, yet not limited by the restrictions of decision-making practices. They have the capacity to be more inclusive and less time bounded, that is, they do have the flexibility to sort things out. More importantly, the process of social learning is purposefully organised. The link between social learning and decision-making is clearly established so that the benefits gained during participants' interactions are directed to a specific outcome.

# Chapter 8
# Further Reflections on Social Learning

The importance of the practice of social learning in civic organisations was discussed in the previous chapter. In their daily routines the members of these associations bring together various groups ranging from Muslims to gays and lesbians. Stories of this kind are not an uncommon feature of multicultural societies. Trapped between strong substantive claims of different groups and a commitment (at least in theory) to universalist principles of a discursively functioning democratic public sphere, these societies experience certain dilemmas in reconciling the conditions of deliberative practice on one hand and providing a meaningful group identity for those who seek recognition on the other hand. The specific requirements of those cultural groups who represent conflicting views pose a challenge to the normative framework of deliberative procedures which hope to universalise specific claims to justice.

In *The Claims of Culture* (2002) Benhabib explores the current dilemmas of multicultural societies. Challenging that cultural formations are insurmountable, hence dialogue and understanding between different cultural identities are not possible, Benhabib maintains that the norms of deliberative practice and the claims of culture are interwoven. She asserts that 'even groups and individuals with deeply held divergent beliefs are motivated to engage in democratic deliberation because there is some convergence at the level of material interests and shared life-forms' (2002: 136). These shared interests in return would stipulate a constructive dialogue 'articulating a civic point of view and a civic perspective of enlarged mentality' (2002: 115).

Benhabib's emphasis on enlarged mentality clearly points to the learning aspect of deliberation. By giving several examples from multicultural societies such as India and France, Benhabib suggests that the learning process, which takes place in the public sphere during civic and electoral processes, would ultimately force groups 'to clarify the bigger political game at stake in their actions' (2002: 119). She maintains that old cultural values and traditions are in transition because the claims of the modern world will eventually require them to reconsider their core commitments. When Shah Bano contested the existing norms of marriage in a Muslim community in a federal court, for instance, her action prompted lively debate among a wide range of organisations including women's groups, government agencies and international development organisations in India. This debate prompted the Muslim community to reform the *Marriage and Divorce Legislation*. The re-evaluation of core commitments within the Muslim community, for Benhabib, is not only a natural progression but also an essential step for the continuing existence of a cohesive community. She contends that 'traditions, world views, and belief systems can only continue as hermeneutically plausible strands of meaning for their members insofar as they can engage in such creative resignification and renegotiation of their own core commitments' (2004: 293).

Benhabib's observations have significant parallels with the findings of this study. The paradigm shift in Islamic politics identified in Chapter 2 testifies to the argument that no matter how strong traditions are the pressures of societal modernisation ultimately force these traditions to shift their boundaries. Two case studies that support this argument are the AKP and the Capital Women's Platform. The AKP largely substituted Islamic values, which previously influenced their political vision, with the liberal idea of individual rights. This marked paradigm shift demonstrates the power of modernisation to facilitate and force social change even within the most traditional groups in modern Turkish public sphere. In Benhabib's sense, it is through resignification and renegotiation of core political values that the AKP has evolved to become a party embraced by a large section of the electorate.

Critics of the AKP, mainly from the Kemalist secular camp, question the sincerity of this poignant shift in Islamic politics. Kemalists claim that the shift is a strategic move aimed at invading the secular system, which in time will reveal the AKP's religious aspirations. This claim has thus far proven to be unfounded. Even if the Kemalist critics are correct in their assumptions of the AKP, the greater significance of the AKP's move is the fact that it has placed a major focus upon individual rights, indicating a commitment to core democratic values. The more the AKP comes to the defence of these values in the public sphere, the greater will be the leverage to broaden democratic aspirations. The hypothesis that the AKP has a hidden agenda and is therefore superficial in its commitment to liberal and democratic values cannot pre-empt the fact that their commitment to these values creates a discourse of its own. This discourse in turn works to broaden the horizon of individuals among different groups leading to an 'enlarged mentality' across society. Discourses of this nature, in this sense, develop a life of their own independent of the motives of participants, leading to two important implications.

Firstly, once a discourse becomes the property of the public sphere, it becomes a binding force for those who subscribe to its terms and conditions. This brings the issue of consistency to the fore. Independent of motives, the more the principles of democratic values are publicly proclaimed, the more difficult it is to breach those principles without losing face. In the case of the AKP, the legacy they have built through proclamation of democratic values has created its own discursive base independent of their motives. It can be argued that losing face does not have binding force in politics. Yet deceptive motives cannot prevail without leading to a public outcry threatening the legitimacy of the government.

Secondly, the fact that the values of a discursive practice generate a social base is indicative of a social learning process. In the case of the Turkish public sphere, public discursive practices embrace democratic principles more than ever. The findings of the Q study reveal a common acceptance by all discourses of the meaning of democratic principles, which shows that the liberal turn in Turkish politics is becoming a common theme. Even though the learning process has had varying consequences for divergent groups, it contributes to development of democratic habits. For instance, in the cases of the Kemalist and Nationalist discourses the Q findings have identified potential inconsistencies that these discourses have displayed. In their attitudes towards application of democratic principles, the gap between what they say and what they mean appears to be obvious. Yet when those principles are accepted and practised as governing principles of civic engagement, either in decision-making processes or as part of an informal deliberation oriented to understanding, they contribute to development of a basis upon which the habits of democratic deliberation flourish. The process of social learning which takes place in those settings nurtures trends and patterns creating a framework for broader acceptance of the democratic ideal, which in turn expands the scope of deliberative activity.

In this sense, the AKP's liberal paradigm has had a clear impact upon fostering democratic behaviour in Turkey. An example of this occurred in August 2004 when the ultra-nationalist MHP sent a letter to 313 generals, including the Chief of General Staff, General Hilmi Özkök, calling on them to issue a warning to the government. The MHP accused the AKP of influencing the judiciary in order to secure release of members of the Kurdish Demokratik Emek Partisi (DEP) – Democratic Labour Party, noting that the Foreign Affairs Minister, Abdullah Gül, had the audacity to meet with 'these convicted separatists'.[1]

The unprecedented action of the MHP received a strong reaction from the press and most of the political parties, which unanimously branded the MHP's letter as a call for a military coup. Among those was Büyük Birlik Partisi (BBP) – Grand Unity Party, which separated from the MHP in 1992. The leader, Muhsin Yazıcıoğlu, and founding members of the BBP, were prominent members of the MHP and their differences with the MHP, specifically in relation to democratic principles, have never been substantial. In response to the MHP's letter, the BBP leader, Yazıcıoğlu, was very critical of the MHP's letter. By distinguishing himself as a democrat, he denounced the MHP's action and stated that there is no room for such actions in a democracy.

One can be easily cynical about the sincerity of Yazıcıoğlu's proclamation of being a democrat and his emphasis on democratic traditions given his party's long running commitment to ultra nationalism with strong authoritarian tendencies. This is, in Robert Dahl's terms (1989), surely a contradiction in terms. Yet, at the least, Yazıcıoğlu's reaction reflects the culture of the day in which democratic values take precedence over a prevailing fashion. Even to contemplate a worst-case scenario that Yazıcıoğlu was hypocritical, it could be assumed that as a matter of consistency he would be forced to reconfigure some of his undemocratic habits. In Elster's sense (1998), this is 'the civilizing force of hypocrisy' through which reasons given to the public rather than base motives would prevail in the public

1 In *Turkish Daily News* 3 August 2004 p 1.

sphere. The final product of this process is expansion of the scope of democratic politics through learning the core principles governing discursive engagements in the public sphere. As Benhabib succinctly states 'the process of "giving good reasons in public" will not only determine the legitimacy of the norms followed; it will also enhance the civil virtues of democratic citizenship by cultivating the habits of mind of public reasoning and exchange' (2002: 115).

The learning process is constitutive of not only better decisions but also establishing a democratic culture in which habits of self-governance prevail. In other words, once a democratic culture created through citizens' learning permeates the public sphere it could generate a capacity for self-correction through which anti-democratic behaviours could be rectified in the process. What has been happening in the larger public sphere among ordinary citizens testifies to this. For instance, in the emotionalism that erupts frequently about the headscarf in the formal political sphere, there is always a noticeable calmness at the street level between secular and religious-minded people. Turam (2007) in her ethnographic study of engagement between Islamists and seculars captures this moment lucidly. She argues that attitudes of a growing number of seculars towards Islam have been changing since the late 1990s. In fact, Turam extends the scope of her analysis to the relationship between the state and Islamists and asserts that 'traditionally hostile fences between Islam and the Turkish state have gradually been replaced by hospitable boundaries' (2007: 37). According to Turam, 'the reorganization of Islam' through some short-term projects in the public and private realms broadened the scope of democratisation in Turkey. She argues that quiet independent of the actual motives and internal dynamics, which can be highly undemocratic at times, these projects nevertheless forced their way through the existing state structures by continuously fine-tuning their private claims in accordance with the liberal claims of the public sphere and the secular demands of the state. Atasoy (2005) also highlights the capacity of Islamic movements for change. Focusing more on the role of global politics and economy, Atasoy contends that, when historically contextualised within the wider relations of global politics the hybrid patterns of social change among Islamic movements displaying 'the contingency, variety and indeed the "modernity" of Islamic politics' becomes apparent (2005: 5).

With this it is possible to return to the main proposal of this study, that, if the social learning aspect of deliberation plays such a fundamental role, then it should be treated as a distinct category analytically rather than subordinated in the terms of decision-making procedures. In divided societies such as Turkey, the need for a formal acknowledgement of deliberation oriented to social learning exhibits a sense of urgency because the process of mutual understanding, rather than the process of decision-making, plays a more significant role in fostering democratic principles. This step is important because, unless social learning is acknowledged in its own right, deliberative theory may fail to produce an effective approach in channelling the scattered habits of democratic practice in the public sphere into the broader framework of the governing rules of public engagement. The key is to distinguish between different rationality requirements for different deliberative settings. Discourses oriented to agreement about decision-making procedures require a level of rationality that discourses oriented to understanding and social learning do not necessarily rely upon.

For instance, the Habermasian criterion that, in order to achieve consensus, all participants should be convinced on the same grounds does not necessarily have the same weight in deliberative procedures oriented to social learning. The purpose of discursive activity determines the kinds of discourses used in deliberative settings. Max Pensky captures this moment in his comment on Benhabib. By pointing to an ambiguity in deliberative democratic theory, Pensky contends that this ambiguity stems from 'an unclarified distinction between two quite different ways of understanding the purpose of discourse' (2004: 264). While discourse as a political practice functions to exchange views and debate, which emphasises 'the horizon-expanding aspect of talking', discourse as a mode of communicative action operates on the basis of deciding what to do, reflecting the characteristics of an institutionalised political speech. Based on this distinction, Pensky concludes:

> If I am correct that public sphere argument cannot reasonably expect cultural members to revise their own core commitments, and that fair bargaining is therefore the more reasonable alternative prior to any attempt at consensus, then we would be looking at a two-stage model in which bargaining (on whatever basis of reasonable argument) would be an appropriate mode of problem-solving in cases pitting a minority culture and the majority culture via the institutionalised legislature, while in the open and contested public sphere, discourses could be far more open, free, interesting, and productive – but precisely because they were not expected to actually decide any specific political or legal problem (2004: 265).

Pensky's suggestion of a two-stage model is based on the distinction between formal and informal ways of deliberating, which represents an initial step towards differentiation of modes of deliberation. Pensky moves in the right direction by pinpointing the fact that discursive activity offers more substance when it does not aim at arriving at a specific decision. Yet Pensky does not develop his suggestion any further. Remaining unanswered is Pensky's main question that how, precisely, are these two kinds of discourse to be thought in their relation. Hence, it is not clear whether his suggestion of a two-track model advocates decoupling social learning moments of deliberation from those of decision-making. My answer to Pensky's question is to liberate the open, free, interesting and productive discourses of the public sphere from the pressures of institutionalised, decision-making oriented discourses, as discussed throughout this study.

Pensky's critique also discusses the dilemma in Benhabib's framework highlighted in Chapter 2. Benhabib provides an intuitive deliberative framework that underlines the importance of continuing contestation and dialogue in the public sphere. In *The Claims of Culture*, Benhabib extends her analysis to multicultural settings and refines her framework, opening the way for a deeper understanding of the relationship between particular cultural claims and the universally claimed properties of democratic deliberation. In her framework, the hermeneutic function of deliberation oriented to understanding and social learning still appears to be captured only within the terms of decision-making procedures. For instance, in response to Bohman and Valadez, Benhabib contends:

> while recognising the empirical logic of democratic deliberation and will-formation processes, we need not forfeit the regulative principle that the logic of public justification requires impartiality, through which the best interests of all considered as equal moral and political beings are taken into account (2002: 145).

Benhabib, following Habermas, insists on the discourse principle which states that the interests of all involved are taken into account. As argued earlier, this principle is viable for decision-making oriented procedures to ensure a fair outcome. It is hard to sustain the case that those procedures oriented to understanding require the same strong criteria. For a hermeneutically inspired deliberative procedure, it is sufficient to rely on the universal pragmatics of speech which presuppose a rational attitude towards differences among participants. The most important aspect of this rational attitude is that it assumes a symmetrical distribution of chances to raise and to challenge claims by participants. In other words, when participants interact with a communicative intent, the presuppositions of speech prevail and regulate their action. Hence the internal rules implicit in the structure of language are sufficient to form a normative basis to regulate deliberative procedures oriented to mutual understanding.

Benhabib insists on the universal application of the strong discourse principle since she does not analytically distinguish between the two different kinds of deliberation and gives prominence to decision-making procedures. As Pensky points out, 'the various kinds of cultural conflict that Benhabib describes all, in the end, involve moral and legal matters that *must be decided*, regardless of whether anyone's horizons are expanded or not' [emphasis in original] (2004: 265). As a result, the social learning aspect of deliberation still remains largely at the background of her theory, therefore prompting further elaboration about its unique qualities and internal dynamics. Benhabib concludes that:

> The critique in question – that a deliberative democracy framework based on discourse ethics contains too many epistemic and affective biases to make it function fairly within intercultural and cross-cultural contexts – is overstated, and that such concerns can be accommodated without forfeiting the essential premises of the model (2002: 145).

It is not immediately obvious how this can be achieved without addressing the double character of deliberation and consequently redesigning deliberative procedures. It is true that 'contentious multicultural dialogues in the public spheres of democracies may result in narrative resignifications and reappropriations of their culture by minority groups' (2004: 292). This resignification process could only be fully appreciated and utilised if those dialogues are set free from the constraints of decision-making procedures and are placed within their own spheres operating at a distinctively different dimension in terms of their logic as well as their institutional design. In her example about the scarf affair in France, Benhabib argues that the voices of Muslim girls were not properly passed to the French public and asks, 'would it not have been more plausible to ask these girls to account for their actions and doings at least to their school communities, and to encourage discourses among the youth about what it means to be a Muslim citizen in a laic French republic?' (2002: 118). The obvious answer to this question is surely, 'yes'. Yet, what is really needed requires more than a 'yes'. These kinds of discursive activities oriented to hermeneutic understanding could make a better contribution to democratic culture if they become a permanent feature of the public sphere claiming their own institutionally designed sphere distinct from decision-making procedures. Thus redesigning the public sphere to open up a formal place for social learning and understanding-oriented deliberative activities is the next challenge for deliberative theory.

**Binary Deliberation**

I have argued for the need for a new structural arrangement in order to rescue the social learning aspect of deliberation from its subordinate status in existing practices. The redesign option itself immediately manifests new challenges to the idea of social learning. Two key and interrelated questions going to the heart of democratic legitimacy arise: First, if social learning is an arena where the function of deliberation is limited to opinion formation with no clear link to decision-making, then the role of social learning in legitimate decision-making remains unclear. An immediate upshot of this ambiguity would be to reduce politics to relational subjectivity in that deliberative activity is narrowed down to mutual accommodation of differences only. The obvious danger here is to relegate the sphere of social learning to a talk shop since the democratic capacity created during the process of understanding and negotiating differences would linger on with no specific purpose in mind.

The second question is, if citizens cannot link their deliberative practice to the decisions made on their behalf, and if there is no clear formula to narrow the gap between citizens and their representatives, then sustaining the level of engagement and deliberative capacity, which flourishe during the social learning oriented practices of citizens, could become doubtful.

It is therefore essential that an alternative framework should not only grant social learning its own formal space, but also show how this space can be integrated into the decision-making phase. I have previously shown the role that social learning played in the theories of Habermas, McCarthy, Benhabib, Dryzek and Young. I have also concluded that, despite their different levels of conceptual engagement with it, none offers a framework based on a systematic analysis of social learning. The lack of such analysis becomes even more pressing in the face of questions that I raised above. In the case of Habermas, for instance, his dual-track model not only subordinates the impact of social learning to the formal realms of decision-making, but also leaves one of the most important questions open, that is, how to sustain citizens' deliberative capacity and their level of engagement within a setting in which the link between their effort and the outcome is ultimately tied to the decisions of a third party? Fragmentation of modern societies undeniably and inescapably creates different layers between the legitimate owners of the decision-making power and the moment of actual decision-making. In this context the discontinuity between the people as the authors of the law and the legislatures who ultimately formulate the law needs to be addressed carefully when this discontinuity manifests itself in the form of a simple but important question: 'why participate if influence can only be achieved indirectly?'

A satisfactory answer to this question should entail measures to enhance the democratic capacity of citizens in different participatory practices within the public sphere. Unless the capacity gained within these practices is visibly and comprehensibly linked to actual decision-making processes, the question of 'why participate' would remain a continuing dilemma for democratic societies. Giving a proper answer, therefore, to this question requires development of a framework which aims to achieve two goals; first, creating a formal sphere for social learning so that it can function in its own terms; second, linking social learning back to the decision-making moments of deliberation in order to create a more sustained and better legitimated deliberative practice.

The Binary Deliberation Model aims at resolving this dilemma. Binary Deliberation envisages deliberative activity, where possible, always structured in a two-phase form in which social learning is separated from actual decision-making process. The first phase is strictly oriented toward understanding specifically to facilitate the broad, inclusive, informal means of deliberation. I refer to it as Structured Social Learning (SSL).

In the second phase, deliberative activity specifically moves towards making decisions. It differs from standard decision-making processes because it builds upon, hence benefits from, the outcomes of the SSL phase. Therefore, the scope of participants' engagement within the Binary Deliberation Model weaves through both phases. The separation, in this sense, is only a temporary step to achieve better decision-making outcomes. In other words, the SSL and decision-making phases work in tandem in a mutually inclusive fashion. Perhaps most importantly, while the decision-making phase benefits from the SSL phase, repeated applications of this model could in turn influence future outcomes within continued SSL phases. That is, each repeated applications of the model could potentially facilitate the development of new and higher levels of social understanding so far as the Binary Deliberation Model is conceived in continuum.

*The Structured Social Learning (SSL) Phase*

Claus Offe has asked an important question, 'Is it conceivable that the "social capital" of trusting and cooperative civic relations can be encouraged, acquired and generated – and not just inherited?' (1999: 87). Offe's question is critical simply because, if democratic theory assumes that the longevity of political systems largely depends on the level of attachment among citizens, then trust certainly plays a central role in the process of building a democratic polity. If decision-making oriented deliberation is prone to switching to the strategic forms of communication, then how to get participants out of this power game cocoon and establish trust between them becomes an immediate priority for deliberative theory. The Structured Social Learning phase of Binary Deliberation model aims at providing a solution to this undertaking.

The SSL phase builds understanding between group members by enhancing communication between them. There are potentially many advantages offered by the SSL process. It is structured in such a way that the process never loses sight of its main purpose, which is to identify values, interests and preferences of individuals, and to learn from them.

An important aspect of deliberative process, cognitive objectivity, can be learned during this process. Talking to other people and being involved in their point of view plays a significant role in establishing cognitive objectivity (Heider 1958). During the SSL phase individuals freely express their values and concerns in a cooperative manner. A key issue is to allow individuals to express their identity freely so that they feel respected, hence more involved in the process. Research in social psychology indicates that reaching an understanding between conflicting parties is most likely to be successful when the process serves as a forum in which the parties are fully satisfied with the level that they are allowed to express themselves (Eggins et al. 2002). Free expression of identities, feelings and thoughts allows participants to establish a link between themselves and the goals of the deliberative process. This link is crucial because it creates a self-defining reference point which works as a yardstick for participants to compare themselves with the broader social context in which they are located. During the process of forming a yardstick, the issues discussed from the ethical and moral perspectives of participants enable them to establish the points of commonality within the group. These commonalities are crucial because the attitude change becomes more likely when participants establish a common reference point with others (Haslam et al. 1996).

The SSL phase could also offset the impact of group polarisation. Eggins et al. argue that the length and frequency of deliberative gatherings sustained over time is an important factor in offsetting the effect of group polarisation. They indicate that group polarisation occurs under conditions where a representation of group identities is insufficient. They examine the impact of group identities over time and conclude that structural factors that ultimately enhance identity have a positive impact upon participants' experience of the process and their capacity to work productively. A corollary to the study is the finding that if participants feel that their contributions are valued, their relationship with others has a more positive spin. This in turn contributes to the process by creating a shared identity. The importance of time is also underlined by the Common In-group Identity Model. Gaertner et al. (1999) show that, after an extended period of contact, people can develop a new and more inclusive category underlining similarities, hence reducing intergroup bias.

In a case study of environmental management, Kelly (2001) highlights the impact of social learning on participants' attitudes and preferences. He reports that the process and facilitation methods organised between landholders, researchers and government staff and based on a participatory learning cycle encouraged participants to be open about their preferences, goals and values. The process, coupled with the impact of having an open and transparent style, produced a high degree of trust among participants.

Therefore, the first phase of Binary Deliberation, the Structured Social Learning process, could hypothetically offer the following potential outcomes:

- *Better understanding, hence trust*: Communication between different groups would break the mental cycle that stereotyping creates. In most cases this process would also generate trust among group members.
- *A sense of belonging, hence shared identity*: Being able to express personal points of view would generate a sense of belonging to the wider community, potentially to develop a shared identity.
- *Satisfaction*: Inclusiveness and equality principles of the process would generate a sense of satisfaction among participants, which could lead to enhanced legitimacy when tied to the decision-making phase.

*The Decision-making Phase*

A properly designed and executed SSL phase could be a springboard for developing trust and satisfaction amongst participants who, upon entering the decision-making phase, are expected to make more informed decisions. The importance of this process lies in the fact that participants, at the end, not only get to know each other better, but also, by reaching a decision together, step into a realm of cooperation and one way or another step out of a realm of mistrust. Eggins et al. show that the positive outcomes produced in an earlier phase are carried over to a subsequent phase in which members of different groups come together to negotiate a collective strategy. The two-phase structure of Binary Deliberation would encourage cooperative behaviour. If the positive sense of cooperation developed during the SSL phase of deliberation is followed by reaching a decision, then participants would be able to link their efforts to a concrete outcome. This link in return would not only make the deliberative process more sustainable over time, but would also increase the chance of achieving a better outcome which represents a common denominator of the choices and opinions of all parties involved. This is a powerful process in the sense that it could create the conditions of communication across the marginal sections of the community. That is, the possibility of reaching an agreement increases when social learning occurs. In other words, the greater the amount of learning achieved, the better potentially is the outcome of decision-making.

In the decision-making phase, the sense of satisfaction developed in the first phase could also lead to another important outcome: the fairness of the process. Research indicates that if participants feel satisfied with the fairness of the process they worry less about the nature of the final decision. Even if it is not in their favour they do not necessarily feel alienated from the process (Tyler 2006, Pruitt et al. 1993). It can be expected that satisfaction with the process should lead to an enhanced level of legitimacy.

The fairness of the process is also crucial to developing 'a new sense of self' among participants as being part of a social group. The group value model suggests that people are more likely to develop a different sense of themselves related to a certain group when they receive fair treatment within this group (Tyler 1989). Furthermore, fair treatment also increases people's commitment to their group (Simon and Sturmer 2003). The effect of developing a sense of social connection with others has been tested in a deliberative setting. In their study of a deliberative poll conducted in the Australian Capital Territory in 2002, on the question of whether or not the ACT should introduce a bill of rights, Eggins et al. (2007) found that exposure to information, fair treatment and social identification can all play a role in better engaging participants in the process. The most important factor is 'when they are treated with respect and given opportunities to discuss issues, ask questions and to air their views in collaboration with other members of a relevant community' (2007: 99).

The most important outcome of the decision-making phase would be a likely change in the attitudes of participants. Intergroup contact theory in social psychology maintains that when individuals engage in positive social interaction with the members of a disliked group, such as making a decision together about a common concern, what they learn from this interaction becomes inconsistent with their general attitude (Pettigrew 1998, Gilbert et al. 1998). This inconsistency ultimately leads to a change in attitudes to justify new behaviour. Therefore, at the end of the second phase, combined with the positive effects of the first phase of Binary Deliberation, it would not be unrealistic to expect a positive shift in attitudes towards members of other groups.

The hypothetical benefits of the second phase of the Binary Deliberation model, the Decision-Making Phase, could then be summarised as follows:

- *Better outcomes*: Since participants would be better informed and more satisfied in relation to the issues they dealt with during the first phase, the quality of decisions in the second phase would be higher in the sense that they would reflect an overall satisfaction among participants.

- *Enhanced legitimacy*: Being consulted in a process in equal terms with others would enhance trust not only in others but also in the political system, hence yielding in enhanced legitimacy.
- *Possibility of a change in negative attitudes*: Meaningful cooperation could further enhance the possibility of a positive change in the attitudes of those who display negative attitudes towards members of a different group.

As stated earlier, the Binary Deliberation Model perceives the Structured Social Learning and decision-making phases working in tandem, that is, they are two distinct spheres of operation, yet they are also mutually inclusive in the sense that the process of Binary Deliberation cannot be assumed fully completed without a full realisation of both phases. In addition to all positive outcomes listed above, what should be valuable in this process is that it is capable of having an influence beyond its boundaries. There is potential for an enhanced level of understanding and trust to be aroused throughout these phases which could then become the foundation for a more sustainable level of participation within the community. As Mutz indicates, studies in social contexts and social networks concur that a participatory social environment renders more participation: 'the more people interact with one another in a social context, the more norms of participation will be transmitted, and the more people will be recruited into political activity' (2006: 96). Similarly, Pettigrew echoes Mutz by asserting that 'intergroup contact and its effects are cumulative – we live what we learn' (1998: 78).

The positive attitudes developed within Binary Deliberation would, therefore, progress beyond the deliberative process and create a more generalised basis for future forms of cooperation. The successful and repeated applications of Binary Deliberation within a singular social sphere could create a continuously upwardly moving spiral of bonding and trust to be the future platforms for ever increasing cooperation within future Binary Deliberation engagements as well as general interaction within the broader social sphere.

# Chapter 9

# Conclusion

The challenge for democratic theory to create a legitimately functioning social order has reached a new point. Under current conditions, the question of how to deal with fundamental value differences is a key issue. The idea of deliberative democracy offers a viable resolution of this challenge. By tying legitimacy of a social order to a discursively functioning framework, in which different perspectives and claims are negotiated through a dialogic process, deliberative democrats have surely opened a new chapter in democratic theory.

This chapter itself is already facing a new challenge. The theory of deliberative democracy has now reached a point where investigation into the internal differentiation of deliberative procedures has become essential. This is particularly true of societies divided on moral and ethical issues. In relation to its internal differentiation, deliberation should be conceptualised in two different stages: social learning and decision-making. Treating deliberation mainly as a decision-making procedure is a common trend among deliberative theorists.

This does not necessarily mean that they ignore or do not acknowledge the social learning component of deliberation. It means that these theorists conceive and argue deliberation within terms of decision-making. These differ substantially from those of social learning, hence subordinating the social learning phase of deliberation to that of decision-making.

This ambiguous treatment of social learning can be rectified by a framework in which social learning and decision-making aspects of deliberation are analytically distinguished. In this framework the social learning mode of deliberation is formally allocated its own dominion in the public sphere, equipped with its own resources and operated under its own terms. The relationship between the two is not mutually exclusive. Quite the contrary; salvaging social learning from the pressures of decision-making would enable its unique resources to flourish freely and enhance the outcome of decision-making procedures. Introduction of a preliminary framework, the Binary Deliberation Model in the previous chapter, aims to offer an alternative to address this issue.

To show the importance of this step in modern Turkey, social, religious and cultural divisions that cut deep into society have been examined. With the help of the Q study, the main contours of different tendencies about one of the most important issues in the Turkish public sphere, the relationships between Islam, democracy and secularism, have been outlined. The Q study has shown that there is a considerable desire for dialogue and mutual understanding between Islamic and secular groups who have traditionally been hostile towards each other. From the Q study it has also emerged that there are both points of convergence and divergence between these groups. These provide clues for a framework for mutual understanding. The significance of deliberation oriented to social learning appears precisely at this point. It is unlikely that these groups will successfully converge on common ground under the auspices of decision-making procedures. This is because priority at this stage is developing an understanding of each other. The BSKP case shows that building a mutual understanding between these groups may be achievable. The experiences of women from different backgrounds in the BSKP, as well as the relationship between the leftist IHD and Islamist Mazlum-Der, signify the genesis of a new form of cooperation in the Turkish public sphere. The paradigm shift towards individual rights-based politics amongst the leftist and Islamist groups played a fundamental role in creating the leverage that inspired mutual cooperation. Dialogue and cooperation between these groups testify that a liberal culture, usually conceived as a prerequisite for the success of deliberative practice, could grow from grassroots movements without necessarily having the support of an established democratic order at large. Eventually it is quite likely that, in time, those movements can influence mainstream political culture.

**Appendix 1   Q study participants profile**

|  | Gender | Age | Religion | Politics | Occupation | Education | Rural/Urban |
|---|---|---|---|---|---|---|---|
| Subject 1 | F | 29 | Secular | Social Democrat | Admin | High School | Urban |
| Subject 2 | M | 39 | Secular/Muslim | Nationalistic | P. Servant | University | Urban |
| Subject 3 | M | 75 | Secular/Muslim | Social Democrat | Retiree | University | Urban/Rural |
| Subject 4 | M | 44 | Secular | Left | Mayor | Primary | Rural |
| Subject 5 | F | 32 | Secular | Left | Academic | Post Grad | Urban |
| Subject 6 | M | 21 | Secular | Socialist | Student | University | Urban/Rural |
| Subject 7 | F | 41 | Secular | Social Democrat | P. Servant | University | Urban |
| Subject 8 | M | 37 | Secular/Muslim | Conservative | Manufacturing | High School | Urban |
| Subject 9 | F | 32 | Secular/Alevi | Social Democrat | Cleaner | Primary | Rural |
| Subject 10 | M | 30 | Muslim | Centre Right | Small Buss | University | Urban/Rural |
| Subject 11 | M | 33 | Muslim | Centre Right | Chemist | University | Urban |
| Subject 12 | F | 21 | Muslim | Liberal Islam | Student | University | Urban |
| Subject 13 | F | 43 | Secular/Muslim | Social Democrat | Social Work | High School | Urban/Rural |
| Subject 14 | F | 40 | Muslim | Feminist | Housewife | Primary | Rural |
| Subject 15 | M | 28 | Secular | Left | Academic | Post Grad | Urban |
| Subject 16 | M | 42 | Muslim | Islamic | P. Servant | University | Urban |
| Subject 17 | F | 52 | Secular | Left | Academic | Post Grad | Urban |
| Subject 18 | F | 42 | Secular | Left | Unionist | University | Urban |
| Subject 19 | F | 40 | Secular/Muslim | None | Social Work | High School | Rural |
| Subject 20 | M | 83 | Secular/Muslim | Social Democrat | Lawyer | University | Urban |
| Subject 21 | M | 50 | Secular | Social Democrat | Retiree | University | Rural |
| Subject 22 | F | 41 | Secular | Left | Retiree | High School | Urban |
| Subject 23 | F | 56 | Secular | Social Democrat | Retiree | University | Urban |

**Appendix 1 continued    Q study participants profile**

| | Gender | Age | Religion | Politics | Occupation | Education | Rural/Urban |
|---|---|---|---|---|---|---|---|
| Subject 24 | M | 25 | Muslim | Nationalist | Unemployed | High School | Rural |
| Subject 25 | F | 27 | Secular/Muslim | Conservative | Unemployed | High School | Urban/Rural |
| Subject 26 | F | 58 | Secular | Social Democrat | Small Buss | University | Urban |
| Subject 27 | F | 33 | Secular/Muslim | Social Democrat | Social Work | High School | Rural |
| Subject 28 | M | 44 | Muslim | Islamic | P. Servant | University | Urban/Rural |
| Subject 29 | M | 40 | Muslim | Islamic | State worker | High School | Rural |
| Subject 30 | M | 50 | Muslim | Islamic | Policeman | High School | Urban/Rural |
| Subject 31 | F | 44 | Secular | Social Democrat | P. Servant | High School | Urban |
| Subject 32 | F | 37 | Muslim | Islamic | Housewife | University | Rural |
| Subject 33 | F | 39 | Muslim | Islamic/Feminist | Researcher | Post Grad | Urban |

## Appendix 2   Q study statements and rankings

| | Statements | KD | ND | LLD | ID |
|---|---|---|---|---|---|
| 1 | Today's oppressive attitudes against Muslims in the name of secularism are rooted in Kemalist ideology. | -5 | -5 | 3 | -1 |
| 2 | Kemalism and secularism cannot be separated from each other. Separating them will mean the end of secularism. If you are secular, you are also Kemalist, or vice versa. | 2 | 3 | -2 | -4 |
| 3 | Secularism is atheism. | -6 | -6 | -3 | -2 |
| 4 | About one thousand female students have been refused entry to the University of Marmara because they dress themselves according to their religious belief. This shows that there is a serious problem with freedom of belief and education in Turkey. | -3 | -1 | 0 | 3 |
| 5 | The state does not want people's consciousness to rise. Nevertheless, may be thanks to the media, people from different backgrounds have started understanding each other better. | -2 | -1 | -2 | -2 |
| 6 | The problem with Islamic law in relation to democracy is that Islamic communities exert social pressure on individuals. This conflicts with the democratic notion of individual freedom and rights. | 4 | 1 | 3 | -2 |
| 7 | The Army is the guarantor of democracy and secularism. | 0 | 4 | -6 | -6 |
| 8 | Today, the biggest obstacle for democracy in Turkey is not Islam, but the political parties, which offer no solution to corruption. | 2 | 2 | 1 | 1 |
| 9 | Islamists are not as tolerant towards atheists as atheists are towards Islamists. | 2 | -2 | 1 | -3 |
| 10 | The differences between us are too deep. We cannot reconcile them by talking. This system will remain as it is in the future. | -4 | -6 | -3 | -5 |
| 11 | In some religious cities, during the Ramadan, people were beaten if they ate or drank during the day. How can I be sure that Islamists will not do the same if they come to power? How can I trust them? | 0 | -1 | 2 | -3 |
| 12 | The debates in media, such as discussion forums on TV channels, are playing an important role in allowing people to understand each other. | -2 | 1 | -1 | -2 |

## Appendix 2 continued      Q study statements and rankings

|   | Statements | KD | ND | LLD | ID |
|---|---|---|---|---|---|
| 13 | Some remarks made by Islamic leaders contributed to increasing the tension between Islamists and Kemalists. An example of this is Mr Erbakan's remark suggesting that one day the deans, who do not allow students with headscarf into the universities, will be forced to salute those students. | 4 | -2 | -2 | -3 |
| 14 | The universities are important places where secular people and Islamists can close the existing gap between the two groups. When we do not allow female students wearing scarf into the universities we also throw them out of the modern world. By doing this we jeopardise the possibility of living together. | -2 | -1 | 1 | 5 |
| 15 | Islam can accommodate different groups including atheists. | -2 | 0 | -4 | 4 |
| 16 | Islam, as a system of law, cannot be compatible with democracy. The role and the place attributed to women by Islamic law, which denies women basic individual rights, is enough to prove this. | 2 | -3 | 1 | -4 |
| 17 | The purpose of religion will be defeated when it is carried over to the public arena. Beliefs are personal matters. They should be kept within the individual sphere. | 6 | 4 | 3 | -5 |
| 18 | Democracy cannot be realised before economic equality is achieved. | 3 | 1 | 2 | -1 |
| 19 | People are less corrupt under *Shari'ah* regime because it induces the fear of God. | -6 | -5 | -5 | -1 |
| 20 | If everybody tries to live according to Islamic rule, a just system can come into existence. | -5 | -4 | -5 | 0 |
| 21 | Whether the state is secular or not should not be dealt with by the Constitution. The state should only act as a guarantor of the freedom of religious practice. There should not be a state institution to organise religious practice. | -1 | -3 | 3 | -1 |
| 22 | The negative image that some extreme Islamic groups have created has been attributed to the whole Islamic community particularly by the media. We have to stop this misrepresentation. | -1 | 0 | -1 | 0 |
| 23 | One cannot claim to be a real Muslim if one does not interpret the Qur'an in light of today's living conditions. | 0 | 0 | -3 | -1 |

## Appendix 2 continued    Q study statements and rankings

|  | Statements | KD | ND | LLD | ID |
|---|---|---|---|---|---|
| 24 | The Qur'an does not praise a particular political system. Islam can fit into any system as long as it is fair. For instance, Islam could fit into a monarchy if the King were fair. | -4 | -3 | -4 | 5 |
| 25 | Whether I cover myself with a scarf or not should not be anyone else's business. This is what I understand from secularism. Everybody should respect different beliefs. | 0 | 4 | 4 | 4 |
| 26 | Turkish people tend to be very tolerant towards people who have similar views. The important thing is to be able to show respect to people who hold different views. | 0 | 0 | 2 | 0 |
| 27 | The important thing is to start from somewhere. If people could start showing respect and tolerance to each other, this would force the state to do the same. | 2 | 1 | -1 | 1 |
| 28 | During Ottoman rule, a variety of ethnic and religious groups lived together. This diversity only became a problem when it was exploited for political purposes. When people form a system of government, whatever the name or the form of it, there should not be a big problem as long as they can agree on basic moral values. | -1 | 0 | -2 | 2 |
| 29 | I trust that secular people and Muslims will come to an agreement when human values are brought onto the agenda. | 1 | 2 | 0 | 2 |
| 30 | The reason behind the reaction to Kemalists is their antagonistic attitude towards Islamic people. The problem can be solved easily if they tried to understand Muslim people rather than attacking and dehumanising them. | -4 | -2 | -1 | 1 |
| 31 | I do not see anything wrong with religious sects. People should be able to get together if they believe in the same thing. Everybody, religious people, atheists etc., should be able to live together in peace within the same nation. | -1 | -1 | -2 | 0 |
| 32 | Recently, Islamic and secular people have been softening their attitudes. It shows that we can solve our problems better when we try to understand each other. | -1 | 5 | -1 | 1 |
| 33 | The military tradition has paralysed the self-reflective capacity of our society. That is why we are still being governed by a mentality which is out of date. | 1 | -4 | 4 | 1 |

## Appendix 2 continued    Q study statements and rankings

|  | Statements | KD | ND | LLD | ID |
|---|---|---|---|---|---|
| 34 | Secularism is the undeniable foundation of religious pluralism and the most important norm for societal peace. We must hold on to it. | 5 | 3 | 0 | -3 |
| 35 | Today, the meaning attributed to democracy has gone beyond understanding that it is only a system of governing. It is being perceived almost like another religion, interfering with people's private spheres. Democracy is not a way of living. It is a way of governing. | -1 | 0 | 0 | 0 |
| 36 | Mustafa Kemal Atatürk is a very important personality who could only be respected. The Kemalism label unfortunately has been stuck on him and is being unfairly used against Muslims. Kemalism has now become a metaphysical concept with a religious-like content. Like democracy, its meaning has been abused and changed. | -3 | -3 | 0 | 1 |
| 37 | In Turkey, more than 80 percent of Islamic people have a moderate line. They cannot be a threat to the secular regime. | 1 | 3 | 1 | 1 |
| 38 | If Turkey has today become more modern than any other Islamic country, it is mainly because law and education have been laicised by being separated from the influence of religion. | 5 | 2 | -1 | -1 |
| 39 | Notwithstanding the claim, our state is not a secular one. Forcing people to declare their religion on their identity cards or having compulsory religious lessons in schools are examples of this. | 1 | -4 | 4 | -2 |
| 40 | The fear of communism and fundamentalism has contributed to inclusion of very undemocratic rules in the penal code against them (142, 141, 163). If they were allowed to develop freely, they would be able to reach new syntheses, thus avoiding today's problems. | 2 | -2 | 5 | 2 |
| 41 | Quite a few female students, who had to take off their scarf to be admitted to universities, later became happy with their new look. Maybe this rule allowed them to do what they really want. | -1 | -1 | -3 | -4 |
| 42 | The solution is mutual understanding. Groups who oppose each other should try to understand each other. | 3 | 3 | 1 | 3 |

## Appendix 2 continued     Q study statements and rankings

| | Statements | KD | ND | LLD | ID |
|---|---|---|---|---|---|
| 43 | The lack of education is the main reason why we are having such problems between secular and Islamic people. People do not like reading and investigating. They believe whatever they hear. | 1 | 6 | 2 | -1 |
| 44 | I am trying to survive economically to be able to feed my children. The debate between Islam and secularism does not interest me. | -3 | -4 | -2 | -3 |
| 45 | To claim that Muslims in Turkey are not allowed to practise their religion is a totally unfair statement. If we do not count the scarf problem in public institutions, there has been no obstacle to Muslims practicing their religion. | 6 | 1 | 1 | -2 |
| 46 | The secularists in Turkey claim that women who wear the scarf cannot be secular. This is not a democratic attitude. | -3 | 2 | 0 | 0 |
| 47 | My wife has been refused a health card only because she wears a scarf. This is against basic human rights and secularism. | -2 | 5 | 5 | 3 |
| 48 | The conflict between secular and Islamic people has been created superficially. The groups who are in control of the state have always created enemies in order to maintain their power. Yesterday it was communism, today it is fundamentalist Islam. | 0 | -1 | 6 | 3 |
| 49 | In a Muslim society, the framework for freedom has to be determined according to Islamic values. | -5 | -5 | -6 | 4 |
| 50 | We have to produce our own model of democracy. The cultural values of eastern countries are different from those in the west. Eastern countries should not be governed by an American model of democracy. | -4 | 4 | 2 | -1 |
| 51 | If the freedom of belief is overemphasised, Muslim people might be affected by ideas that are dangerous for the secular regime. | -2 | -2 | -4 | -5 |
| 52 | Respect for individual rights, the fundamental principle of democracy and secularism, exists in Islam. | 0 | -2 | -4 | 2 |
| 53 | I support our President who defends the supremacy of law. We can only solve our democratic problems by creating a real system of law in our country. | 5 | 1 | 3 | 1 |

## Appendix 2 continued    Q study statements and rankings

| | Statements | KD | ND | LLD | ID |
|---|---|---|---|---|---|
| 54 | The state is not supposed to carry a religious identity. Its task should only be to govern people. It should not question its people on the basis of their religious identities. | 4 | 5 | 4 | 5 |
| 55 | A state taking measures to help the practice of religious freedom should not be against secularism. Quite contrary, a secular system requires this. | 0 | 1 | -1 | 2 |
| 56 | The state should lead the reconciliation process. It should not treat some of its citizens as enemies. | 1 | 2 | 2 | 2 |
| 57 | We have no other choice to solve our problems but dialogue. However, we have to be careful of the tone of the dialogue, which should favour a rational, non-antagonistic style that respects others. | 3 | 1 | 1 | 6 |
| 58 | The fundamental condition is respect for others. If we achieve this at the grassroots level, then we can solve the problems created and imposed from above. | 4 | 0 | 0 | 4 |
| 59 | We have to find out what is common among us rather than focusing on differences. For instance, we have to emphasise the importance of education at the universities instead of arguing about the scarf controversy. | 3 | 6 | 6 | 3 |
| 60 | In a secular society everybody should abide by the law. If the law bans wearing the scarf in public institutions, the rule should be respected. | 3 | 0 | -5 | -6 |
| 61 | We should trust our people whether they are Kurds, Turks, Laz, Alevi, whether they wear a scarf or not. The more divisions are created in the name of state protection, the more divided we become. This is the real danger. | 1 | 2 | 5 | 6 |
| 62 | The state must trust its people. We are here for our country and the state. I served in the Army and fought against Kurdish separatists in the east. Today, the state considers me a fundamentalist threat because my wife wears a scarf. | -1 | -3 | -1 | 0 |
| 63 | If a law breaches a basic individual right, it can be disobeyed. | -3 | -1 | 0 | 0 |
| 64 | The Islamists are only softening their views because of strong resistance shown against them by the Army and Kemalists. | 1 | 3 | -3 | -4 |

*Notes*: The KD: Kemalist Discourse; the ND: Nationalist Discourse; the LLD: Liberal left Discourse; the ID: Islamic Discourse.

# Bibliography

Adanalı, H. 2000. Kelam: İslam Toplumunun Rasyonelleşme Süreci. *İslamiyat*, III, 1, 55-70.

Akdere, İ. and Karadeniz, Z. 1996. *Türkiye Solunun Eleştirel Tarihi-1: 1908-1980*, İstanbul, Evrensel Basım Yayın.

Akman, A. 2002. Milliyetçilik Kuramında Etnik/Sivil Milliyetçilik Karşıtlığı, in *Milliyetçilik*, edited by Bora, T. İstanbul, İletişim, 81-103.

Alkan, M. 2001. Resmi İdeolojinin Doğuşu ve Evrimi Uzerine Bir Deneme, in *Tanzimat ve Meşrutiyetin Birikim*, edited by Alkan, M. İstanbul, İletişim, 377-409.

Alper, M.Ö. 2000. *İslam Felsefesinde Akıl-Vahiy Felsefe-Din İlişkisi*, İstanbul, Ayışığı Kitapları.

Anderson, N.H. 1968. Likeableness Ratings of 555 Personality Trait Words, *Journal of Personality and Social Psychology*, 9, 272-279.

Arkoun, M. 1994. *Rethinking Islam*, Oxford, Westview Press.

Arslan, A. 1996. *İslam Felsefesi Üzerine*, Ankara, Vadi Yayınları.

Arslan, A. 1999. *İslam, Demokrasi ve Türkiye*, Ankara, Vadi Yayınları.

Atacan, F. 2000. 28 Subat 1997: Türk-Islam Sentezinin Sonu, in *Mübeccel Kıray İçin Yazılar*, Istanbul, Bağlam Yayınları, 113-138.

Atacan, F. 2003. *AKP versus SP*; paper presented at the CERI&IFEA Conference in Paris, December.

Atasoy, Y. 2005. *Turkey, Islamists and Democracy: Transition and Globalization in a Muslim State*, London, I.B. Tauris.

Aydın, M. 1994. Kur'an ve İnsan, in *Birinci Qur'an Sempozyumu*, edited by Ersin M.A., Ankara, Bilgi Vakfı Yayınları.

Aydın, S. 2001. Iki Ittihat Terakki; in *Tanzimat ve Meşrutiyetin Birikimi*, edited by Alkan, M. İstanbul, İletişim, 117-129.

Aydın, S. 2002. Sosyalizm ve Milliyetçilik: Galiyefizm'den Kemalism'e Türkiye'de Üçüncü Yol Arayışları, in *Milliyetçilik*, edited by Bora, T. İstanbul, İletişim, 438-483.

Baas, L.R. 1979. The Constitution as Symbol; The Interpersonal Sources of Meaning of a Secondary Symbol, *American Journal of Political Science*, 23, 101-120.

Belge, M. 2001. Mustafa Kemal ve Kemalism; in *Kemalism*; edited by İnsel, A. İstanbul, İletişim, 29-44.

Belli, M. 1988. Milli Demokratik Devrim; in *Sosyalizm ve Toplumsal Mücadeleler Ansiklopedisi*, Istanbul, Yön.

Benhabib, S. 1987. The Generalised and the Concrete Other; in *Women and Moral Theory* edited by Kittay and Meyers, New Jersey, Rowmann and Littlefield, 154-177.

Benhabib, S. 1992a. *Situating the Self*, Oxford, Polity Press.

Benhabib, S. 1992b. Models of Public Space: Hannah Arendt, The Liberal Tradition, and Jurgen Habermas, in *Habermas and the Public Sphere*, edited by Calhoun, C, Cambridge, MIT Press, 73-99.

Benhabib, S. 1996. *Democracy and Difference: Contesting the Boundaries of the Political*, Princeton, Princeton University Press.

Benhabib, S. 2002. *The Claims of Culture: Equality and Diversity in the Global Era*, Princeton, Princeton University Press.

Benhabib, S. 2004. On Culture, Public Reason and Deliberation: Response to Pensky and Peritz, *Constellations*, v11, No 2, 291-299.

Bernstein, R. 1983. *Beyond Objectivism and Relativism: Science, Hermeneutics, and Praxis*, Oxford, Blackwell.

Bernstein, R. (ed.) 1985. *Habermas and Modernity*, Cambridge, Polity.

Billard, S. 1999. How Q Methodology Can Be Democratised; *Feminism and Psychology*; v 9(3), 357-366.

Block, J. 1961. *The Q-sort Method in Personality Assesment and Psychiatric Research*, Springfield IL, Charles C. Thomas.

Bohman, J. 1996. *Public Deliberation: Pluralism, Complexity and Democracy*, Cambridge, MIT Press.

Bohman, J. (ed.) 1997. *Deliberative Democracy: Essays on Reason and Politics*, Cambridge, MIT Press.

Bohman, J. 1998. The Coming of Age of Deliberative Democracy, *The Journal of Political Philosophy*, 6, 400-425.

Bora, T. 2003. Nationalist Discourses in Turkey, *The South Atlantic Quarterly*, 102; 2/3, 433-451.

Bora, T. and Canefe, N. 2002. Türkiye'de Popülist Milliyetçilik; in *Milliyetçilik*, edited by Bora, T. İstanbul, İletişim, 635-663.

Brown, S. 1980. *Political Subjectivity: Applications of Q methodology*, in *Political Science*, New Haven, Yale University Press.

Brown, S. 1993. A Primer on Q Methodology, *Operant Subjectivity*, 16, 91-138.

Bulaç, A. 1991. *Din ve Modernizm*, İstanbul, Endülüs Yayınları.

Bulaç, A. 1995. *Modern Ulus Devlet*, İstanbul, İz Yayıncılık.

Bulaç, A. 2001. *Din Devlet ve Demokrasi*, Ankara, Zaman.

Çaha, Ö. 1999. İslam ve Demokrasi, *İslamiyat*, v2, no:22.

Çaha, Ö. and Aras, B. 2000. Fetullah Gülen and His Liberal Turkish Islam Movement, *Middle East Review of International Affairs*, 4, 30-42.

Calhoun, C. (ed.) 1992. *Habermas and the Public Sphere*, Cambridge, MIT Press.

Can, K. 2002. Ülkücü Hareketin İdeolojisi; in *Milliyetçilik*, edited by Bota, T. İstanbul, İletişim, 663-706.

Çetinsaya, G. 2001a. Kalemiyeden Mülkiyeye Tanzimat Zihniyeti, in *Tanzimat ve Meşrutiyet'in Birikimi*, edited by Alkan, M. İstanbul, İletişim, 54-72.

Çetinsaya, G. 2001b. İslami Vatanseverlikten İslam Siyasetine in *Tanzimat ve Meşrutiyet'in Birikimi*, edited by Alkan, M. İstanbul, İletişim, 265-277.

Dahl, R. 1989. *Democracy and its Critics*, New Haven, Yale University Press.

Davison, R. 1977. Nationalism as an Ottoman Problem and the Ottoman Response, in *Nationalism in a Non-National State: The Dissolution of the Ottoman Empire*, edited by Haddad and Oschsenwald, Colombus, Ohio University Press.

Deringil, S. 2002. *İktidarın Sembolleri ve İdeoloji*, Istanbul, Yapı Kredi Yayınları.

Deveaux, M. 2003. A Deliberative Approach to Conflicts of Culture, *Political Theory*, v31, n6, 780-807.

Donner, J.C. 2001. Using Q Sorts in Participatory Processes: An Introduction to the Methodology, in *Social Analysis: Selected Tools and Techniques*, Washington, The World Bank, 24-50.

Dryzek, J. 1990. *Discursive Democracy: Politics, Policy and Political Science*, Cambridge, Cambridge University Press.

Dryzek, J. 2000. *Deliberative Democracy and Beyond: Liberals, Critics, Contestations*, Oxford, Oxford University Press.

Dryzek, J. 2005. Deliberative Democracy in Divided Societies: Alternatives to Agonism and Analgesia, *Political Theory*, v 33, n 2, 218-242.

Dryzek, J. and Holmes, L. 2002. *Post-Communist Democratisation: Political Discourses Across Thirteen Countries*, Cambridge; Cambridge University Press.

Eggins, R., Haslam, S.A., Reynolds, K. 2002. Social Identity and Negotiation: Subgroup Representation and Superordinate Consensus, *Personality and Social Psychology Bulletin*, 28, 887-899.

Eggins, R., Reynolds, K., Oakes, P., Mavor, K. 2007. Citizen Participation in a Deliberative Poll: Factors Predicting Attitude Change, *Australian Journal of Psychology*, 59-2, 94-100.

El Fadl, A.K. 2004. Islam and the Challenge of Democracy, in *Islam and the Challenge of Democracy*, edited by Cohen, J. and Chasman, D., Princeton, Princeton University Press.

Elster, J. 1998. *Deliberative Democracy*, London, Cambridge University Press.

Esposito, J. and Voll, J. 1996. *Islam and Democracy*, New York, Oxford University Press.

Esposito, J. and Voll, J. 2004. Cohen J, Chasman, D (eds), Princeton, Princeton University Press.

Fearon, D.J. 1998. Deliberation as Discussion; in *Deliberative Democracy*, edited by Elster, J, London, Cambridge University Press.

Fennema, M. and Maussen, M. 2000. Dealing with Extremists in Public Discussion: Front National and 'Republican Front' in France, *The Journal of Political Philosophy*, v8, n 3, 379-400.

Findley, C. 1980. *Bureaucratic Reform in the Ottoman Empire: The Sublime Porte, 1789-1922*, Princeton, Princeton University Press.

Fishkin, J. 1991. *Democracy and Deliberation*, New Haven, Yale University Press.

Fishkin, J. 1995. *The Voice of the People: Public Opinion and Democracy*, New Haven, Yale University Press.

Fraser, N. 1992. Rethinking the Public Sphere: A Contribution to the Critique of Actually Existing Democracy, in *Habermas and the Public Sphere*, edited by Calhoun, Cambridge, MIT Press, 109-142.

Fung, A. 2003. Recipes for Public Spheres: Eight Institutional Design Choices and Their Consequences, *The Journal of Political Philosophy*, v11, n3, 338-367.

Gadamer, H.G. 1975. *Truth and Method*, Newyork, Seabury Press.

Gadamer, H.G. 1979. The Problem of Historical Consciousness, in *Interpretive Social Science: A Reader*, edited by Rabinow P. and Sullivan M.W, Berkeley, University of California Press, 73-103.

Gartner, S.L. Dovidio, J.F. Rust, M.C. Niez, J.A. Banker, B.S. Ward, C.M. Mottola, G.R. Houlette, M. 1999. Reducing Intergroup Bias: Elements of Intergroup Cooperation, *Journal of Personality and Social Psychology*, 76, 388-402.

Gellner, E. 1981. *Muslim Society*, Cambridge, Cambridge University.

Gellner, E. (ed.) 1994. *Conditions of Liberty: Civil Society and Its Rivals*, London, Hamish Hamilton.

Gellner, E. 1997. The Turkish Option in Comparative Perspective, in *Rethinking Modernity and National Identity in Turkey*, edited by Bozdogan S. and Kasaba R, Seattle, Washington University Press, 233-244.

Gilbert, D., Fiske, S., Lindzey, G. 1998. *The Handbook of Social Psychology V2*, Boston, McGraw-Hill, 576-579.

Glaser, B. and Strauss, A. 1967. *The Discovery of Grounded Theory: Strategies for Qualitative Research*, Chicago, Aldine Publications Co.

Göle, N. 2000. *İslamın Kamusal Yüzleri*, İstanbul, Metis.

Göle, N. 2002. Islam in Public: New Visibilities and New Imaginaries; *Public Culture*, 14(1), 173-90.

Güler, İ. 2002. *Politik Teoloji Yazıları*, Ankara, Kitabiyat.

Gündem, M. (ed.) 1998. *Abant Toplantıları-1: İslam ve Laiklik*, İstanbul, Gazeteciler ve Yazarlar Vakfı Yayınları.

Habermas, J. 1984. *The Theory of Communicative Action I*, Boston, Beacon Press.

Habermas, J. 1987. *The Theory of Communicative Action II*, Boston: Beacon Press.

Habermas, J. 1990. *Moral Consciousness and Communicative Action*, Cambridge, MIT Press.

Habermas, J. 1992. Further Reflections on the Public Sphere; in *Habermas and the Public Sphere*, edited by Calhoun, Cambridge, MIT Press, 421-462.

Habermas, J. 1994. *Justification and Application*, Cambridge, MIT Press.

Habermas, J. 1995a. *Postmetaphysical Thinking*, Cambridge: MIT Press.

Habermas, J. 1995b. Reconciliation Through the Public Use of Reason:Remarks on John Rawls' Political Liberalism, *Journal of Philosophy*, XCII:3, 109-131.

Habermas, J. 1996. *Between Facts and Norms*, Cambridge, MIT Press.

Habermas, J. 1998a. Reply to Symposium Participants; in *Habermas on Law and Democracy*, edited by Rosenfeld M. and Arato A, California, University of California Press, 381-453.

Habermas, J. 1998b. *The Inclusion of the Other: Studies in Political Theory*, Cambridge, MIT Press.

Habermas, J. 2001a. *The Postnational Constellation: Political Essays*, Cambridge, MIT Press.

Habermas, J. 2001b. From Kant's 'Ideas' of Pure Reason to the 'Idealizing' Presuppositions of Communicative Action: Reflections on the Detranscendentalized 'Use of Reason', in *Pluralism and the Pragmatic Turn*, edited by Rehg, W. and Bohman, J., Cambridge, MIT Press, 11-40.

Halliday, F. 2003. *Islam and The of Confrontation*, London, I.B. Tauris.

Haslam, S.A., McGarty, J., Turner, J. 1996. Salient Group Membership and Persuasion: The Role of Social identity in Validation of Beliefs, in *What is Social About Cognition in Small Groups*, edited by Nye, J.L. and Brower, A.M., Thousand Oaks, SAGE, 29-56.

Heider, F. 1958. *The Psychology of Interpersonal Relations*, New York, J. Wiley and Sons.

Honneth, A, 1995. *The Fragmented World of the Social: Essays in Social and Political Philosophy*, Albany, State University of New York Press.

Huntington, S.P. 1996. *The Clash of Civilizations and the Remaking of the Modern World*, New York, Simon and Schuster.

Iqbal, M. 1986. The Principle of Movement in the Structure of Islam, in *Liberal Islam: A Source Book*, edited by Kurzman C., New York, Oxford University Press.

Kabuli, N. 1994. *Democracy According to Islam*, Pittsburgh, Dorrance.

Karaömerlioğlu, A. 2001. Tek Parti Döneminde Halkçılık, in *Kemalism*, edited by İnsel, A. İstanbul, İletişim, 272-284.

Karpat, K. 1972. The Transformation of the Ottoman State, 1789-1908, *International Journal of Middle East Studies*, 3 (3), 243-281.

Karpat, K. 1982. Millets and Nationality: The Roots of Incongruity of Nation and State in the Post-Ottoman Era; in *Christians and Jews in the Ottoman Empire*, edited by Braude B. and Lewis B., New York, Holmes and Meyer, 141-170.

Karpat, K. 2001. The *Politicisation of Islam*, New York, Oxford University Press.

Kasaba, R. 1988. *The Ottoman Empire and the World Economy: The Nineteenth Century*, Albany, SUNY Press.

Kayalı, H. 1997. *Arabs and Young Turks: Ottomanism, Arabism, and Islamism in the Ottoman Empire, 1908-1918*, Berkeley, University of California Press.

Kelly, D. 2001. *Community Participation in Rangeland Management*, Canberra, Rural Industry Research and Development Cooperation.

Khan, A. 1986. *Islam, Politics and the State*, Kuala Lumpur, Ikraq.

Khurshid, A. 1976. *Islam: Its Meaning and Message*, London, Islamic Council of Europe.

Kittay, E.F. and Meyers, T.D. (eds) 1987. *Women and Moral Theory*, Totowa, N.J., Rowman and Littlefield.

Koçak, C. 2001. New Ottomans and the First Constitutional Government, in *Tanzimat ve Meşrutiyet'in Birikimi*, edited by Alkan, M. İstanbul, İletişim, 72-88.

Köker, L. 2000. *Modernleşme, Kemalizm ve Demokrasi*, İstanbul, İletişim.

Köker, L. 2001. Kemalizm/Atatürkçülük: Modernleşme, Devlet ve Demokrasi; in *Milliyetçilik*, edited by Bora, T. İstanbul, İletişim, 97-119.

Koloğlu, O. 2001. Abdulhamid'in Siyasal Düşüncesi, in *Tanzimat ve Meşrutiyet'in Birikimi*, edited by Alkan, M. İstanbul, İletişim, 273-277.

Kurzman, C. (ed.) 1998. *Liberal Islam: A Source Book*, New York, Oxford University Press.

Kushner, D. 1977. *The Rise of Turkish Nationalism*, London; Frank Cass.

Kymlica, W. 1996. Two Models of Pluralism and Tolerance, in *Toleration: An Elusive Virtue*, edited by Heyd, D., Princeton, Princeton University Press, 81-105.

Lewis, B. 1968. *The Emergence of Modern Turkey*, London, Oxford University Press.

Little, D. 1988. The Western Tradition, in *Human Rights and the Conflict of Cultures: Western and Islamic Perspectives on Religious Liberty*, edited by Little, D., Kelsay, J., Sachedina, A., South Carolina, University of South Carolina Press, 13-32.

Macedo, S. (ed.) 1999. *Deliberative Politics: Essays on Democracy and Disagreement*, New York, Oxford University Press.

Mackie, G. 2003. *Democracy Defended*, New York, Cambridge University Press.

Mackie, G. 2006. Does Democratic Deliberation Change Minds?, *Politics, Philosophy and Economics*, 5, 279-303.

Mansbridge, J. 1980. *Beyond Adversary Democracy*, New York, Basic Books.

Mardin, Ş. 1962. *The Genesis of Young Ottoman Thought: A Study in the Modernisation of Turkish Political Ideas*, Princeton, Princeton University Press.

Mardin, Ş. 1990. *Türkiye'de Toplum ve Siyaset*, İstanbul, İletişim.

Mardin, Ş. 1991. *Türk Modernleşmesi*, İstanbul, İletişim.

Mardin, Ş. 2006. Turkish Islamic Exceptionalism Yesterday and Today: Continuity, Rupture and Reconstruction in Operational Codes, in *Religion and Politics in Turkey*, edited by Çarkoğlu, A. and Rubin, B., London, Routledge, 3-24.

Mazıcı, N. 2002. 27 Mayıs, Kemalizmin Restorasyonu mu? In *Kemalism*, edited by İnsel, A. İstanbul, İletişim, 555-569.

McCarthy, T. 1978. *The Critical Theory of Jürgen Habermas*, London, Hutchinson.

McCarthy, T. 1991. *Ideals and Illusions*, Cambridge, MIT Press.

McCarthy, T. 1992. Practical Discourse: On the Relation of Morality to Politics, in *Habermas and the Public Sphere*, edited by Calhoun, C., Cambridge, MIT Press, 51, 73.

McCarthy, T. 1998. Legitimacy and Diversity: Dialectical Reflections on Analytic Distinctions; in *Habermas on Law and Democracy: Critical Exchanges*, edited by Rosenfeld, M. and Arato, A, California, University of California Press, 115-157.

McKeown, B. Thomas, D. 1988. *Q Methodology*, California, Sage Publications.

Mert, N. 2001. Türkiye'de Merkez Sağ Siyaset: Merkez Sağ Politikaların Oluşumu, in *Türkiye'de Sivil Toplum ve Milliyetçilik*, İstanbul, İletişim, 45-83.

Mortimer, E. 1982. *Faith and Power: The Politics of Islam*, London, Faber and Faber.

Mutlu, Y. 2003. Interview with the author on 2 December 2003 in Ankara.

Mutz, D. 2006. *Hearing the Other Side: Deliberative versus Particpatory Democracy*, Cambridge, Cambridge University Press.

Norris, P. and Inglehart, R. 2004. *Sacred and Secular: Religion and Politics Worldwide*, Cambridge, Cambridge University Press.

Outhwaite, W. (ed.) 1994. *Habermas: A Critical Introduction*, California, Stanford University Press.

Parla, T. 1993. *Ziya Gökalp, Kemalizm ve Türkiye'de Korporatizm*, İstanbul, İletişim.

Parla, T. and Davison, A. 2004. *Corporatist Ideology in Turkey: Progress or Order*, Syracuse, Syracuse University Press.

Pensky, M. 2004. Comments on Seyla Benhabib, The Claims of Culture, *Constellations*, v 11, n 2, 258-266.

Pettigrew, T. 1998. Intergroup Contact Theory, *Annual Review of Psychology*, 49, 68-85.

Plagemann, G. 2001. Türkiye'de İnsan Hakları Örgütleri: Farklı Kültürel Çevreler, Farklı Örgütler: in *Türkiye'de Sivil Toplum ve Milliyetçilik*, İstanbul, İletişim, 361-397.

Pruitt, D.G., Peirce, R.S., Zubek, J.M., McGillicuddy, N.B., Welton, G.L. 1993. Determinants of Short-Term and Long-Term Success in Mediation, in *Conflict Between People and Groups*, Chicago, Nelson Hall, 60-75.

Rabinow, P. and Sullivan, W. (eds) 1979. *Interpretive Social Science: A Reader*, Berkeley, University of California Press.

Rawls, J. 1973. *A Theory of Justice*, Cambridge, Belknap Press.

Rawls, J. 1993. *Political Liberalism*, New York, Columbia University Press.

Rawls, J. 1995. Reply to Habermas, *Journal of Philosophy*, XCII:3, 132-80.

Rehg, W. and Bohman, J. 2001. *Pluralism and the Pragmatic Turn*, Cambridge; MIT Press.

Rosenfeld, M. and Arato, A. 1998. *Habermas on Law and Democracy*, Berkeley, University of California Press.

Roy, O. 1994. *The Failure of Political Islam*, Massachusetts, Harvard University Press.

Şalcı, Z. 2003. Interview with the author on 2 December 2003 in Ankara.

Sanders, L. 1997. Against Deliberation, *Political Theory*, 25, n 3, 347-376.

Sharif, A. 1999. *Democracy, The Rule of Law and Islam*, London, Aspen.

Simon, B. and Sturmer, S. 2003. Respect for Group Members: Intragroup Determinants of Collective Identification and Group Serving Behaviour, *Personality and Social Psychology Bulletin*, 29, 183-193.

Somel S.A. 2001. Osmanlı Reform Çağında OsmanlıcılıkDüşüncesi, in *Tanzimat ve Meşrutiyet'in Birikimi*, edited by Alkan, M. İstanbul, İletişim, 88-116.

Stepan, A. 2001. *Arguing Comparative Politics*, New York, Oxford University Press.

Stephenson, W. 1935. Technique of Factor Analysis, *Nature*, 136, 297-297.

Stephenson, W. 1953. *The Study of Behavior: Q-technique and its Methodology*, Chicago; Chicago University Press.

Stephenson, W. 1985. Perspectives on Q Methodology, *Operant Subjectivity*, 8: 83-87.

Sunstein, R.C. 2002. The Law Of Group Polarisation, *Journal of Political Philosophy*, v 10, 175-195.

Surush, A.K. 2000. *Reason, Freedom and Democracy in Islam*, New York, Oxford University Press.

Temo, İ. 1987. *İbrahim Temo'nun İttihad ve Terakki Anıları*, İstanbul, Arba.

Thomas, D.B. 1979. Psychodynamics, Symbolism and Socialization, *Political Behaviour*, 1, 243-268.

Thomas, D.B. and Sigelman, L. 1984. Presidential Identification and Policy Leadership: Experimental Evidence on the Reagan Case, *Policy Studies*, 12, 663-675.

Thompson, J. and Held, D. (eds) 1982. *Habermas Critical Debates*, London, Macmillan.

Tuksal, H. 2000. *Kadın Karşıtı Söylemin İslam Geleneğindeki İzdüşümleri*, Ankara, Kitabiyat Yayınları.

Tuksal, H. 2003. Interview with the author on 4 December 2003 in Ankara.

Tuncay, M. 2000. *Türkiye'de Sol Akımlar-I (1908-1925)*, Istanbul, BDS Yayınları.

Turam, B. 2007. *Between Islam and the State*, Stanford, Stanford University Press.

Türköne, M. 2002. 3 Kasım: Bizans Düştü, *Türkiye Günlüğü*, n 70, 262.

Türköne, M. 2003. *Siyasi İdeoloji Olarak İslamcılığın Doğuşu*, Ankara, Lotus.

Tyler, T. 1989. The Psychology of Procedural Justice: A Test of the Group Value Mode, *Journal of Personality and Social Psychology*, 57, 830-838.

Tyler, T. 2006. *Why People Obey the Law*, New Gaven, Yale University Press.

Ünüvar, K. 2001. İhyadan İnşaya; in *Tanzimat ve Meşrutiyet'in Birikimi*, edited by Alkan, M. İstanbul, İletişim, 129-143.

Uyanık, M. 1999. *İslam Siyaset Felsefesinde Sivil İtaatsizlik*, Istanbul, Kaknüs Yayınları.

Warnke, G. 1987. *Gadamer: Hermeneutics, Tradition and Reason*, Cambridge, Polity Press.

Warnke, G. 2001. Taking Ethical Debate Seriously; in *Pluralism and Pragmatic Turn*, edited by Rehg, W and Bohman, J., Cambridge, MIT Press, 295-319.

Weymouth, L. 2002. A Devout Muslim, A Secular State, *Washington Post*, online (www.washingtonpost.com/wp-dyn/articles/A30603-2002Nov8.html) accessed: 15 November 2002.

Yaran, C.S. 2001. *İslam ve Öteki: Dinlerin Doğruluk, Kurtarıcılık ve BiraradaYaşama Sorunu*, İstanbul, Kaknüs Yayınları.

Yavuz, H. and Esposito, J. 2003. *Turkish Islam and the Secular State*, Syracuse, Syracuse University Press.

Young, I. 2000. *Inclusion and Democracy*, Oxford, Oxford University Press.

Young, I. 2001. Activist Challenges to Deliberative Democracy, *Political Theory*, v 29, n 5, 670-690.

Zurcher, E. 1993. *Turkey: A Modern History*, London, Tauris.

# Index